MOST
EVIL
II

ZODIAC CASE SOLVED

MOST
EVIL
II

Presenting the Follow-up Investigation
and Decryption of the 1970 Zodiac Cipher
in Which the San Francisco Serial Killer
Reveals His True Identity

STEVE HODEL

THIS IS A GENUINE VIREO BOOK

A Vireo Book | Rare Bird Books
453 South Spring Street, Suite 302
Los Angeles, CA 90013
rarebirdbooks.com

FIRST TRADE PAPERBACK ORIGINAL EDITION

Set in Georgia
Printed in the United States

10 9 8 7 6 5 4 3 2 1

Publisher's Cataloging-in-Publication data

Hodel, Steve, 1941 -
Most evil : presenting the follow-up investigation and decryption of the
1970 Zodiac cipher in which the San Francisco serial killer reveals his
true identity / by Steve Hodel.
338 pages
ISBN 978-1-942600-45-9
Includes bibliographical references and index.

1. Serial murders—California. 2. Serial murder investigation—California.
3. Serial murderers—California. 4. Serial murderers—United States—
Biography. 5. Serial murders—United States. I. Title.

HV6248.H462 H63 2015
364.15/23/0979461—dc23

For The Victims, Living And Dead,
and SFPD Patrolman Eric Zelms,
Killed In The Line Of Duty On January 1, 1970

ON A BALMY SUMMER day in June of 1936, George Hill Hodel, a tall, handsome man of twenty-eight, stood on the campus of UCSF, raised his right hand into the air, and, with his classmates, took the following Hippocratic Oath:

> *"I swear by Apollo the physician, and Aesculapius, and Health, and All-heal, and all the gods and goddesses, that, according to my ability and judgment, I will keep this Oath and this stipulation.*

> *...I will give no deadly medicine to anyone if asked, nor suggest any such counsel; and like manner I will not give to a woman a pessary to produce abortion. With purity and with holiness I will pass my life and practice my Art.*

> *...Into whatever houses I enter, I will go into them for the benefit of the sick, and will abstain from every voluntary act of mischief and corruption; and, further from the seduction of females or males, of freemen and slaves.*

At the completion of those ceremonies, he was bestowed with the respected and time-honored title of Medical Doctor. His life was now dedicated to the preserving and healing of human life. He was now charged with one of man's highest callings, and it would now be his duty forthwith to assist in the removal of pain and suffering from his humankind.

George Hill Hodel, MD San Francisco Medical School photo, 1935.

CONTENTS

INTRODUCTION

THIS IS THE SEQUEL to *Most Evil: Avenger, Zodiac, and the Further Serial Murders of Dr. George Hill Hodel,* published by Dutton Penguin Group in September 2009. During the past five years, some of the investigative findings included here have been discussed both on my author website[1] and in my sequel *Black Dahlia Avenger II* (Thoughtprint Press, 2012; updated in 2014.)

For those readers who might not be familiar with that work, I have decided to include some of the relevant Zodiac information, in the addendum to this book.

From the back cover of *Most Evil* (Dutton, 2009):

> When veteran LAPD homicide detective Steve Hodel discovered that his late father had known the victim in the infamous Black Dahlia murder case in 1947 Los Angeles, the ensuing three-year investigation became the New York Times bestseller Black Dahlia Avenger. Publication led directly to the discovery of a cache of hidden documents, covered up for decades, that confirm George Hodel had long been law enforcement's number one suspect in Elizabeth Short's grisly death. A lurid murder mystery that had endured for more than fifty years was finally solved.
>
> But for Steve Hodel, that revelation was only the beginning. With twenty-five years of experience

investigating homicides as an LAPD detective, Hodel's instincts told him that a man capable of bisecting Elizabeth Short's body, arranging it in a gruesome and public tableau, and taunting the police and the public with notes and phone calls, did not begin or end his killing career with the Black Dahlia. A chance encounter in the wake of Black Dahlia Avenger's publication led Steve to consider a question as preposterous as it is compelling:

Twenty years after shocking the world in Los Angeles, could Dr. George Hill Hodel have returned to terrorize California as the killer known as Zodiac?

In *Most Evil* (2009), I presented my four-year follow-up investigation (2005 to 2009) pointing to the possibility that my father, Dr. George Hill Hodel, might have committed more crimes in Chicago, Illinois; Manila, Philippines; and Riverside, California, as well as the seven crimes in the San Francisco Bay area attributed to "Zodiac" in 1968 through 1969.

Unlike my Black Dahlia investigation, I did not claim that these out-of-state, out-of-country, and Zodiac crimes were "solved."

In the conclusion (*Most Evil*, 281-2), I wrote:

> *...As a homicide investigator who has been called upon to collect sufficient evidence to press formal charges and ultimately convince a jury, I realize that the chain of evidence linking my father to Zodiac and the Chicago Lipstick murders is largely circumstantial. But, as was found in the case of the Black Dahlia investigation, I believe that detectives possess and are still holding forensic evidence that links Dr. Hodel to the Zodiac killings and possibly even to one or more of the sixty-year-old Chicago "Lipstick Murders."*

> *...As with* Black Dahlia Avenger, *I expect new witnesses will come forward, new evidence will come to light, new links will be established.*

Here, I present the anticipated new witnesses, new evidence, and new linkage.

The new findings are dramatic and compelling and, for most readers (my jury), I believe they will likely move them across the evidentiary threshold from *Most Evil's* strong circumstantial case to "beyond a reasonable doubt," which is the proof required to arrive at a guilty verdict.

As I write this introduction it is August 2015.

In November of 2014, I mailed letters to the concerned law enforcement agencies (San Francisco Police Department, Solano and Napa Sheriffs, and Vallejo Police Department) requesting a confidential meeting with their cold case detectives.

In that letter, I offered to present, on my time and my dime, a three-hour PowerPoint presentation to provide them with an overview of all of the evidence that I believe links my father, Dr. George Hill Hodel, to their unsolved crimes—collectively known as the Zodiac Murders.

My purpose was to convince law enforcement to proceed with an attempt to obtain confirmed Zodiac DNA.

I originally made this offer (absent the new and increasingly compelling evidence found in this edition) back in 2009. At that time, I informed law enforcement that I was in possession of my father's full DNA profile and it was available for comparison when and if they obtained a confirmed Zodiac DNA sample.

The general public, along with a few self-appointed Zodiac "experts" and most journalists, remains under the impression that Zodiac DNA exists and that various suspects have been eliminated because their DNA did not match that of the actual suspect.

These "eliminations," seen in some crime documentaries and news bulletins, are not coming from official police sources. Why? Because the investigating officers know that the partial DNA samples in their possession remain unconfirmed and cannot be represented as actual Zodiac DNA.

My request to brief detectives in the following month or two had but one purpose—to convince them that there exists a strong likelihood that they can solve and clear five cold case murders and two cold case attempted murders by simply obtaining Zodiac DNA.

It was my hope that at least one of the four jurisdictions would take the necessary step to reexamine the two dozen or more as-yet-untested pieces of Zodiac evidence and obtain that confirmed DNA.

If they had succeeded in obtaining actual DNA, then those samples can be compared to the full DNA profile that is in my possession and include or exclude George Hill Hodel as the Zodiac Killer.

In the chapters that follow I continue to build on the existing circumstantial evidence linking Dr. George Hill Hodel to Zodiac.

However, it is not until a closing chapter of this book, with its decryption of the original Zodiac cipher, that we are presented with Zodiac's Rosetta stone.

So confident that he was a master criminal with what he considered an absolutely "crackproof" coded cipher, the megalomaniac Zodiac codified his signature using his real name.

The following investigation picks up where I left off with the publication of *Most Evil* in 2009.

—*Steve Hodel*
August 2015

CHAPTER 1

I WILL BEGIN MY follow-up investigation by reintroducing and adding to a list of MO and crime signatures used by Dr. George Hill Hodel in the forties and compare them to those used by the so-called Zodiac, who began his "urban reign of terror" some twenty years later, in the late sixties.

While a few of the thirty modi operandi (MO) and crime signature patterns (listed below) could be considered generic if isolated, in combination they become extremely rare. In my twenty-four years with the Los Angeles Police Department, I investigated more than three hundred separate homicides.

None of those murders included the signatory acts and exceptionally rare MO of mailing mocking, taunting notes to the press and police, not to mention sending personal threats to the victim's parents—mailed directly to their home address.

In fact, I am unable to find a single modern-day serial killer prior to Zodiac's 1966 Riverside killing [Cheri Jo Bates] who has used the specific MO of taunting the police and press with letters containing obvious misspellings— with only one exception, Dr. George Hill Hodel, in the forties, calling himself the "Black Dahlia Avenger." (Prior to those crimes we have to go back another sixty years to 1888 and London's Jack the Ripper.)

George Hodel was employed as a reporter for both the *L.A. Record* and *San Francisco Chronicle* newspapers. In both the Black Dahlia Avenger and Zodiac crimes, law enforcement suspected the killer might have had ties to or prior employment with their local newspapers.

In *BDA*, *BDA II*, and *Most Evil*, I addressed many other specific links to handwriting characteristics, as well as surrealist connections to art, literature, music, and film. In 2010, a California Department of Justice Questioned Document Expert examined George Hodel's handwriting and compared it to known Zodiac letters and, while not being able to positively connect him, stated, "We are unable to eliminate George Hodel as the writer/author of the Zodiac letters." (At that time, the DOJ requested I provide them with additional lowercase samples of my father's handwriting, which to date remain unavailable or nonexistent.)

As stated in *Most Evil*:

> *George Hodel was a prolific serial killer whose signature is visible not in any single method of murder, type of victim, or specific killing ground, but rather as a series of complex arrangements, installations, and obscure references to art, culture, and film that, taken together, reveal a chilling and never-before-documented variety of serial murder: murder as a fine art.*

Black Dahlia Avenger/Zodiac MO and Crime Signature Comparisons

The following crime signatures were used by both the Black Dahlia Avenger and Zodiac:

✓ Serial Killer

✓ Created his own marketing/public relations campaign along with inventing and providing newspapers with a pseudonym for them to use in headlining his crimes and his "reign of terror." (Black Dahlia Avenger and Zodiac.)

✓ Contacted and taunted press by telephone after crimes.

✓ Contacted and taunted police by telephone after crimes.

✓ Used press as his instrument to terrorize public, promising, "There will be more."

✓ Drew crude picture of a knife dripping blood and mailed the drawing to press.

✓ Brought precut lengths of clothesline and used them to bind and tie victims during crimes.

✓ Mailed more than a dozen notes to press and police feigning illiteracy, using misspelled words and disguised handwriting.

✓ Mailed cut-and-paste notes to press and police.

✓ Mailed typewritten letter describing his actions to police.

✓ Placed excessive postage and multiple stamps on the taunting notes he mailed to press and police.

✓ Addressed press mailings, "To the Editor."

✓ Mailings sent on particular "anniversary dates" related to crimes.

✓ Packaged and mailed personal items belonging to his murdered victims to the press to prove he was the killer.

✓ Told victims and press he was "Going to Mexico."

✓ Used both a knife and a gun(s) in his separate crimes.

✓ Included puns and word games in his mailings.

✓ Continued to send in mailings to press and police months and years after original crimes.

✓ Egomaniacal personality demanded constant media publicity and front-page coverage under threat of additional killings.

✓ Identified himself as an "Avenger," claiming he was wronged by the female victim or that he was getting revenge for being spurned and ignored by the victim.

✓ Informed the public that the crime was "justified" or was "divine retribution."

✓ Stabbed several victims with a long-bladed jungle or bayonet-style knife.

✓ Wrote taunting messages at the scene either on the bedroom wall, a nearby telephone post, a door panel of victim's vehicle, or the victim's body.

✓ Manually ripped away band from a men's wristwatch and left both band and watch at separate crime scenes, on or near the victim's body.

✓ Left men's white handkerchief either at the scene near the body, or used it to wipe away fingerprints from inside the victim's vehicle or from the knife left at the crime scene.

✓ Geographically preselected crime scene locations by plotting coordinates on a map; then randomly murdered victim(s) who by happenstance entered his "killing zone," or

✓ Geographically preselected crime scene locations by plotting coordinates on a map, then had unwitting victim (taxi driver) drive him to that specific location, where victim was then shot and killed, or,

✓ Forcibly kidnapped female victim, strangled her to death, and dismembered the body with surgical skill and precision. Then posed the body parts in public view at a specific location (street name) that provided a taunting clue related to the crime or suspect.

✓ Brutal assault and overkill, particularly savage with his female victims.

✓ Telephoned and/or sent sadistic note to victim's parents after brutal murder of their daughter.

One new discovery (our thirty-first listed here) that is specific to both Avenger and Zodiac MOs, unrecognized by me until only recently, is that both used the same unique signature in one of their mailed taunts to the press: "a friend." (Note that both Avenger and Zodiac signed it using a small letter "a.")

Mailed to the Newspaper Editor by Black Dahlia Avenger

Black Dahlia Avenger 1947

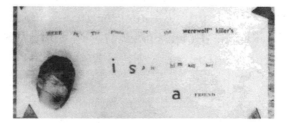

Fig. 1.0

Mailed to the Newspaper Editor by Zodiac

Zodiac February 14, 1974[2]

Fig. 1.1

These thirty-one MO/signatures in both Dr. George Hill Hodel's crimes as the Black Dahlia Avenger and in Zodiac's

---

2   Zodiac's "a friend" note was mailed to the press on February 14, 1974, which was the twenty-sixth anniversary of the Black Dahlia Avenger's murder of Gladys Kern in Los Angeles, slain by him on February 14, 1948.

crimes are so unusual, so distinctive, that it defies logic that they would have been committed by two separate killers.

Perhaps a detective, noting the use of three or four of these identical signatures, might consider the possibility of a "copycat"—but never thirty-one.

As we begin to review the new evidence, it is important that we recognize that we are not simply rounding up and reviewing "one of the usual suspects."

Rather, we are starting off with a man that can only be described as "a prime Zodiac suspect." (Based on the previous evidence presented in *Most Evil*, coupled with these identical signatures, I would have to say, *the* prime suspect.)

Dr. George Hill Hodel, like Zodiac, was an urban terrorist and a killing machine who taunted both the press and the police with repeated mailings and threats to "kill more." Their signature acts are identical down to the minutest details.

I agree with author Michael Connelly's LAPD Detective III Harry Bosch, when it comes to murder investigations, "There are no coincidences."

I submit these two serial killers were the same man.

What follows are my further proofs.

CHAPTER 2

"I am one-hundred percent certain that the book cover sketch [Great Crimes of San Francisco] I drew back then [in 1974] was based on material that was directly related to the crime."

—*Neal Adams*
Comic-Con, San Diego
July 23, 2014

Cover Sketch by Neal Adams, 1974

Original Source Traced to SFPD Police Composite Drawing

Fig. 2.0

Artist/Illustrator Neal Adams
1974 Zodiac Book Cover Sketch

THANKS TO THE ABOVE statement from artist/illustrator Neal Adams and some further digging, we now have the answers to the several questions I initially raised in *Most Evil* back in 2009 related to the then-unidentified sketch, which appeared to be a dead-ringer for my father. I quote from *Most Evil*, Chapter 16, page 191:

> *...Because of the sketch's striking similarity to my father (including his black, horn-rimmed glasses) I was determined to find its source. Was I looking at an artist's imaginary rendition of a reproduction or an actual police drawing from official files? If the Zodiac composite was simply the publisher's decision to take "creative license," then why place it on an official SFPD Police Bulletin connected to an otherwise completely factual true crime story? On the other hand, if the composite was an official police drawing, why had it not surfaced earlier?*

Five years later, we finally have a definitive answer to those questions!

And, those answers come directly from the original source—Neal Adams, the man that drew the original Zodiac book cover sketch.

George Hodel in 1974 is here compared to Zodiac as represented on paperback cover of 1974 Great Crimes of San Francisco *(Ballantine Books, 1974).[3]*

Fig. 2.1

A Chance Meeting Provides the Answer

ON WEDNESDAY, JULY 23, 2014, I received a telephone call from a personal friend, artist/illustrator Scott Gandell. Scott told me he was at his booth at the 2014 Comic-Con Festival in San Diego, California.

At the four-day convention, he chanced to meet fellow artist/illustrator Neal Adams, who drew the illustrated Zodiac face for the cover of the 1974 true crime book, *Great Crimes of San Francisco* (Ballantine Books, 1974).

Scott, being familiar with the facts and history of the drawing as presented in *Most Evil*, seized the moment to take Neal Adams aside and question him as to what he remembered about his 1974 book cover Zodiac sketch.

While Adams could not recall the specific original source more than forty years later, he did say, "I am one-hundred

---

3   Cover artist Neal Adams remained unknown and was not identified until after publication of *Most Evil*.

percent certain that the sketch I drew back then was based on material that was directly related and somehow connected to the crime."

Adams told Gandell that under no circumstances would he have simply created his own imaginary suspect. Rather, his drawing of the Zodiac suspect, as rendered on that book cover, definitely was inspired by outside source material directly related to the official police investigation.

Based on Scott's conversation with Neal Adams, we have now established, 1) The picture was drawn by Neal Adams and, 2) Adams did not create the likeness from his own imagination, but based it on an official Zodiac investigation source that he saw between 1969 and 1973.

Neal Adams Source Material—"Sonoma Composite" Misnamed

IN *MOST EVIL*, IN addition to the known SFPD Police Bulletin on Zodiac, I included a second supposed image, the so-called "Sonoma Police Composite." It had surfaced with little documentation other than a reference on the respected Zodiac website "This is the Zodiac Speaking," run by Jake Wark. Jake included the composite with a comment that stated simply, "It is unknown why Sonoma County would issue a Zodiac sketch, as no Zodiac crimes are acknowledged in that area."

I included the "Sonoma Composite" because of the physical likeness it shared to both the SFPD composite and the *Great Crimes of San Francisco* cover.

Denver Post Staff Artist/Illustrator Joe Barros

IN *MOST EVIL*, I asked a second question: "Why would the artist who drew the book cover composite place it on an official San Francisco Police Bulletin?" I believe we now have the answer: Because the 1969 SFPD Zodiac suspect composite was the source for Neal Adams' original drawing.

Thanks to a forty-three-year-old article from the *Vallejo Sunday Times-Herald*, by then-staff reporter Dave Peterson, we have our answer. Peterson's piece appeared on February 28, 1971, with the headline "New Zodiac Art Work Is Criticized."

SFPD Police Composite Sketch

Redrawn by Denver Post *Artist Joe Barros*

Two new sketches of Zodiac, above, the Bay Area "code killer" done by Joe Barros, staff artist of the Denver Post. He depicts Zodiac with and without glasses. Barros sees Zodiac as fatter-faced, with a higher forehead, and "prettier" than in the San Francisco Police artist's sketch. — AP Wire-photos

Fig. 2.2

The article included both the original SFPD composite and a revision (see Fig. 2.2) drawn by Joe Barros, a staff artist for the *Denver Post*.

SFPD Homicide Bureau Chief Inspector Lieutenant Charles Ellis, commenting on Barros' revision of the original SFPD composite, said he believed that his department's police artist rendition was "more accurate."[4]

The following is an excerpt from an online eBay art sale bio on Joe Barros:

> ...*Joseph "Joe" Barros (1921-2011) was an American artist, painter, and illustrator who, for more than thirty years, was the chief illustrator for the* Denver Post *newspaper. In addition to his newspaper work, Barros illustrated numerous books, many featuring western settings, including* Place Names of the Medicine Bow National Forest *(by Mel Duncan) and* Prairielands of My Heart *(by Clyde Brundy). Barros achieved some notoriety in the early seventies when he created police-type composite sketches of the Zodiac Killer based upon descriptions and the sketches in the San Francisco police files. His sketches were published across the country by the AP wire services.*[5]

---

4   Several of the Zodiac witnesses who saw the Barros drawing informed the journalist-illustrator that his drawing, more accurately resembled Zodiac than the police composite."

5   www.worthpoint.com/worthopedia/joe-barros-original-art-illustration-238859720

Evolution of the SFPD Composite Sketch

SFPD sketch—Good? (1969)

Fig. 2.3.1

Joe Barros SFPD sketch—Better? (1971)

Fig. 2.3.2

Neal Adams SFPD sketch—Best? (1973)

Fig. 2.3.3

I now believe the "official source" for Neal Adams' Zodiac drawing originates from this 1971 *Sunday Times-Herald* article and possibly additional Associated Press-circulated articles showing Barros' 1971 composite.

It appears that Adams combined the SFPD and Barros composites into his own Zodiac likeness, which would appear on the cover of a true crime book just three years later.

This also answers why Adams placed his cover drawing on a likeness of a SFPD Bulletin! The police drawing was his original source.

| George Hodel 1974 | Adams composite | Barros composite | Hodel 1962 | SFPD composite 1969 |

Fig. 2.4

Above we see comparisons of Dr. George Hill Hodel to the Barros and Adams Zodiac drawings and the 1969 SFPD composites. All three renditions show Zodiac as he appeared in 1969, so in the 1974 Hodel photo one must subtract or "youthen" George Hodel by five years and in the 1962 picture, one must add, or age him, some seven years.

The evidence is undeniable—Neal Adams' likeness of Zodiac, based on his review of the official SFPD composite drawing and a merging with Barros' sketch, is a near picture-perfect likeness to Dr. George Hill Hodel's physical appearance in 1969.

Sunday Times-Herald: "New 'Zodiac' Art Work Is Criticized," by Staff Writer Dave Peterson on Sunday, February 23, 1971

REF
INFO

Sunday Times·Herald
SOLANO AND ‧ NAPA COUNTY'S MORNING NEWSPAPER

VALLEJO, CALIF.—HOME OF MARE ISLAND NAVAL SHIPYARD—SUNDAY, FEB. 23, 1971

New 'Zodiac' Art Work Is Criticized

By DAVE PETERSON
Times-Herald Staff Writer

SAN FRANCISCO — The belated new sketches of Zodiac the slayer of at least five persons in the Bay Area, leave San Francisco homicide investigators cold — and not from fear.

Lt. Charles Ellis, Homicide Bureau chief, said the Denver newspaper artist who drew them obviously tried to "add some expression" to the composite sketches done by the San Francisco police artist.

Pot Chief Inspector Ellis said the Denver artist had not interviewed the eyewitnesses who saw Zodiac when he killed cabbie Paul Stine the night of Oct. 10, 1969, in Presidio Heights.

'MORE ACCURATE'

Ellis was confident that the sketches of his artist, checked repeatedly with the eyewitnesses, are more accurate.

As for Zodiac himself, Ellis said it's possible the homicidal maniac has been committed or incarcerated. Nothing has been heard from him since he sent a Halloween card to a San Francisco newspaper reporter last Oct. 8.

Or the "horrorscope killer" could have shipped overseas on a merchant vessel or some other way, Ellis agreed.

SEES CAPTURE

But Ellis remains confident that Zodiac will be captured eventually in what the officer calls "one of the greatest crime hunts" in the nation.

Two San Francisco police officers still spend much of their time on the case, Ellis said. Hundreds of persons have been investigated, including servicemen and sailors, without solving the case.

Zodiac will be a prime subject for consideration at a conference in Los Angeles Thursday of a number of investigators watching the usual number of bizarre murders in California recently, Ellis indicated.

This composite sketch of Zodiac is considered an excellent likeness by San Francisco police. It was drawn from the observations of five eyewitnesses at the scene of the murder of a San Francisco cabbie, and confirmed by a San Bernardino woman who escaped from Zodiac's car last March north of Modesto.

NON-CIRCULATING

Two new sketches of Zodiac, above, the Bay Area "code killer" done by Joe Barros, staff artist of the Denver Post. He depicts Zodiac with and without glasses. Barros sees Zodiac as fatter-faced, with a higher forehead, and "prettier" than in the San Francisco Police artist's sketch. — AP Wirephoto.

Fig. 2.5

1969 SFPD Zodiac Composite Bulletin
on Paul Stine Murder

SAN FRANCISCO POLICE DEPARTMENT

NO. 90-69   WANTED FOR MURDER   OCTOBER 18, 1969

ORIGINAL DRAWING   AMENDED DRAWING

Supplementing our Bulletin 87-69 of October 13, 1969. Additional information has
developed the above amended drawing of murder suspect known as "ZODIAC".

WMA, 35-45 Years, approximately 5'8", Heavy Build, Short Brown Hair, possibly with
Red Tint, Wears Glasses. Armed with 9 MM Automatic.

Available for comparison: Slugs, Casings, Latents, Handwriting.

ANY INFORMATION:
Inspectors Armstrong & Toschi
Homicide Detail   THOMAS J. CAHILL
CASE NO. 696314   CHIEF OF POLICE

Fig. 2.6

Journalist Duffy Jennings Correction—For the Record

IN MY 2009 BOOK, *Most Evil*, when I still didn't know the
source of the *Great Crimes of San Francisco* cover, I wrote
the following (Chapter 16, page 191):

> ...If the composite was an official police drawing, why
> had it not surfaced earlier?

I found the answer with the help of a confidential source who contacted the author of the essay on Zodiac in Great Crimes of San Francisco, Duffy Jennings. *Jennings, a former* San Francisco Chronicle *crime reporter, confirmed, "the composite originated from law enforcement," but couldn't recall the specific agency. Since the sketch includes the correct date (October 18) and the number (90-69) of a known San Francisco Police Department Bulletin, it would appear that this composite originated from the files of the SFPD.**

I then footnoted the above paragraph as follows:

*Despite Jennings' acknowledgment and the fact that it is an almost picture-perfect likeness to George Hodel, I still have some doubts about this third composite. When I attempted to locate editor Dean W. Dickensheet, I discovered that he died in the nineteen-nineties. Further attempts to confirm recollection that this was an official police composite are being made through Dickensheet's original publisher.

A year later, with the publication of *Most Evil*'s paperback edition (Berkley, 2010), I added an Author's Note identifying the cover artist as Neal Adams, and indicating that Duffy Jennings was apparently mistaken in his recollection that it came from law enforcement.[6]

Let Me—For the Record—Correct That Statement

MR. DUFFY JENNINGS, THE former *San Francisco Chronicle* reporter, was not mistaken in his belief that the "composite originated from law enforcement." He was, in fact, correct. While it was not drawn by law enforcement, it did "originate from law enforcement" as it was rendered from an original SFPD composite.

---

6   Several readers have emailed me questioning why I used a "confidential source" to check with Mr. Jennings, as opposed to contacting him directly. In 2007-2008, I was conducting a sub-rosa investigation and I, 1) did not want a former *San Francisco Chronicle* reporter to know that the author of *The Black Dahlia Avenger* was actively investigating Zodiac, and 2) had signed a confidentiality agreement with Dutton Publishing and the book's contents were embargoed.

Seen below is my Author's Note as published in Most Evil (Berkley, 2010) paperback edition, which was printed one year after the original hardcover edition at Dutton.

Author's Note

In the original Dutton hardcover publication, a second un-identified "SFPD Composite Bulletin" was included and mistakenly identified as being my "original source." It was not. That second drawing, initially believed to have been drawn by an unidentified SFPD police artist, contained an even stronger almost "picture-perfect" likeness of George Hodel. This second composite originally appeared on the cover of a book entitled, *Great Crimes of San Francisco* (Ballantine Books, 1974). The book was an anthology of true crimes all of which occurred in the Bay Area. Included in the book was a chapter on the Zodiac serial murders, written by Duffy Jennings, a former *San Francisco Chronicle* reporter. Mr. Jennings confirmed that, "the composite originated from law enforcement," but could not recall the specific agency. Since the drawing was posted on a SFPD Wanted Bulletin using the actual Zodiac case number and crime date, it appeared obvious that the source was SFPD.

However, in October 2009, immediately after the hardcover was published, the actual source of this second composite drawing was identified. Mr. Jennings was mistaken in his recollection. I discovered that the drawing had not come from law enforcement, but rather from Neal Adams, a civilian artist-illustrator, who drew the composite for the book cover. For complete details and background related to this second composite, see my Web site blog entries at www.stevehodel.com/evidenceroom.

Fig. 2.7

We now have the answers to questions I initially posed in *Most Evil*.

We now know with certainty that the striking likeness to my father's person, as drawn by Neal Adams on the 1974 cover of *Great Crimes of San Francisco*, was his rendition and merging of the official 1969 police composite with the 1971 Barros composite.

Based on the evidence at hand, I believe the Zodiac suspect composites have gone from SFPD's sketch (good) to illustrator Joe Barros' revision (better), to Neal Adams' drawing (best).

CHAPTER 3

SFPD's Donald Fouke Memorandum

A GREAT DEAL OF controversy has emerged in the past decade over an SFPD internal memo written by one of the first uniform patrol officers to arrive at the scene of cabdriver Paul Stine's murder on October 11, 1969.

SFPD Officer Donald Fouke (the memo writer) and his partner, Officer Eric Zelms, were in the second patrol car to arrive at scene. Stine, the cabbie, was shot in the head and it was initially treated by SFPD as a random robbery/murder until Zodiac identified himself as the shooter.

To fully understand why the original events are so hotly contested, let us first establish their chronology. (Times are approximate):

October 11, 1969 10:00 p.m.: Teenage witnesses call in a "robbery in progress" across the street from their residence at Washington and Cherry Streets in San Francisco's Presidio Heights District. Responding uniform officers broadcast an initial description of the robber as a "male black," which is quickly corrected to a "male white." The victim, cabdriver Paul Stine, is pronounced dead at the scene. Cause of death: gunshot wound to head, execution style. The shooter is described leaving the scene on foot northbound toward the Presidio.

October 11, 1969 10:10 p.m.: SFPD patrol units search for the robber in the immediate area, including the Julius Kahn

Playground. He can't be found. Inspectors Dave Toschi and Bill Armstrong of SFPD Homicide arrive at the scene and take control of the investigation.

October 13, 1969: Zodiac sends letter to the *San Francisco Chronicle* taking credit for the Stine murder, and to prove he is telling the truth, includes a swatch of Stine's bloody shirt, which he tore from Stine's body after the murder (a fact confirmed by SFPD). The letter ridicules the police for their poor search methods while looking for him in the park.

October 13, 1969: SFPD police artist obtains description of the robber from teenage witnesses, and original sketch is distributed to law enforcement agencies and the press.

October 18, 1969: Police composite updated and revised, now identifying suspect as Zodiac. Changing age upward to "thirty-five to forty-five years old," and adding the further characteristic of "short brown hair possibly with red tint."

November 8, 1969: Zodiac sends taunting "dripping pen" card to *San Francisco Chronicle*.

November 9, 1969: Zodiac sends six-page letter to *San Francisco Chronicle*, claiming seven murders. Says he looks like the police composite, "only when I do my thing, the rest of the time I look entirle [sic] different."

In letter, Zodiac provides extensive description of his and police activities on the night of the Stine murder and highlights a section of the letter with arrows, demanding that the *Chronicle* "must print in paper."

November 12, 1969: The *Chronicle* complies with Zodiac's demand and prints portions of the letter, including the highlighted "must print" section, which read:

> *ps. 2 cops pulled a goof abot 3 min after I left the cab.*
>
> *I was walking down the hill to the park when this cop car pulled up & one of them called me over & asked if I saw any one acting supicisous* [sic] *or strange in the last 5 to 10 min & I said yes there was this man who was running by waveing* [sic] *a gun & the cops peeled rubber & went around the corner as I directed them & I disappeared into the park a block & a half away never to be seen again.*

Zodiac went on to add, "Hey pig doesn't it rile you up to have your noze rubed [*sic*] in your booboos?"

Page 3, Zodiac November 9, 1969 Mailing
"Must print in paper"

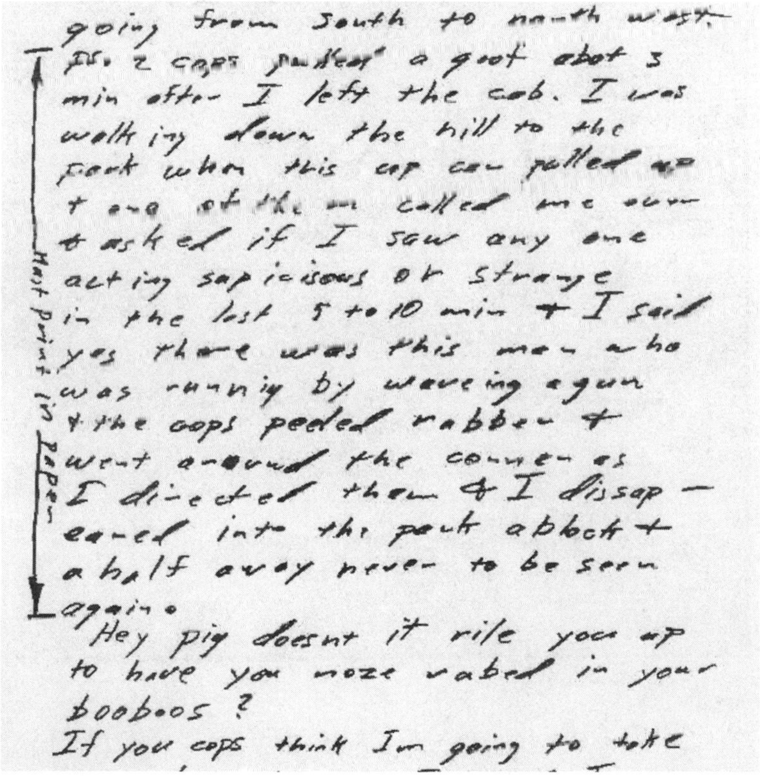

going from South to north west.
ps. 2 cops pulled a goof abot 3
min after I left the cab. I was
walking down the hill to the
park when this cop car pulled up
& one of them called me over
& asked if I saw any one
acting supicisous or strange
in the last 5 to 10 min & I said
yes there was this man who
was running by waveing a gun
& the cops peeled rubber &
went around the corner as
I directed them & I dissap-
eared into the park a block &
a half away never to be seen
again.
Hey pig doesnt it rile you up
to have you noze rubed in your
booboos?
If you cops think I'm going to take

Must Print in Paper

Fig. 3.0

November 12, 1969: On the very same day as the above Zodiac letter appears in the newspaper, Officer Donald Fouke writes a memorandum to Inspectors Toschi and Armstrong.

Here is an actual copy of the November 12, 1969, Fouke memorandum, which had been kept secret for thirty-three years until revealed and published in author Robert Graysmith's second book, *Zodiac Unmasked*, in 2002.

Original Fouke Memo, November 12, 1969

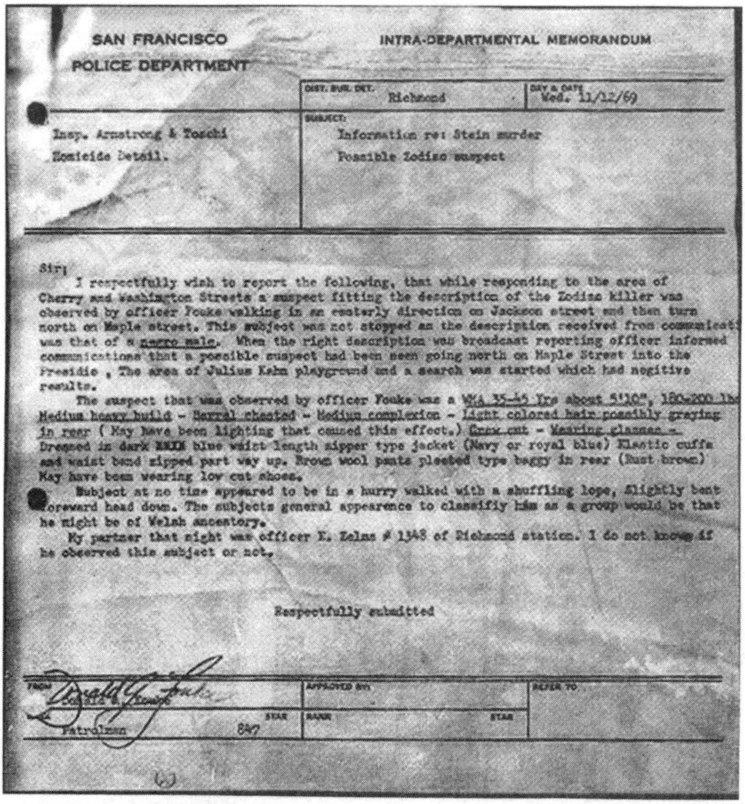

SAN FRANCISCO POLICE DEPARTMENT — INTRA-DEPARTMENTAL MEMORANDUM

DIST. BUR. DET.: Richmond — DAY & DATE: Wed. 11/12/69

Insp. Armstrong & Toschi
Homicide Detail.

SUBJECT: Information re: Stein murder
Possible Zodiac suspect

Sir;

I respectfully wish to report the following, that while responding to the area of Cherry and Washington Streets a suspect fitting the description of the Zodiac killer was observed by officer Fouke walking in an easterly direction on Jackson street and then turn north on Maple street. This subject was not stopped as the description received from communicati[ons] was that of a negro male. When the right description was broadcast reporting officer informed communications that a possible suspect had been seen going north on Maple Street into the Presidio, The area of Julius Kahn playground and a search was started which had negitive results.

The suspect that was observed by officer Fouke was a WMA 35-45 Yrs about 5'10", 180-200 lbs Medium heavy build - Barrel chested - Medium complexion - Light colored hair possibly graying in rear (May have been lighting that caused this effect.) Crew cut - Wearing glasses - Dressed in dark XXXX blue waist length zipper type jacket (Navy or royal blue) Elastic cuffs and waist band zipped part way up. Brown wool pants pleated type baggy in rear (Rust brown) May have been wearing low cut shoes.

Subject at no time appeared to be in a hurry walked with a shuffling lope, Slightly bent foreward head down. The subjects general appearence to classifiy him as a group would be that he might be of Welsh ancestory.

My partner that night was officer E. Zelms # 1348 of Richmond station. I do not know if he observed this subject or not.

Respectfully submitted

FROM: Donald A. Fouke
Patrolman — STAR 847

APPROVED BY: — REFER TO:

Fig. 3.1

In follow-up questioning and in television interviews through the years, Officer Fouke made it clear that "at no time did he and his partner, Officer Eric Zelms, ever stop and speak with the suspect."

Fouke, to this day, maintains that he was driving and only glanced over at the man on the sidewalk as he slowed down slightly. Fouke estimates it was "maybe a five- to ten-second look."

In one television interview, Officer Fouke was asked whether the man's age fit the robber's description (thirty-five to forty-five years old). He said "it was more to the high-end of that range."

I find several statements in the original Fouke Memo troubling. Let's examine them together:

1. The facts as reported in his memo instantly catapult Fouke into the most important Zodiac witness on record. As a veteran officer, he is a professional and most reliable witness, yet to my knowledge, there exists no public mention of Officer Fouke seeing and obtaining this extremely detailed Zodiac description back in 1969. Why not?

2. Fouke's description is amazingly detailed. How is this possible, considering it was dark (10:00 p.m.) that he (driver, not passenger) could obtain such a thorough description from just a ten-second drive by?

3. Fouke writes, "The subject's general appearance, to classifiy [*sic*] him as a group, might be of Welsh ancestry." To my mind, Welsh ancestry might be determined or suspected from hearing an individual speak (think Richard Burton or Anthony "Hannibal Lecter" Hopkins) but from a passing glance in the night? Hard to fathom.[7]

---

7   Were one to hear George Hodel speak for the first time, they very likely might think he was Welsh. His voice was one of his most distinctive characteristics. He possessed a cultured, meticulous speech, which he took full advantage of, and it served him well as a young radio announcer.

4. The timing of the memo is highly suspect. Written and dated on the very same day the *San Francisco Chronicle* printed Zodiac's claim that he was stopped by two uniform cops and cleverly sent them on a wild-goose chase, allowing him to escape. Why would Zodiac not simply say, "They drove right past me"? By writing his memo on the same day the public is informed of "the stop," it sounds like Fouke is giving Detectives Toschi and Armstrong a formal, written rebuttal to that very day's major news article. ("No, we didn't stop him, just drove by him.")

5. Lastly, and to my mind, the most incredible statement in the entire memo is: "My partner that night was officer E. Zelms #1348 of Richmond Station. I do not know if he observed this subject or not."

How is it possible that, after discovering you might have just seen and are able to provide a detailed description of a suspected killer, and offering follow-up details and participating in a composite sketch (supposedly with your partner), you don't know what your partner saw?

You have become the most important witness in the search for Zodiac, and a month later, you haven't even spoken to your partner about what he saw in what will become the most important event in your entire police career?

Below is a second diagram of the Fouke Memo in which I have highlighted some of the aforementioned unanswered questions.

SFPD Officer Donald Fouke Memo

Insp. Armstrong & Toschi Homicide Detail

Wed. 11/12/69

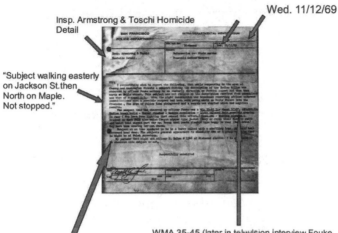

"Subject walking easterly on Jackson St.then North on Maple. Not stopped."

"My partner that night was officer E. Zelms #1348 of Richmond station. I do not know if he observed this subject or not."

WMA 35-45 (later in television interview Fouke states "age closer to high-end--45 yrs.") 5-10", 180-200, Medium heavybuild- Barrel chested- Medium complexion- Light colored hair possibly graying in rear (May have been lighting that caused this effect.) Crew cut- Wearing glasses. Dark blue waist length zipper type jacket, Navy or royal blue. Elastic cuffs and waist band zipped part way up. Brown wool pants pleated type baggy in rear (Rust brown) May have worn low cut shoes. The subjects general appearance to classifiy [sic] him as a group, might be of Welsh ancestry.

Fig. 3.2

In the decades after Zodiac's crimes, new information has come out, answering many, if not all, of the questions I raised.

Multiple sources directly contradict Officer Fouke's written statement on November 12, 1969. I won't recount all of them, but will present the two that I consider most important.

If these new interviews are to be believed, then they establish, without doubt, that officer Donald Fouke lied to his superiors and that Zodiac, as he claimed in his November 12, 1969 letter, was telling the truth: that he spoke to officers

Fouke and Zelms "face-to-face." If true, then the accuracy of Fouke's detailed description, along with his "Welsh ancestry" statement, becomes much more understandable.

Robert Graysmith/Inspector Toschi Interview

AUTHOR AND EX-*SAN FRANCISCO* Chronicle cartoonist Robert Graysmith was the first to publish the Fouke Memo in its entirety in his second Zodiac book, *Zodiac Unmasked.*

In that book, he quotes SFPD Lead Inspector Dave Toschi's seeming confirmation that Fouke and Zelms did stop and talk to Zodiac and that detectives "did everything we could to keep it quiet so they [Fouke and Zelms] wouldn't be hurt by the police commission or embarrassed."

According to Robert Graysmith's *Zodiac Unmasked*:

> ..."Zodiac," [Fouke] said to a television producer, was "walking toward us at an average pace, turned when he saw us, and walked into a private residence [on Jackson Street]."
>
> Toschi disagreed. "Zodiac disappeared," he said. "'Into the brush, somewhere in the park,' is what Fouke said, not into a residence, not whatsoever. Fouke clocked the encounter at no more than five to ten seconds. **We felt that Zelms and Fouke had stopped Zodiac, and did everything we could to keep it quiet so they wouldn't be hurt by the police commission or embarrassed.**[8] I remember I talked to Don [Fouke] on the side. He was all teary-eyed. 'Jesus Christ, Dave, my God, it was the guy,' he said. I said, 'Yeah, it was, Don, but he could've killed you so easy. If you had gotten out of your vehicle, unassuming, he could have blown you and Eric [Zelms] away. You gotta consider that.' **We had them do a sketch,**[9] sent our sketch artist out there, and got the composite."[10]

---

8   Author's note: Emphasis mine
9   Author's note: Emphasis mine
10   Berkley Publishing Group, 2002. Page 23.

Dr. Howard Davis/Diane Zelms Interview

DR. HOWARD DAVIS HOLDS a Ph.D. in Philosophy and has been researching Zodiac for decades. He is the author of the 1997 book *The Zodiac/Manson Connections* and is a regular contributor to Tom Voigt's zodiackiller.com website, which I have previously referred to as "Zodiac Central."

Rookie Officer Eric Zelms was slain in the line of duty, just eleven weeks after he and his partner Officer Fouke responded to the Paul Stine murder. (See summary to follow.)

Nearly ten years ago, in August, 2005, Dr. Davis conducted a remarkable interview with the fallen officer's widow, Diana Zelms. Dr. Davis has graciously allowed me to reproduce that interview in full. Here it is:

> ...Diane said that Eric closely followed the Stine murder on television. He told her that when he and Fouke saw a WMA they quickly decided to question him. He said that they spoke to this man 'face-to-face!' The man was polite, calm, and answered all of their questions. There was nothing suspicious about him. They then quickly left to continue their search for a BMA as had been broadcast in the APB.
>
> Officer Zelms confessed to his wife that when they realized the man they had talked to was the Zodiac they absolutely did not know what to say or do. They understood what the full ramifications would be if it became known that San Francisco police officers had confronted but failed to capture the Zodiac Killer! She was told in all confidence that Fouke made the final decision to say they only drove by a WMA, and he was not stopped because they were looking for a BMA.
>
> It would seem that Fouke knew that he and Zelms had spoken to Zodiac 'face-to-face' and he wanted to protect a rookie officer. It would be quite unthinkable that the senior officer did not know if his partner had

seen the WMA, as Fouke wrote in his memo and has said in some interviews. Zelms admitted to his wife in private that he cooperated with Fouke because he didn't want to get a negative report and possibly lose his job in light of the heavy criticism from some quarters about the failure of the SFPD to capture the Zodiac; if what had happened were to get out the effects would have been devastating.

Retired detective Dave Toschi is quoted as saying to Graysmith that they (SFPD) "felt that Zelms and Fouke had stopped Zodiac and did everything we could to keep it quiet so they wouldn't be hurt by the police commission or embarrassed." Toschi said that Fouke said, in tears, "it was the guy" and that they had both officers "do a sketch."

...

Zelms also mentioned to his wife that Zodiac appeared quite ordinary in size and stature. He was not physically imposing enough to stand out in any way.

Diane said that privately her husband was deeply distressed about the entire matter. He carried the Zodiac composite with him, which was a good resemblance of the man he spoke to, in case he ever saw him again. He admitted to her that when he realized he had spoken to the Zodiac Killer "face-to-face" he became filled with fear. He realized then how close he had come to death."

Howard Davis adds:

Young Eric Zelms did not know that the grim reaper was less than three months away. He was shot three times at around one a.m. on New Year's Day 1970 and died a hero leaving a young widow, an infant son, and family to grieve his passing.[11]

Clearly, someone is lying as to what happened between Zodiac and Officers Fouke and Zelms on the night of October 11, 1969.

11   Interview of Diane Zelms (Widow of Officer Eric Zelms). Interviewed by Dr. Howard A. Davis. Interview Date: August 2005. web.archive.org/web/20091104130217/http://thezodiacmansonconnection.com/index.htm

In 2008, Dr. Davis posted the following email from Diana Zelms on his website.[12]

From: Diana Zelms
Sent: Friday, May 16, 2008 13:01
To: author@thezodiacmansonconnection.com
Subject: Zodiac Killer

Dear Howard

    I want to confirm that you and I did speak on the phone several times concerning the Zodiac Killer and that what I told you that my husband Eric Zelms told me was true. After we spoke, I saw the new movie that came out and read the two books that are out and was very upset about the lies told in the books and how they turned things around to extract the truth. For the record I want to say that everything I told you was true.

        Sincerely,
        Diana Zelms

Fig. 3.3

On the one hand, we have the statements of Zodiac, Lead Homicide Inspector Dave Toschi, and the widow, Diane Zelms, all of whom confirm there was a "face-to-face" conversation.

On the other, we have Officer Fouke, a respected veteran uniformed officer, who maintains to this day "there was no stop, just a five- to ten-second drive-by."

I leave it to you the reader to decide for yourself just exactly who is lying.

SFPD Officer Eric Zelms—Rest In Peace

FOR THOSE OF YOU who have read my previous writings, you are likely familiar with one of my favorite sayings, "Synchronicity happens!"

Today is January 1, 2015. I am close to sending my manuscript to my editor. These are the last words I will be writing before sending my manuscript to my editor.

---

12   web.archive.org/web/20091104130217/http://thezodiacmansonconnection.com/index.htm

What I was unaware of until last night was the fact that today is the forty-fifth anniversary date of the senseless murder of San Francisco Police Officer Eric Zelms.

The shooting was described in a feature article in the June 1970, Official Detective Stories *magazine:*

New Year's Eve Slaying Tragedy in San Francisco . . .

DRAGNET FOR THE KILLERS OF A HERO ROOKIE COP

by BRYAN WILLIAMS
Special Investigator for OFFICIAL DETECTIVE STORIES

Only 22, Eric Zelms was one of the new breed of policemen—educated, eager, and utterly dedicated to a career in law enforcement. But a trigger-happy punk, not content with wounding the young officer, fired a coup de grace shot which ended that career a mere 349 days after it began . . .

Fig. 3.4

The 1970 magazine article, written by Bryan Williams six months after the actual crime, gives all the details the tragic story. Here is an overview:

Eric Zelms was just twenty-two years old. In the early morning hours of January 1, 1970, he was just two weeks short of completing his first year on the job.

He was married to Diane, age nineteen, and had an infant son.

Zelms and his partner, Officer Richard Bodisco, age twenty-five and a three-year veteran, normally worked out of the Richmond Station, but because it was New Year's Eve they were assigned to San Francisco's Tenderloin District.

Both officers, in uniform, decided to have dinner at one of San Francisco's favorite restaurants, Oreste's, located at the bottom of Nob Hill.

They entered the restaurant, and Officer Bodisco walked to the back to use the restroom, while Zelms waited for him near the maître d' stand.

A minute later, a witness came running into the restaurant and informed Zelms there was "a man breaking into the shop next door."

Zelms took off out the door. Within moments his partner exited the restroom and was looking for Zelms when he heard two nearby gunshots. Somebody ran into the restaurant yelling, "A cop's been shot."

Officer Bodisco ran next door and found his partner Zelms on the ground. He saw two young men running down the slope of Jones Street, heading for Market Street.

Bodisco drew his revolver, but was unable to fire at the fleeing suspects because of innocent citizens on the sidewalk, so he yelled out for the two men to "halt" and fired two shots into the air.

The suspects jumped aboard a passing streetcar and escaped.

Bodisco quickly talked to the witnesses who saw the shooting and put out an immediate description of "two young, male blacks, wearing dark clothing."

Responding officers captured both men in separate arrests. Zelms' shooter, later identified as Vincent Fredericks, age twenty-nine, from Los Angeles, engaged a second patrol unit (SFPD officers Gallager and Sullivan) in an exchange of gunfire and was wounded before being taken into custody.

Frederick's accomplice, Michael Webster, age twenty, was arrested after being seen by officers a short distance from the shooting, pretending to wait for a bus.

In separate statements to the press, both men admitted being involved. But Fredericks said "it was all an accident" when he struggled with the officer, and Webster told reporters "it was all a bad dream," and he ran away, frightened.

I quote from Bryan Williams' 1970 article in *Official Detective Stories* magazine:

> *...On January 6, 1970, five days after the tragedy on Jones Street, a solemn funeral was held for Patrolman Eric Zelms. The mourners included the Mayor of San Francisco and every prominent city official. The funeral chapel was filled to overflowing and officers from more than a dozen northern California police departments were there to pay last respects to the heroic officer.*
>
> *Six days later, a stonecutter painstakingly inscribed the name of Eric Zelms in the marble of the foyer of the San Francisco Hall of Justice. The name of Eric Zelms was the seventy-fifth to be placed on this honor roll of police officers who gave up their lives in the line of duty.*
>
> *...*
>
> *The grand jury next returned an indictment formally charging Vincent Fredericks and Michael Webster with the murder of Eric Zelms, plus charges of assaulting police officers.*
>
> *The murder charge is a capital offense and could result in the death penalty at the San Quentin Prison gas chamber."*

According to the Officer Down Memorial Page, the two defendants were tried and convicted of the murder of Officer Zelms and both received a prison sentence of "eight to ten years."[13]

 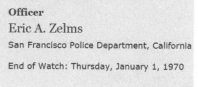

Officer
Eric A. Zelms
San Francisco Police Department, California
End of Watch: Thursday, January 1, 1970

Fig. 3.5

Hero's burial was accorded Ptl. Zelms (insert), fatally shot while trying to prevent burglary. San Francisco police line up (below) for his funeral march.

Fig. 3.6

My belated condolences to Diane Zelms and all and any surviving Zelms family members. Thank you Eric Zelms for giving the ultimate service and sacrifice to your city.

May you rest in peace.

13   www.odmp.org/officer/14665-officer-eric-a-zelms

CHAPTER 4

The *Chronicle* Connection[14]

BAY AREA INVESTIGATORS HAVE often speculated that Zodiac seemed to have a special relationship with the *San Francisco Chronicle*. According to the book *Great Crimes of San Francisco*, "Zodiac began his publicity campaign with several Bay Area papers, but he soon began to concentrate on one: the *San Francisco Chronicle*."

Many experts suspect that Zodiac had a direct, personal connection to the newspaper. Perhaps he was related to someone who worked at the *Chronicle* or had once been an employee himself.

Zodiac's Halloween card of October 22, 1970 (Letter #17) was addressed directly to "Paul Averly, *San Francisco Chronicle*." In his final letter (#25, dated April 24, 1978), Zodiac took the time to acknowledge Herb Caen, one of San Francisco's most beloved columnists, as though they were old friends. He wrote:

> *This is the Zodiac speaking, I am back with you. Tell herb caen [sic], I am here. I have always been here. That city pig toschi [sic] is good but I am bu [sic] smarter and better he will get tired then leave me alone. I am waiting for a good movie about me. who will play me. I am now in control of all things.*
>
> *—yours truly*

On the surface, Zodiac's message can be taken as just another taunt to San Franciscans, reminding them that he's a local boy and still on the prowl. But the person who carefully composed these letters and risked being discovered isn't someone who says things casually. Everything that issues from his complex, enigmatic, psychotic mind alludes to a deeper meaning as he plays his dangerous double game—relying on his superior intellect to outsmart the police while at the same time feeding his massive ego that demands that he leave subtle clues to his identity.[15]

In the earlier biographical summary of my father's life, I mentioned his experiences as a young journalist, first in Los Angeles as a crime reporter for the *Los Angeles Record*, then later, while he was living and attending medical school in San Francisco. It was during this time that he was employed as a columnist for the *San Francisco Chronicle*.

San Francisco Chronicle Columnists George and Emilia Hodel with Son, Duncan, Circa 1932

Fig. 4.0

---

15   In 1978, several months after the receipt of this letter, a controversy arose when it was learned that Inspector Toschi had anonymously written himself some "fan mail" letters and sent them to a friend at the *San Francisco Chronicle*. This caused some to wonder if the "I am back" letter was genuine. Toschi adamantly denied writing the Zodiac letter and was backed by command staff on the SFPD. On July 16, 1978 an article appeared in *The New York Times* headlined, "Police Officials on Coast Deny Insp. Forged Zodiac Letters." I quote in part from that article, "Police officials have emphatically denied reports that Insp. Dave Toschi, who has investigated the Zodiac Killer case for nine years, ever was suspected of forging the latest letters attributed to the murder.... Mr. Toschi was reassigned from homicide to the pawn shop detail Monday after admitting that he used fake names to write self-flattering fan mail to a former *San Francisco Chronicle* columnist."

Beginning on Valentine's Day, February 14, 1932, George and (his first wife) Emilia Hodel wrote a weekly Sunday column in the *San Francisco Chronicle* titled "Abroad In San Francisco." The following insert printed next to their first co-bylined article, "Little Italy, Like Naples, Leans Over Azure Bay; Breath of Mediterranean," shows how George and Emilia Hodel were introduced to San Franciscans back in 1932:

> *Editor's note—This series of articles, by George and Emilia Hodel, deals with the foreign colonies of San Francisco. The various foreign quarters—Chinatown, the Latin Quarter, Little Greece, and the rest are veritable cities within a city. There are more than twenty of them, with a combined population of over 190,000. Each Sunday you will explore, with the Hodels, one or another of these colonies.*
>
> *The foreign populations of San Francisco have merged their interests inseparably with those of all San Francisco. In many respects life in the "colonies" is indistinguishable from that of the entire American scene. Nevertheless, each group has brought over with it its old-world heritage—customs, festivals, philosophies, foods.*
>
> *The old ways have in many cases been carefully preserved, and each now lends its special color to the life of San Francisco.*

Each subsequent Sunday, George and Emilia described the sights, sounds, customs, and tastes of another ethnic enclave within the city. These included Italy, Yugoslavia, Portugal, Spain, Fisherman's Wharf, Greece, the Danes, Norway, Sweden, Russia, Japan, Germany, Chinatown, and France. Accompanying the articles were photographs showing traditional dress and interviews by George Hodel featuring a prominent citizen.

Exhibit 81a

Fig. 4.1

Exhibit 81b is a collage of the series of articles.

Fig. 4.2

After reading the "Abroad in San Francisco" series of articles, one comes away with two distinct impressions of George Hodel. One, he was a man who loved things that were different and exotic. Two, he was an acute observer who saw everything and remembered every detail.

George Hodel left the *Chronicle* in 1932, after writing some fourteen articles over a five-month period. Herb Caen, some nine years younger than George, didn't begin writing for the newspaper until 1938.

Herb Caen went on to become the *Chronicle*'s greatest journalist and wrote about the city he loved for almost sixty years. While my father encouraged San Franciscans to explore the cultural diversity of their own city, Caen spoke to them much more directly. His message: Let's laugh at ourselves and the vagaries of our time and in the process learn to accept one another in our splendid diversity.

While Herb Caen was likely completely unaware of George Hodel, I suspect George followed Caen's career with interest. Given the enormity of his ego, he probably considered himself to be Caen's predecessor. As he read Caen's column, he probably thought to himself, "I've been there and done that, said that before you."

In his cryptic message to Caen, the author adopts a familiar tone. It no longer sounds like the Zodiac pontificating, but former *San Francisco Chronicle* columnist George Hodel talking to a colleague, as he says:

> *I am back with you. Tell herb caen, I am here. I have always been here.*

(END OF CHAPTER 16 EXCERPT)

Zodiac's "I Am Back" Letter

Mailed to San Francisco Chronicle, *April 24, 1978*

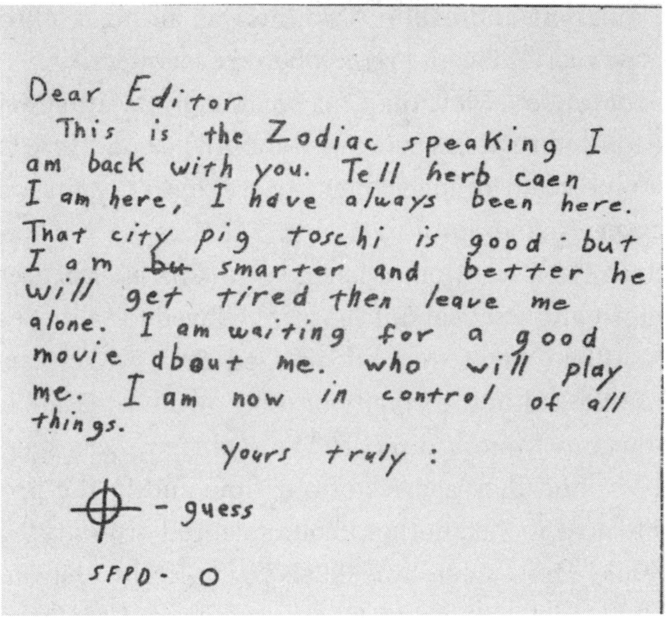

Dear Editor
This is the Zodiac speaking I
am back with you. Tell herb caen
I am here, I have always been here.
That city pig toschi is good · but
I am ~~but~~ smarter and better he
will get tired then leave me
alone. I am waiting for a good
movie about me. who will play
me. I am now in control of all
things.
        Yours truly :
    ⊕ - guess

    SFPD - O

Fig. 4.3

THIRTY-FIVE YEARS LATER, DISAGREEMENT prevails within the Zodiac law enforcement community as to whether the "I am back" letter was actually written by Zodiac.

Some believe it may have been a forgery, and a few have gone as far as to suggest that SFPD homicide detective David Toschi, who remained in charge of the Zodiac investigation in 1978, may have written the letter to the *San Francisco Chronicle* "for personal reasons."

Based on these rumors, Inspector Toschi remained under a cloud for some time, was transferred out of, then back into, the homicide detail.

I have seen no evidence to substantiate that Inspector Toschi forged the letter. To my knowledge, his department has never come out and accused him of the act. The suggestions and innuendo could have come from politically-motivated individuals within the police department.

Several document experts have separately included and excluded Zodiac as being the author of the "I am back" letter. Sherwood Morrill of California Identification and Investigation Bureau (CII) is Zodiac's leading document expert and SFPD's "go-to guy on Zodiac handwriting." He believes the 1978 letter was legitimate and "was written by Zodiac."

I am in total agreement with Morrill and absent any hard evidence to the contrary, will treat it (and several other disputed letters) as being legitimate Zodiac documents.

The SFPD Inspector Toschi Fiasco

SFPD Inspector Dave Toschi 1976

Fig. 4.4

Working a high-profile murder case can be hazardous to one's health and, more importantly, to one's reputation. Just ask former SFPD Inspector Dave Toschi.

On October 11, 1969, Toschi and his partner, Bill Armstrong, were the "on-call" homicide detectives and happened to catch what they thought was a fairly routine crime—an armed robbery of a taxi with shots fired. The victim, taxi driver Paul Stine, died from a gunshot wound to the head, which made it a robbery/murder, a less common crime, as most cabbies handed over the twenty dollars and kept their lives.

In all likelihood, Stine's murder would have remained just another cold case—worked for a month or two, no leads, then filed and forgotten among the hundreds of other unsolved murders from the streets of San Francisco in the sixties.

But that was not to be. The killer himself would ensure that he would be on page one of the *San Francisco Chronicle* for decades to come.

The following article, an excellent summary of the Toschi Fiasco by staff reporter David Johnston, appeared in the *Los Angeles Times* on July 12, 1978:

Los Angeles Times

LARGEST CIRCULATION IN THE WEST, 1,034,329 DAILY, 1,332,873 SUNDAY

ᵗS—PART ONE   128 PAGES   WEDNESDAY MORNING, JULY 12, 1978   CC †

EXCITED BY SEEING NAME IN S.F. SERIAL
Zodiac Officer Demoted Over Letters

Inspector David R. Toschi pictured in 1976

Detective Demoted for Writing Letters

Fig. 4.5

Excited by Seeing Name in San Francisco Serial

Zodiac Officer Demoted Over Letters

By David Johnston
Times Staff Writer

SAN FRANCISCO—The crack homicide detective who alone for nine years has pursued the mysterious Zodiac Killer has been demoted from the homicide division to the pawn shop squad for writing letters over fictitious signatures to a newspaper seeking favorable comment about himself.

Inspector David R. Toschi readily admitted writing the letters to Armistead Maupin, whose fictional newspaper serial, "Tales of the City," was a popular feature in the San Francisco Chronicle in 1976-77.

However, Toschi denied Maupin's suggestion that he also wrote an April 24 letter from the Zodiac, the first communication in four years from the mystery man suspected of six random shootings in 1969-70.

Police Chief Charles R. Gain said he demoted Toschi for writing the letters to Maupin. Gain said the authenticity of the latest Zodiac letter is now in question. He would not comment on whether police think Toschi wrote it but said there is no evidence that he did.

Other sources, however, confirmed an "investigation into whether Toschi wrote the latest Zodiac letter is under way."

"It was a very foolish thing to do," Toschi said of the letters to Maupin. "I am ashamed of it."

Toschi said he wrote the letters to Maupin, using a fictitious name, only because he was excited to see his name in the serial and wanted it to continue.

Maupin, in a prepared statement, said he considered the letters "harmless" and sent them to the police only after he noticed "certain similarities between the tone of the letters (to him) and the tone of the latest Zodiac letter."

Maupin, who brought the matter to the police eighteen months after he got the letters, called a press conference Tuesday.

But he refused to answer any questions and said that a story about Toschi and the letters will appear in New West magazine's issue. He denied the episode was a publicity stunt.

Asked by reporters if he was the Zodiac, Toschi dismissed the idea as absurd. Toschi, who turned forty-seven Tuesday, has been a policeman here for twenty-five years and a homicide investigator for eighteen years. Usually, a department spokesman said, homicide detectives work in pairs, but Toschi worked alone on the Zodiac case.

The Zodiac was the name the gunman gave himself in a series of cryptic letters, some written in code, that he sent to the Chronicle and two other newspapers when he was terrorizing the Bay Area.

Zodiac claimed in one letter to have killed ten persons.

The April 24 letter to the Chronicle said Zodiac is "back with you. Tell Herb Caen [the Chronicle columnist] I am here. I have always been here. That city pig Toschi is good, but I am smarter and better...he will get tired then leave me alone. I am waiting for a good movie about me. Who will play me. I am now in control of all things," the letter continued.

Toschi had once said he would eventually catch Zodiac because he was smarter than the killer.

Sherwood Morrill, retired chief of the questioned documents section of the California Bureau of Criminal Identification, who examined all the Zodiac letters, said he is certain the April 24 letter was from "the real Zodiac."

Morrill added that *"if Toschi wrote the last one, he's the Zodiac—he wrote them all."*

But Morrill said he thought, instead, that Toschi was being framed.

"My suspicion is that somebody is after Toschi," Morrill said.

Robert Prouty, who now heads the questioned documents section, said he believes the April 24 letter was written by someone other than the real Zodiac.

In separate reportage, San Francisco Police Chief Charles Gain showed no objectivity when he publicly described his veteran detective, Dave Toschi, as:

> *a disturbed personality because of his craving for publicity that results in a lack of objectivity on the part of the investigator.*

San Francisco Chronicle columnist Herb Caen responded immediately to Chief Gain's comment, leading off his regular column with the following advice to the Chief:

> *Police Chief Gain should stand in a corner (preferably the intersection of Third and Market) for saying that "Inspector Dave Toschi is a 'disturbed personality'" because he likes publicity. That is merely a human frailty Chiefie. You know. Like wearing a toupee...*

Herb Caen Article Defending Inspector Toschi July 20, 1978

San Francisco Chronicle July 20, 1978

HERB CAEN

Something Like This

POLICE CHIEF Gain should stand in a corner (preferably the intersection of Third and Market) for saying that Inspector Dave Toschi is "a disturbed personality" because he likes publicity. That is merely a human frailty, Chiefie. You know. Like wearing a toupee . . . Don't invite to your next initiative: Howard Jarvis and Paul Gann. The latter reportedly has Had It Up To Here with Howard's hankering for the spotlight, and his "lack of seriousness" in seeing that the spirit of Prop. 13 is carried out . . . I suppose you saw Jerry Jarvis (Brown and Howard) on the front pages yesterday, urging landlords to lower their rents. Hellzbellz, a lot of the tenants I keep hearing from would settle simply for not getting an increase. Rents have been raised all over the place since Election Day. On the landlords' side, how can they reduce rents till they find out how much their property tax is being cut? Fair's feh . . . Justlikethat, Jerry Brown's reelection campaign is $75,000 richer. That's the amount Ann and Gordon Getty raised by means of a banquet in their storybook mansion in Presidio Heights Monday night (150 people paid $500 each).

★   ★   ★

Fig. 4.6

Herb Caen was not the only notable San Franciscan coming to Toschi's defense.

Feinstein Says Toschi's Being 'Crucified'

DIANNE FEINSTEIN, THEN-PRESIDENT OF the San Francisco Board of Supervisors, declared in a July 15, 1978, *Chronicle* article, "It's appalling. Toschi is being crucified." She went on to say that Toschi's removal from the Homicide Division was "outrageous police personnel policy" and he "was being unjustly crucified by the department, without substantiation in a way that I have never seen another case handled."

Ms. Feinstein was elected mayor of San Francisco the following year and served two terms. In 1992 she was elected as a US Senator from California and remains in that position to this day.

Serial Novelist Armistead Maupin—"Tales of the City," New West Magazine Expose—A Toschi Takedown

Observe due measure, for right timing is in all things the most important factor.
– Hesiod, Greek didactic poet (~800 BC)

I TOTALLY AGREE WITH Hes. "Timing is everything." Especially when it comes to the 1978 Fall of the House of Toschi.

In 1976, novelist Armistead Maupin's "Tales of the City" was published as a fictional serial, which ran in the *San Francisco Chronicle*. (Due to their popularity, the stories were later published as separate novels and adapted for television.)

As research for one of his fictional characters, Maupin wanted to meet with a real-life homicide detective and get a sense and understanding of how a big-city detective acted and operated.

Maupin contacted *Chronicle* crime reporter Bob Popp, who hooked him up with one of San Francisco's most famous— Inspector Dave Toschi. By then, Toschi was into his seventh year of tracking the infamous serial killer known as Zodiac.

Here is how Maupin describes his first meeting with the Inspector back in 1976, excerpted from the July 31, 1978 *New West* magazine article, "Tales of the Zodiac Letters," page 51:

> *My first contact with Inspector Dave Toschi was in late summer, 1976, when I was still writing a fictional serial called "Tales of the City" in the* San Francisco Chronicle. *I had decided to juice it up with a murder-mystery sub-plot, a suspense element that would ensure daily readership.*
>
> *...*
>
> *Dave Toschi...turned out to be nothing less than a reporter's dream: He was personable, talkative and colorful. His dialogue, far from being pedantic or bureaucratic, seemed to come straight from a B-grade detective movie.*
>
> *...*
>
> *When I left the Hall of Justice that afternoon I was armed with more cops-and-robbers color than I had bargained for. Not only had Toschi proudly shown me his special upside-down Colt Cobra holster (Steve McQueen supposedly saw it and had it copied for Bullitt), but he had readily granted me permission to feature him as a real-name character in "Tales of the City." He was to make several "guest appearances" as the friend and mentor of my fictitious detective, Inspector Henry Tandy. (Tandy, like Toschi, was hot on the trail of his own murderer, a fiend named Tinkerbell, who sprinkled his victims with blue glitter.)*

In the *New West* magazine article, Maupin informs us that, in 1976 after receiving three separate "fan mail" letters from women praising not his storytelling, but rather, Inspector Toschi's appearance, he became suspicious and went on to determine that all three letters had been written on the same typewriter, and in his mind, by one person: Inspector Toschi.

From "Tales of the Zodiac Letters," page 53:

> *...Both Zodiac and his official pursuer used the same device for the promotion of their careers—cornball letters to the* Chronicle.
>
> *So I phased Toschi out of "Tales of the City"—that is, until the last episode of Book One on New Year's Eve, 1976, when (quite perversely, I admit) I brought him back to nab the mythical Inspector Tandy in the act of confessing to the Tinkerbell crimes. Tandy, it evolved, had committed the murders himself in order to become the superstar of the SFPD. "You're nothing as a cop in this town," he bellowed, "if your crime doesn't hit it big with the media."*

It was not until April 26, 1978, (nearly a year and a half later) with the publication of the "I am back" Zodiac letter and a friend reading the letter to Maupin over morning coffee that the novelist informs us he had his epiphany:

From "Tales of the Zodiac Letters," page 53:

> *...It was one of those moments when clocks seem to stop ticking.*
>
> *It's inaccurate to say that the letter rang a bell. A veritable carillon was clanging in my head. Principally— and most blatantly—there was the plug for Toschi: that city pig Toschi is good. Then there was the corny Bogartesque, tough-cop-versus-tough-crook phraseology, as well as the reference to* Chronicle *columnist Herb Caen and the ultimate bid for movie stardom.*

As an arson investigator might say, this is the point of origin of the grass-fire that will burn out of control for the next three months. The accelerant? A spark from the mind of a novelist who sees and believes that what he has written as fiction may have come true.

Author Maupin immediately reports his suspicions to both the *San Francisco Chronicle* and to command officers on the SFPD. He further provides his proof, in the form of the "fan letters" written nearly two years prior.

What did Maupin suspect?[16]

1. Inspector Toschi wrote (forged) three "fan mail" letters and sent them to the *Chronicle*, praising himself and signing fictitious names.

2. Inspector Toschi may have forged the Zodiac "I am back" letter, ostensibly written and mailed to the *Chronicle* in April 1978.

3. Inspector Toschi may have forged the Zodiac "Exorcist" letter ostensibly written and mailed to the *Chronicle* on January 30, 1974.

4. His own "Tinkerbell" sub-plot "coming to life" with the possibility that a real-life homicide detective (Toschi) might be Zodiac?

In support of point four, I quote the following reference from Maupin's *New West* magazine article of July 31, 1978. (Found on page 1 of the article, in the boxed author description.) To my ear it has a slight sprinkling of sarcasm, with a hint of "I told you so."

> *Editor's note—Armistead Maupin is the author of* Tales of the City, *to be published August 23 by Harper & Row. The Tinkerbell subplot discussed in this story was removed from his book by his editor on the grounds that it was too outlandish to be believable.*

---

16   Regarding the author Maupin, "suspect" may be too strong a word as relates to two, three, and four. However, he had to have at least considered the possibility. We do know that after Maupin reported his suspicions to SFPD's Internal Affairs, they did in fact suspect Toschi might have written the letters, as they surreptitiously collected and ordered their Questioned Document Expert to compare Toschi's handwriting samples to the known Zodiac letters. Toschi was officially eliminated as not being the author of both Zodiac letters, and the 1974 "Exorcist" letter was reconfirmed as being authentic. The "I am back" letter remains in dispute. (Top Zodiac handwriting expert Sherwood Morrill authenticated it, while others still disagree.)

The Toschi Fiasco—Bottom Lines

Here are my thoughts and takeaway on the 1978 Toschi/ Maupin exchange:

- Inspector Dave Toschi, in writing the 1976 "fan letters" in praise of himself, committed an incredibly stupid act. He knows this and has paid a high price for his actions.

- I see author Armistead Maupin's actions in the whole affair as both opportunistic and self-promoting. Though he may have been well intentioned, still, in 1976 he used Toschi's public popularity to enhance his readership, and then two years later, very publicly, threw him to the wolves. His motives in revealing the "fan letters" and then immediately soliciting and writing a large magazine article, all within a three-month period, are suspect. Especially with the *New West* magazine's front page announcement that read, "*Tales of the City* to be published August 23, by Harper & Row."

- The real damage came by way of the contamination of hard evidence in the ongoing Zodiac investigation. I hold both Toschi and Maupin to blame for this. By their actions both men put two important Zodiac letters, the 1974 "Exorcist" and the 1978 "I am back" in question. The real evidence has been tainted and made "guilty by association" with the "fan mail" letters, a completely separate act, which occurred nearly two years prior to the receipt of the 1978 Zodiac letter.

- As I indicated previously, I have no doubt and am in complete agreement with document expert Sherwood Morrill's findings that the 1978 letter was written by Zodiac.

Let's now move forward and see if we can find any additional connections between Zodiac and Herb Caen other than those I've already presented at the beginning of this chapter.

CHAPTER 5

"Tell Herb Caen I am here. I have always been here."
—Zodiac, (in a letter to San Francisco Chronicle
on April 4, 1978)

Herb Caen, Kenneth Rexroth, and George Hodel

I AM NOW FORCED to question my original 2009 observation in *Most Evil*: "While Herb Caen was likely completely unaware of George Hodel..."

New facts would suggest otherwise. It appears highly likely that Herb Caen and George Hodel knew each other at least casually through mutual San Francisco acquaintances. If they didn't have a direct link, there is, at most, no more than one degree of separation.

Let's examine the evidence.

I recently discovered a book, *Our San Francisco*, published by Diablo Press in 1964. Its beautiful photographs depict the city's people, landscapes, and seascapes of the bay. Five prominent photographers took the pictures, and five prominent San Francisco authors wrote the text. Two of those five authors were Herb Caen and Kenneth Rexroth.

While the two men may not have been bosom buddies, there most certainly would have been some interaction between the contributors.

Our San Francisco

(Diablo Press 1964, San Francisco)

Fig. 5.0
Arrows highlight Herb Caen and Kenneth Rexroth as two of the five authors for the text.

Author Bill Morgan, in his book *The BEAT Generation in San Francisco: A Literary Guidebook* (City Lights Publishers, 2003), writes:

Black Cat Café 19.
710 Montgomery

One of the earliest bohemian cafes in North Beach, the Black Cat Café opened in this building in the early thirties in the heart of the old Barbary Coast. The Black Cat was reborn as a fine French brasserie at the corner of Kearny and Broadway for a short time, but the funky original was located here in the beautiful old Canessa Park Building. Clientele of the original Black Cat were **Herb Caen**, *Truman Capote,* **Kenneth Rexroth**,[17] *Janet and Charles Richards, William Saroyan, John Steinbeck, and*

---

17 Author's note: Emphasis mine

a host of bohemians in black berets and corduroy pants. As some wag said, the place didn't attract writers with drinking problems, but drinkers with writing problems.

In the fifties, it became a gay club with drag shows and witty cross-dressing skits by Jose Sarria, whose stage name was "The Empress Norton." Ferlinghetti remembers a piano player wearing an old top hat, and a pug dog sitting on top of the upright piano. Alcoholic Beverage Control agents shut down the Black Cat for good on Halloween night, 1963. It has now been recognized as the true birthplace of Gay Pride, where gays were invited to "come out" and be themselves. This was truly revolutionary in the fifties.

Both Caen and Rexroth frequented the Black Cat Café in the thirties, so it's hard to imagine they didn't socialize with each other way back then. I'm confident we can add George Hodel to the list of those attending the Black Cat since he was very likely a friend to Kenneth Rexroth while attending medical school and working as a reporter for the *San Francisco Chronicle* during those years (1928 to 1936).

Kevin Starr, former state librarian and author of the magnificent eight-volume *California Dream* series, offers more insights into the stature of Kenneth Rexroth.

The below excerpt is from his book, *Golden Dreams: California in an Age of Abundance, 1950-1963* (Oxford University Press, 2011). In a discussion about Ginsberg and the obscenity trial for the reading of his poem, *Howl*, Starr transitions to Rexroth:

...The very genre that Howl *represented, a publicly declaimed jeremiad, was initially established by Rexroth, a longtime resident of San Francisco with extensive connections to the Provincial establishment and as such*

a civic and literary principle distinct from the Beats. Rexroth also established the genre of public performance of poetry to jazz accompaniment, most notably in his sweeping jeremiad "Thou Shalt Not Kill," a eulogy for the Welsh poet Dylan Thomas, who succumbed to alcoholism in November 1953.

From Rexroth's perspective, it was not the booze that killed Thomas, but the very same corporate capitalist military/industrial culture—led, as Rexroth put it, by the sons of bitches in Brooks Brothers suits—that had wiped out practically every major American poet of the twentieth century. "Thou Shalt Not Kill" constituted an outspoken denunciation from the Left during an era of Cold War McCarthyism and was especially effective when Rexroth read it to jazz as part of the Cellar series of poetry and jazz readings he had organized, some of them released as LPs by Fantasy Records. By combining jazz and poetry, Rexroth was emphasizing poetry as a flexible and open-ended idiom, declamatory and spontaneous in the manner of Walt Whitman and jazz, yet possessed as well of an inner logic and discipline.

The following excerpts are from "Rexroth's San Francisco Journalism," by Ken Knabb:[18]

In early 1960 the San Francisco Examiner (a Hearst newspaper) offered Kenneth Rexroth a job writing a weekly column. He accepted. By May 1961, the column had proved popular enough that he was asked to do two and sometimes even three per week.

The association was an odd one. Although Rexroth was by that time a well-known figure in the Bay Area, he was known primarily as a political and cultural radical, and even (somewhat misleadingly) as "the godfather of the Beat Generation." But he was willing to work for the Examiner as long as they gave him complete freedom *to write whatever he wanted. They did so until mid-1967, when they fired him after he wrote a particularly scathing article on the American police. He then shifted to the* San Francisco Bay Guardian *(1967-1972) and* San Francisco Magazine *(1967-1975).*

Altogether he wrote over 800 columns for these three publications. I've read them all with fascination and often with astonishment at his practical knowledge of so many facets of life. Individually, most of them are admittedly rather slight productions. But as an ensemble I think they add up to a social document and critical commentary of remarkable range, including many topics not treated in such detail elsewhere in his writings. He reviews jazz concerts, classical music, opera, films (though he usually hates them, he likes Tom Jones and loves Cacoyannis's Electra*), Chinese theater, Shakespeare, Strindberg, Beckett, and Ionesco; discusses literature, art, architecture, city planning, fishing, camping, drugs, and French versus California wines, and engages in heated polemics about civil rights, the Vietnam War, the Harlem and Watts Riots, and numerous other political issues of the day.*

Here is a short biography of Kenneth Rexroth from the *Encyclopedia of American Poetry: The Twentieth Century* (Fitzroy Dearborn Publishers, 2001) edited by Eric L. Haralson.

Born in South Bend, Indiana, 22 December 1905. Attended the Art Institute, Chicago; Art Students' League, New York; conscientious objector during World War II; Forest Service patrolman in Washington State, farm worker, factory hand, and seaman, 1920s; active in libertarian and anarchist movements, San Francisco, California, 1930s and 1940s; orderly, San Francisco County Hospital, 1939-45; painter, individual shows in Los Angeles, New York, Chicago, San Francisco, and Paris; San Francisco correspondent, The Nation, *from 1953; columnist, San Francisco Examiner, 1958-*

1968, San Francisco Magazine, *and* San Francisco Bay Guardian, *from 1968; teacher, San Francisco State College, 1964, and University of Wisconsin, Madison; part-time Lecturer, University of California, Santa Barbara, from 1968. Received Guggenheim fellowship, 1948; Shelley Memorial Award, 1958; Amy Lowell fellowship, 1958; American Academy grant, 1964; Fulbright fellowship, 1974; National Endowment for the Arts grant, 1977; member, American Academy. Died in Montecito, California, 6 June 1982.*

Kenneth Rexroth published over forty books during his lifetime.

Based on the foregoing biographical documentation, it is clear that Herb Caen and Kenneth Rexroth, both highly respected San Francisco columnists of long standing (both over forty years), living and writing about their beloved city, certainly had to have known each other, and at the least, were aquainted with each others writings.

The same can be said about Kenneth Rexroth and George Hodel. Both were true bohemians. Kindred spirits. A couple of rebels, struggling to survive during the tough Depression days of the thirties.

George was driving a Yellow Cab and working as a part-time columnist for the *San Francisco Chronicle*, as he worked his way through premed and then at the UCSF Parnassus Medical School campus, just a mile from the Presidio.

Kenneth was active in leftist causes as he wrote, painted, and attempted to rouse the rebels in the North Beach district and at the Black Cat Café. Based on his biography, it appears that Kenneth began his job as an orderly at San Francisco General Hospital within a year or two of George, a young intern, completing his residency at the same hospital.

As we are about to discover, the acquaintance of George Hodel and Kenneth Rexroth is not speculation. It is fact.

Emilia Hodel—*San Francisco News* Art/Drama Critic

IT IS MOST LIKELY that George Hodel and Rexroth met in San Francisco in the early thirties. Possibly when George and his then-wife, Emilia Hodel, were writing their column, "Abroad in San Francisco," for the *Chronicle*.

San Francisco Chronicle Columnist Emilia Hodel Circa 1932

5.1

After separating from George, Emilia would then marry Franz Bergmann, a well-known San Francisco artist and muralist.

Bergmann completed several large murals at San Francisco's 1939 Golden Gate International Exposition at Treasure Island. At the same time Bergmann was painting his mural, George Hodel was treating patients at the fairgrounds hospital.

Bergmann's completed mural became quite controversial, as local clergy complained that his depiction of Christ was "overly stern and foreboding and lacked spirituality and compassion." Other members of the committee of the Temple of Religion at the Exposition had also received complaints "that the artist had pictured Moses as being totally bald."

According to an *Oakland Tribune* article of March 7, 1939, Bergmann reluctantly climbed a tall ladder "and with his paints and brushes, with a few deft strokes, altered the nose and changed slightly the expression of the eyes, and then clambered back to the ground."

Bergmann was quoted as saying, "I do not see why my conception was challenged, but I believe that there will be no more criticism now. I think the figure still shows that Christ was primarily in my heart when I executed the work." (It is my belief that the muralist drew the line on his artistic license by refusing to add hair to his bald Moses.)

Emilia continued to write for several of the local newspapers and in the forties became the Art and Drama critic for the *San Francisco News*.

**1946 *San Francisco News* Byline Showing
Emilia Hodel as Their Art Critic**

Fig. 5.2

In April 1952, Emilia and Franz were both seriously injured in a car accident. Both would recover, and she continued writing for *The San Francisco News* and *The San Francisco News-Call Bulletin* into the sixties. Emilia Hodel's career as a San Francisco columnist spanned more than thirty years.

Full article reproduced below.

Sausalito News[19]
April 17, 1952

Four Injured in Waldo Crash.

A well-known San Francisco artist and his wife, a drama critic for a San Francisco newspaper, received serious injuries in a head-on crash on the Waldo grade last Saturday night. Two other persons also received minor injuries in the accident.

Franz Bergmann, 54, painter and ceramist, and Mrs. Bergmann, 40, who writes under the name of Emilia Hodel, were taken to Ross Hospital after their car collided head-on with a truck. Bergmann suffered four broken ribs, a compound fracture of the left leg, and possible skull fracture. Mrs. Bergmann, whose condition was reported critical, suffered deep shock, severe head cuts, and a broken kneecap. Hospital attendants said yesterday that her condition was satisfactory.

John C. Campbell, fifty-one, a Boyes Springs carpenter, who was driving the truck, and his wife were treated for minor cuts and bruises.

According to highway patrol officers, Bergmann was driving south when Campbell's truck glanced off the east bank and veered into oncoming traffic. Campbell was booked in the county jail on charges of drunk driving with bodily injury. Bail was set at one thousand dollars.

---

19   cdnc.ucr.edu/cgi-bin/cdnc?a=d&d=SN19520417 ... ---en--20--1--txt-txIN----

Sadly, Emilia Hodel-Bergmann committed suicide with an overdose of pills in July 1987, after her retirement to Daly City, just seven miles south of her beloved San Francisco.

Based on some of the statements found in the material we are about to review, the possibility exists that George could have originally met Kenneth by way of introduction from my mother, Dorothy Huston Hodel.

Prior to their marriage in 1940, both Dorothy and George were regular visitors to the popular Esalen Hot Springs in Big Sur. Esalen was also a favorite retreat of Rexroth and his Northern California friends, including Henry Miller, who lived in Big Sur.

Kenneth Rexroth, two years older than George, died in 1982. George, relocating to San Francisco in 1990, would outlive him by some seventeen years, taking his life (another overdose by pills) in 1999, at the advanced age of ninety-one.

The 1950 Secret DA Hodel/Black Dahlia Files

HODEL-BLACK DAHLIA CASE FILE NO. 30-1268

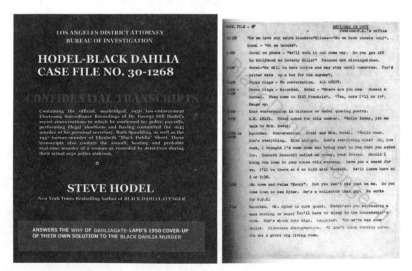

Fig. 5.3

To those not familiar with the Los Angeles District Attorney's Hodel-Black Dahlia case files, let me here provide a short introduction. The relevance to our present discussion will become apparent.

In 2014, I published the complete *Hodel-Black Dahlia Case File No. 30-1268* (Thoughtprint Press, 2014) as a separate book. The subtitle of that book reads:

Confidential Transcripts

Containing the official, unabridged, 1950 law enforcement electronic surveillance recordings of Dr. George Hill Hodel's secret conversations in which he confessed to: police payoffs, performing illegal abortions, and having committed the 1945 murder of his personal secretary, Ruth Spaulding, as well as the 1947 torture-murder of Elizabeth "Black Dahlia" Short. These transcripts also contain the assault, beating, and probable real-time murder of a woman—as recorded by detectives during their actual 1950 police stakeout.

From *Case Files* page 2:

> ...The statements and admissions made by Dr. George Hill Hodel are also verbatim taken from the pages of the DA's transcription of the secret wire recordings.
>
> The tape recordings were obtained during a joint DA/LAPD Task Force stakeout comprised of eighteen detectives. The electronic surveillance was ongoing 24/7 over a five-week period from February 15, 1950, through March 27, 1950, (1,872 man hours) and was terminated only because Dr. Hodel, after being tipped-off, then fled his residence.

*As of that date, detectives had recorded forty-one
wire spools of Dr. Hodel's personal conversations. The
DA's original summary resulted in 146 pages....*

From DA *Case Files*, Author's Preface:

Author's Preface

THE DA'S HODEL-BLACK DAHLIA TRANSCRIPTS

As you begin to read the following summaries, It is important to understand that the detective's entries that make-up these 146-pages of transcriptions are nothing more than *their personal log*. In these files, [with a few fortunate exceptions] we are only reading brief "headlines" as to what was contained in each of the separately recorded conversations.

The officers entries, made in real time, summarize only *bits and pieces* of each conversation. Consequently, we are only receiving a few sentences of a total conversation.

Unfortunately, the actual 41 wire recordings have "disappeared" from LAPD custody, and it is almost certain that the missing recordings containing the complete conversations were destroyed and will never become available.

It is also important to understand that the modern day LAPD had nothing to do with the original investigation *and had no idea that Dr. George Hill Hodel was ever named as a suspect, let alone that he had confessed on tape to committing the crimes. Today's LAPD first learned of both Dr. George Hodel's existence and these transcripts only AFTER the publication of BDA in 2003.*

Today's LAPD had no knowledge that these DA Transcripts existed. All of the evidence connecting George Hodel to the crimes as well as these transcripts was removed from LAPD files a long time ago, probably in the 1950s or 1960s.

Like, LASO Undersheriff, James Downey had told his Chief of Detectives, Gordon Bowers, when speaking about George Hodel and LAPD solving the case, "...it will never come out."

Also, keep in mind as you read these transcripts that we owe their existence solely to one honest [and very cautious] detective.

It was Lt. Frank B. Jemison who was assigned by the 1949 Grand Jury to reinvestigate the Black Dahlia and other *Lone Woman Murders*. He did it, and he solved it. When he was then ordered by his superiors to "shut it down and turn over all the files, tape recordings and transcripts to LAPD's Chief of Detectives, Thad Brown, he did that too.

But, it was Lt. Jemison's final act that changed the course of history and permitted the public to ultimately discover the truth.

Prior to turning over all the materials to LAPD, as ordered, Lt. Jemison made a copy of his complete investigation, including the Hodel transcripts, and secretly locked all of the documents away in the DA's vault, where they remained unopened and untouched for six-decades. This was his insurance. Unbeknownst to all the top brass in both the DA's office and the LAPD, *Lt. Jemison kept a second set of books.*

Here then, thanks to an honest and careful cop, are those books!

In the summary pages that follow I have reduced the original 146-page transcript down to just 15 pages for easier readability. Included in those pages are extracts of what I consider to be the most relevant statements and admissions along with my personal notations.

For historical purposes and the hardcore researchers, [and in case I have missed something that an eagle-eyed armchair detective might find] *the complete unedited Hodel- Black Dahlia Transcripts follow and are reproduced here exactly as they were copied from the original 146-pages.*

I have also included Chapter 9, *DA Investigators Jemison and Morgan* from my earlier publication, *Black Dahlia Avenger II* (Thoughtprint Press 2012) so that my readers may have a complete historical understanding of the critical role each of these two lawmen played in the original investigation, and in Morgan's case, his resurfacing and very active role in my 2002 investigation, *some fifty-years later.*

Finally, I will also include the six-page transcript Lt. Frank Jemison conducted with my mother on March 22, 1950, which was the direct cause of my father's immediate flight from the U.S. to avoid arrest and prosecution—*just five days later.*

Fig. 5.4

*Below are author-prepared photos and original DA/LAPD
document showing secret microphones installed on
February 15, 1950, by crime lab technicians.*

D.A./LAPD Electronic Surveillance of Dr. George Hodel-1950

On February 18, 1950, Dr. George Hodel became the Los Angeles D.A. investigators "prime suspect." Detectives from both the D.A. and LAPD surreptitiously entered Dr. Hodel's Hollywood mansion and installed two live microphones inside the walls; one near the master bedroom, the other in the library area. Phone lines were run from the residence to the basement of the Hollywood Police Station, just 2 miles away. Eighteen (18) detectives, assigned to separate four-hour shifts, monitored Dr. Hodel's conversations (live not phone) 24/7, for the next forty-days. On March 28, 1950, George Hodel unexpectedly fled the country, forcing the DA/LAPD surveillance teams to end their joint "stakeout."

Franklin House 5121 Franklin Ave 1950

Dr. George Hodel inside residence 1950

L.A.P.D. Hwd Police Station circa 1950

Distance of Hodel residence to Hollywood Police Sta 1.7 miles (2.4 miles driving time approximately 5 minutes.

Electronic Surveillance installed Hodel residence on 2/15/50

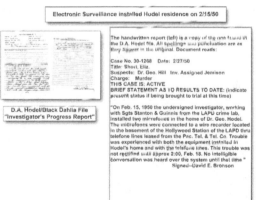

D.A. Hodel/Black Dahlia File
"Investigator's Progress Report"

The handwritten report (left) is a copy of the one found in the D.A. Hodel file. All spellings and punctuation are as they appear in the original. Document reads:

Case No. 30-1268   Date: 2/27/50
Title: Short, Eliz.
Suspects: Dr. Geo. Hill   Inv. Assigned Jemison
Charge: Murder
THIS CASE IS: ACTIVE
BRIEF STATEMENT AS TO RESULTS TO DATE: (indicate present status if being brought to trial at this time)

"On Feb. 15, 1950 the undersigned investigator, working with Sgts Stanton & Guinnis from the LAPD crime lab, installed two mircrofones in the home of Dr. Geo. Hodel. The microfones were connected to a wire recorder located in the basement of the Hollywood Station of the LAPD thru telefone lines leased from the Pac. Tel. & Tel. Co. Trouble was experienced with both the equipment installed in Hodel's home and with the telsfone lines. This trouble was not rectified until approx 2:00, Feb. 18. No intelligible conversation was heard over the system until that time "
Signed--David E. Bronson

Fig. 5.4.1

Here are author-prepared photos and diagrams showing locations in which microphones were installed inside the Sowden/Franklin house by DA/LAPD Detectives.

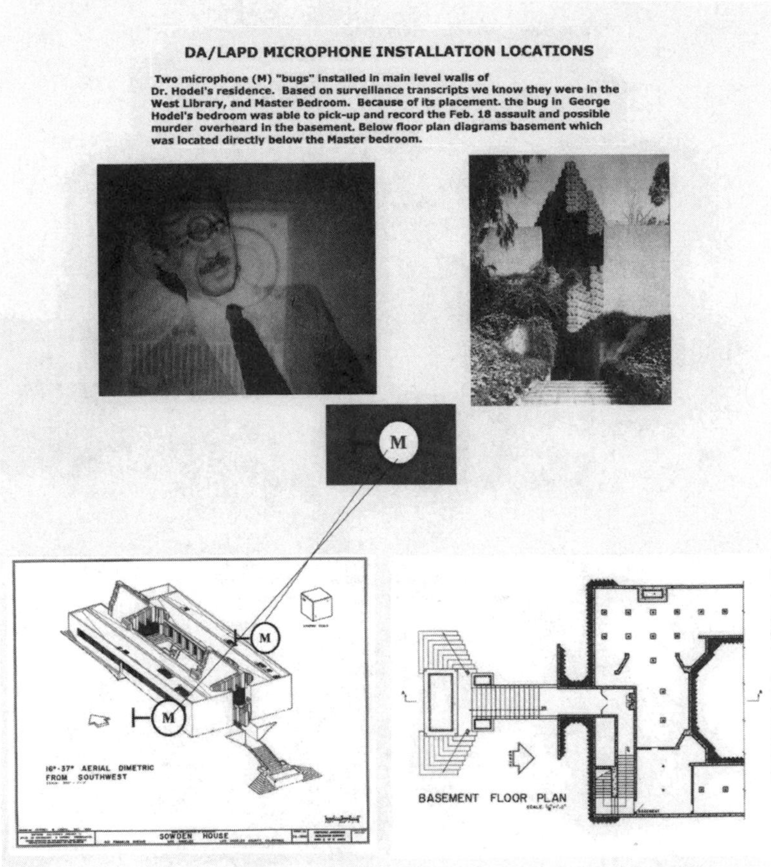

Fig. 5.5

Photograph shows some of the original DA transcripts pages
(146 total) from the 1950 Hodel stakeout.

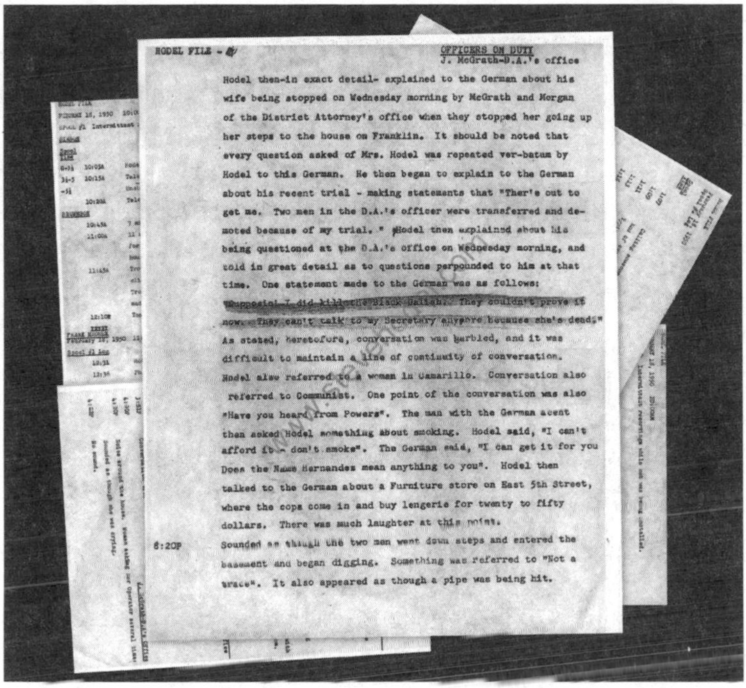

Fig. 5.6

Now that we know the what and why of the DA/LAPD
Hodel-Black Dahlia transcripts, let us examine the recordings
from one specific afternoon during the actual stakeout.

The electronic stakeout is only in its fourth day. The DA
and LAPD have just (the previous evening, February 18)
recorded George Hodel in conversation with another man
(later identified by me as Baron Ernst von Harringa).

In that conversation, Hodel detailed to the Baron how
he killed his personal secretary, Ruth Spaulding, by forced
overdose of pills, as well as admitting to the murder of
Elizabeth "Black Dahlia" Short and "payoffs to police."

Just minutes after those admissions, both Hodel and the
Baron are heard going downstairs to the basement. Then

a pipe is heard striking an object, and a woman screams out. More blows and a second scream, then silence. This is followed by George telling the Baron "to not leave a trace."

In all probability, what the detectives just heard and recorded was a murder in progress. (Incredibly, the stakeout detectives, though only a few minutes away, did nothing.)

George Hodel and Kenneth Rexroth in Conversation

(Beginning on page 9 of the police transcripts.)

Dr. George Hill Hodel Seated on Office Desk at Residence, 1950; Kenneth Rexroth

Fig. 5.7

The below conversation is between George Hodel and Kenneth Rexroth. It is February 19, 1950, early afternoon at the Hodel residence. Rexroth has just arrived and the two men are talking in the living room (and home office). Detectives begin to record just as George dials and speaks to his ex-wife

Dorothy, with Rexroth standing nearby. (At the time of this recording, we three sons and our mother were residing in a small apartment, above the bait shop on the Santa Monica Pier, an absolute paradise for us three brothers, ages seven, eight, and ten.)

Here is that recorded conversation as written by detectives. One should keep in mind that they are only writing parts of the conversation and that the sound quality is frequently poor and difficult to hear. Spelling is unchanged and is as it appears on the transcripts.

February 19, 1950 2:00-4:00 p.m..

2:05P: RECORDED. CONVERSATION. HODEL AND MRS. HODEL. "Hello dear. How's everything. Kids alright. How's everything else? Oh, yes dear, I thought I'd come down and bring that to you that you asked for.

"Kenneth Rexerall[20] called me today, your friend. Should I bring him down to your house this evening. Have you a snack for us I'll be there at 6 or 6:30 with Kenneth. We'll leave here at 5 or 5:30."

2: 12P: Sit down and relax "Kenny." But you can't pin that on me. So you come down to see Ryder. He's a collector that guy. He works for NBC.

2:14P: RECORDED. Mr. Ryder is sure queer.
Hodel: "Are you addressing a mass meeting or what? You'll have to sleep in the housekeeper's room. She's about this high." *Laughter.* "Oh we've had some dillys." Discusses chiropractors. "I don't think Dorothy cares. She has a great big living room."

2:25P: Jimmy Fitzsimons made notes. "Where are these things? What's the name of the poem?" Sounds of auto crash in street.

2:29P: Both leave and return.
Kenny: Exfloius immortality.
Hodel: "What have been doing besides writing."
Kenny: "Traveling."

---

20   Detectives wrote it phonetically, pun intended, it is in fact—Rexroth.

2:31P: Hodel: "Did you get to Cine and the Orient."

Kenny: "No, went to England." Unable to hear—*laughter*.

Kenny: "You can make a lot of money in Paris. I was in Western Europe about 1 year."

2:38P: Hodel: "Did they pay your expenses." *Laughter*.

Hodel: "Was it hard making ends meet."

Kenny: "No, not so bad."

Hodel: "He's a sexual character. Probably decayed bodies caused the rancid odors and back ground setting in the orient, in Hong Kong" Hodel discusses Chinese food.

2:40P: Peter Chang on Sunset Strip has the best. Was big shot in China.

Kenny: "You can't believe the terrible food situation in England."

2:45P: Hodel: "They gave a banquet and I had an interpreter and the American Guard." *Laughter*. "It takes a couple months to get thru to Hankow.

Kenny: "I always wanted to see Central Asia, but the war has been going on since the 30's."

Hodel: "Jean Lamb spent several years in Peiping. His reports would be on desks of Chinese war lords as soon as on the desk of the Ambassador. He was a staff officer. He then was employed by a War Lord. 100's of cases of wrist watches. It was bribery on a big scale. They had internal war. He was ushered in and here was a yellow silk drapery. He spoke Chinese perfectly. He met Prime Minister Hang Chow."

2:55P: Jean became a great power and spent 7 years there. He was out here. I tried to negotiate with him.

Hodel: "They have a special variety of pictures."

Kenny: "Yes."

3:30P: HODEL AND KENNY CONVERSE. Hodel: "Will you have tea or sherry?

Kenny: "Tea" *Sipping of tea sound*.

Kenny: "This man is a heart special. He is Dr. Roth. I was to the doctor in San Diego."

Hodel: "Read thru this, then we can discuss it more intelligently." *Hodel laughs*. "It has some coverage. I'm selling my art collection Monday and Tuesday, and I'm then taking of for Asia."

Kenny: "I am in process of breaking up with my wife of 15 years. No children."

Hodel: "I have 3 boys. You'll see them later. Dorothy lives here a while, and then takes off."

Kenny: "What about "M.""

Hodel: "She is on staff of San Francisco Chronicle. Art Editor, Had a serious operation."

3:45P: *Laughter.*

Hodel: "How were they? They had great masses of hair those whores."

Hodel: "Rosey at 555 Hyde St., San Francisco, was a whore but a honey."

Kenny: "I knew a tall one-black hair like Hollywood Black hair, pale pale gray eyes. I took her home. I thru her in the bath tub—she was drunk. I massaged her, rubbed her under the belly. I got 2 or 3 phone calls. She got mixed up with some bad people. She called and said the Psychiatrist was treating her. I guess I am spoiled (Sounded tight) Dames I know all turn out to be psychiatrists with pale gray eyes."

K. "Dr. Burns would object to your help but he gave 400 to 600 penicillin, but the real help will come from you." Hodel- "Wouldn't he object to you coming to my care." K. "No, as you specialize in heart and you are my friend." (Recorded)

4:00P: Hodel: "Well alright."

THIS ENDS THE HODEL/REXROTH RECORDING.

For the most part the exchange speaks for itself. Nothing earthshaking, the two men speak of travel, where to get the best local Chinese food, and good whores they have known.

Apparently, Kenneth is in LA to give a talk or lecture, as George asks, "Are you addressing a mass meeting or what?"

Based on their conversation, I do not get the impression that they were particularly close friends.

Perhaps they were intellectual kindred spirits? George says to Kenneth, "Read thru this then we can discuss it more intelligently." (Hard to tell if the "this" is a piece of writing, a poem, or a medical brochure?) Clearly, Kenneth wanted George to provide him with some medical care. (Again, difficult to determine what type—venereal disease or heart condition? Rexroth mentions receiving penicillin, which works for the former, but not the latter.)

In George's phone call to Dorothy, with Kenneth standing next to him, he distinctly says, "Kenneth Rexroth, *your friend*, [emphasis mine] called me today. Shall I bring him down to your house this evening?"

Kenneth does ask an interesting and rather revealing question to George when he says, "What about M?" (That would be "Em," Emilia Hodel, George's ex-wife. Kenneth here is obviously using a personal and affectionate term for her, indicating the two of them are/were close.)

George responds, "She is on staff of the *San Francisco Chronicle*, Art Editor. Had a serious operation." (I expect Dad simply misspoke and got his San Francisco newspapers mixed up. As we have read during this time period (1950), "Em" was working as art and drama critic for the *San Francisco News*.)

I believe that these interpersonal links of George Hodel to the three veteran San Francisco columnists: Herb Caen, Kenneth Rexroth, and Emilia Hodel, puts a much finer point to the 1974 "I am back" letter sent to the *Chronicle* by Zodiac:

"Tell Herb Caen I am here. I have always been here."

The letter is a taunt and a clue. Zodiac is informing Caen that he is back in San Francisco and has always been there. Both are true for Zodiac and George Hodel, the former *San Francisco Chronicle* columnist.

CHAPTER 6

"The Sniper"—Zodiac's Manuscript for Murder?

I N ALL THREE OF my earlier books, *BDA*, *BDA II*, and *Most Evil*, I examined what I believe was George Hodel's primary signature, or MO: to plagiarize his crimes and reenact them using characters, dialogue, and actions copied directly from preexistent art, literature, and film.

From the world of art, he included what I have earlier deemed "The Man Ray Nexus," including several of Man Ray's best-known paintings and photographs, making them part of his actual crime scene. (Man Ray's *Minotaur, The Lovers, Juliet in Stocking Mask*, and a 1943 painting, *L'Équivoque*. In the latter painting, the surgeon Hodel, with scalpel in hand, copied Man Ray's unique geometrical figure from the painting and carved it directly into the right thigh of his victim, Elizabeth "Black Dahlia" Short.)

From literature, he spliced and added characters and scenes from Richard Connell's *The Most Dangerous Game*, Edgar Allan Poe's "The Gold Bug", and Thomas De Quincey's two essays, "On Murder Considered as One of the Fine Arts,",and "The Avenger."

In one of his boldest moves, in the summer of 1943, just three weeks after the popular radio show *Suspense Theatre* broadcast "The White Rose Murders" from Hollywood's

Columbia Square Playhouse Studio, George Hodel committed what became known as "The White Gardenia Murder."

The actual copycat crime, committed just six weeks after the fictional radio play aired, followed the script page by page.

The radio play, introduced by "The Man in Black" as "a study in homicidal mania," featured the beautiful Maureen O'Hara. She is probably best remembered for her role as the mother in the holiday classic *Miracle on 34ᵗʰ Street*, which was released in 1947, just three months after the Black Dahlia murder.

"The White Rose Murders" radio mystery play, written by the then-popular mystery novelist/screenwriter Cornell Woolrich, ran thirty minutes. It told the story of a "homicidal maniac" who frequented downtown dance halls where he met, danced with, and wooed women, then lured them out into the night to be beaten and strangled to death.

As his own calling card, he left a carefully posed "white rose" next to each of his victims' bodies. In the vernacular of the day, the police detective described him as "a chain killer." When the story opened, the city was being held in terror. The unidentified suspect had just slain his fourth victim.

George Hodel reenacted the fictional mystery on July 26, 1943, just twenty days after the broadcast, when he picked up what is believed to be his first "Lone Woman Murder" victim, Mrs. Ora Murray. The dapper George, suave and sophisticated, approached her at the downtown ballroom, where he literally swept Ora off her feet. They danced, and he introduced himself to her as "Paul, a businessman down from San Francisco for the weekend."

He invited her to "see Hollywood." She accepted and he drove her to a remote golf course where he brutally beat and strangled her to death. Following the radio script to the letter, he then placed a white gardenia flower next to the body. (Choosing a white gardenia to replace the white rose was clearly a touch of creative license. This crime, the first of the LA Lone Woman Murders is detailed at length in *BDA*.)

Films from which I believe George Hodel plagiarized characters and scenes for his real-life crimes include *The Most Dangerous Game* (RKO, 1932), *Charlie Chan at Treasure Island* (20th Century Fox, 1939), and *Spellbound* (Selznick International, 1945), with a screenplay by Ben Hecht and a surreal dream sequence by Salvador Dalí.

The abovementioned films, and how they link to my father's crime, have been extensively referenced in my earlier works. See *BDA*, *BDA II*, and *Most Evil* for details.

However, there is one film I overlooked for decades, and I am noticing it only now. It is *The Sniper*, filmed in 1951 and released in theaters in 1952.

After analyzing the movie, I genuinely believe *The Sniper* was very likely George Hodel's primary inspiration for the San Francisco Bay Area serial killings attributed to Zodiac two decades later.

The Sniper (Columbia Pictures, 1952)

Fig. 6.0.1   Fig. 6.0.2

The Sniper Poster Showing San Francisco Victims in Serial Killer's Gun Sights

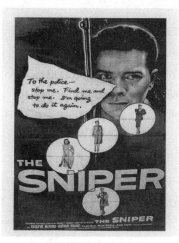

Fig. 6.1

The Story Line

THE FILM WAS SHOT on location, mostly in San Francisco, in 1951.

It opens with a woman caught in the crosshairs of a riflescope. We are quickly introduced to Eddie Miller, the sniper, who has recently been paroled from prison after serving a two-year sentence for "assaulting and beating a woman."

Eddie is a misogynist who hates all women. While the "why" is not entirely explained, we do learn that his hatred is based in rejection. Consequently, he is easily set off, either by a woman making fun of him or by just seeing a loving couple walking hand-in-hand or kissing in public.

In rapid succession, we witness Eddie, the sniper, kill four different women from various rooftop and high-ground positions.

His first victim is a customer on his dry-cleaning delivery route. After flirting with him at her home, she rejects Eddie and makes him aware that she considers him as just a "delivery boy." He stalks her to a nightclub where she performs as a singer, waits for her to finish her gig, then takes her out as she exits the club.

And so it goes through the film. Victim two is a woman he meets in a bar who gives him her home address, but then rejects him. He shoots her through a window from a rooftop across from her apartment. Victim three is a San Francisco socialite who provides her home address during a television interview. Victim four is a woman walking hand-in-hand in the park with her boyfriend.

There is a fifth victim, a male. Eddie shoots him not out of hatred, but because the man, tethered to a rope high above him while working on a smokestack, looks down to see Eddie with a rifle about to shoot another woman on the street below. The witness yells out to warn passersby and Eddie shoots to silence him.

The film is extremely sympathetic to Eddie's psychopathic condition and provides him with his own one-man chorus in the name of Dr. James Kent, the police psychiatrist, played by actor Richard Kiley. Dr. Kent regularly informs his police detective counterparts and the mayor that the suspect "needs help and psychiatric treatment, not prison." The doctor informs them and that he believes the sniper will "keep killing over and over as long as his cartridges last."

Sniper Eddie Miller Taking Out Witness on Smokestack

Fig. 6.2

Film Clip Showing San Francisco Headlines:
"SECOND WOMAN SNIPER VICTIM"
"RIFLE FIEND KILLS AGAIN"
"SNIPER STRIKES IN DAYLIGHT"

Fig. 6.3

As the serial murders continue, San Francisco becomes increasingly terrorized. SFPD officers are assigned to rooftops as the police round up the usual suspects. But Eddie just keeps on killing and, in a desperate cry for help, sends the following handwritten note to the *San Francisco Chronicle*.

The Sniper's "Stop Me" Note to *San Francisco Chronicle*

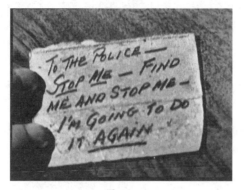

Fig. 6.4

Chicago "Lipstick Killer": "Stop Me Before I Kill More" Note

Lipstick printed sign on post near building where body of Suzanne Degnan was dismembered, discovered yesterday.

Fig. 6.5

George Hodel wrote "Stop Me" or "I will kill again" notes as part of his signature MO in his role as an "urban terrorist" in each of the separate cities he held hostage, during his more than two-decade crime sprees. Those cities included: Chicago, Los Angeles, Riverside, and the San Francisco Bay Area.

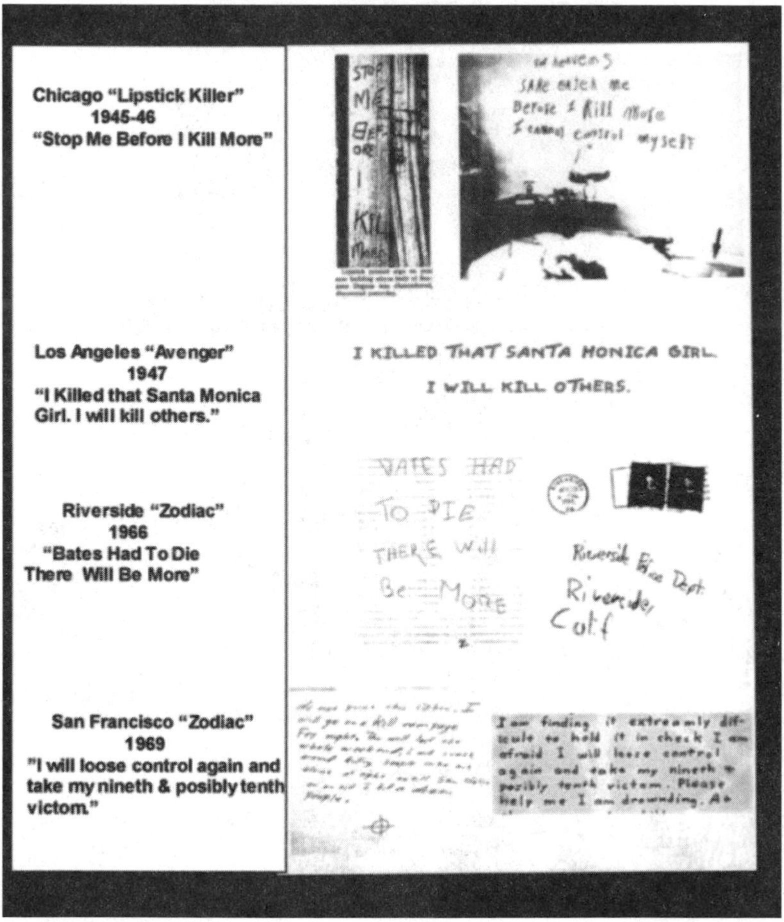

Fig. 6.6

The streets of San Francisco, with their vertical-noir look, were the perfect location to film *The Sniper*.

Below photos show a few of the film's outdoor scenes, which include: (1) San Francisco Cable Car, (2) Coit Tower[21] on Telegraph Hill, (3) Buena Vista Park in the Haight-Ashbury District, (where victim number four was shot and killed, while walking with her boyfriend), and (4) North Beach District, where police have sealed off the area, in hopes of capturing the sniper.

1951 Streets of San Francisco Scenes from *The Sniper*

Fig. 6.7

For those familiar with Zodiac's MO and crime signatures nearly two decades later, the comparisons to *The Sniper* become apparent:

- Serial killer shooting random victims

- Misogynist who hates all women and wants to destroy them

- Shoots victims on public streets and in public parks

21   Father, during his medical school years (1932 to 1936) and while working part-time as a young reporter for the *San Francisco Chronicle*, rented a small residence on Telegraph Hill, literally in the shadow of Coit Tower. On one of my visits to see him and June in San Francisco, circa 1995, he had me drive them by the house from his youth, which was still standing, and he fondly remembered his time there as a young medical student.

- Holds San Francisco in terror with repeated savage murders

- Sends hand-printed note to police pleading to be caught, "Stop Me I'm Going to Kill Again."

- Zodiac imitates story line claiming to be recently out of prison. (Sniper paroled, Zodiac claims he "escaped.")

- Zodiac adopts *The Sniper*'s riflescope with crosshairs as his signature and a "clue" to his inspiration and identity

The Sniper Cast—One Degree of Separation from George Hodel

THE SNIPER WAS FILMED mostly on location in San Francisco, with some of the interiors shot on a Columbia Studios sound stage in Los Angeles.

It was a Stanley Kramer production, directed by Edward Dmytryk from a screenplay and story by Harry Brown, with music composed by George Antheil.

The film starred veteran actor Adolphe Menjou as Lt. Frank Kafka. (As it has been often said, "You can't make this stuff up.")

The sniper role went to actor Arthur Franz, a real-life WWII hero and POW cast perfectly in the part of a mentally deranged ex-soldier and prison parolee. Franz had just started his acting career two years earlier where he debuted as Lt. "Mace" Willard in the 1948 movie *Jungle Patrol*.

Actor Richard Kiley, also just beginning his acting career, played the role of the police psychiatrist Dr. James G. Kent.

Character actor Charles Wagenheim had a minor role in the film as the sniper's boss, Mr. Alpine, who owns a dry-cleaning business.

As indicated previously, I had not been aware of the film until the summer of 2014, which is when I ordered the DVD for a "first look." I watched the movie in its entirety, then went to the bonus material, which included a running commentary on the film by San Francisco writer Eddie Muller.

In addition to being a mystery writer, Eddie is also known as "The Czar of Noir." As an expert on all things noir, he has contributed numerous articles and video commentaries on more than a dozen classic films.

I immediately replayed *The Sniper*, this time with Eddie's running commentary. As he points out at the beginning of his narration, it is only fitting he provide the commentary, a native San Franciscan with only one syllable separating his name from the star. (Eddie Muller vs. the sniper Eddie Miller.)

Muller's trivia and details convinced me to take a deeper look, not only at the story line similarities (which I was becoming increasingly convinced my father had lifted directly from *The Sniper* for his 1969 "remake" as Zodiac), but also to search for subtler, long-forgotten pieces of the puzzle.

What I discovered were the many examples of the real-life cast and crew's one degree of separation from Dr. George Hill Hodel.

Let's take a look.

Edward Dmytrk (1908-1999), The Director

JUST A YEAR YOUNGER than George Hodel, he was the son of Russian-Ukrainian immigrants, like George. He spent two years of his boyhood in San Francisco before moving south to be raised in Los Angeles. Also like George, Edward was identified at a young age as being intellectually gifted.

In 1923, both Edward and George, based on their superior California public school test scores, were independently selected to participate in what would become one of the world's most famous (and highly controversial) psychological studies.

"The Genetic Studies of Genius" was created by Stanford University's Dr. Lewis Terman, who had created the Stanford-Binet IQ test and was considered at that time to be one of the world's leading psychologists. The young geniuses who participated in his study became known as "Terman's Termites."

The following 1995 *Los Angeles Times* article written by Richard C. Paddock is worth including in its entirety. It is totally on-point in describing both the study and Edward's participation as a young boy of just thirteen.

Los Angeles Times   July 30, 1995
by Richard C. Paddock

The Secret IQ Diaries : They Were Guinea Pigs in the Longest-Running Psychological Study Ever, Their Identities Largely Kept a Mystery. Now in Their 80s, the 'Children' of Lewis Terman Are Still Defining What It Really Means to Be A Genius.

The boy who would grow up to direct "The Caine Mutiny" was a 13-year-old student at Lockwood Street School on the fringes of Hollywood when he was discovered by Lewis M. Terman, the inventor of the modern-day IQ test. It was 1922, and the Stanford University professor had dispersed a small flock of assistants to test children around the state.

Even now, nearly three-quarters of a century later, 86-year-old Edward Dmytryk can sit in his Encino home, encircled by the memorabilia of his movie career, and evoke that first milestone in his life: getting out of class, riding the Yellow Car to school district headquarters Downtown to sit in a row of desks with other kids and take the great psychologist's newfangled test. He didn't know what he was part of then, but he was in his element.

"The testing went on for three straight days," he recalls. "I was excused from school. And I loved it. A lot of the things [on the test] were puzzles. They'd give you a seven-integer number and tell you to say it backward right away."

The test was a three-day lark for Dmytryk, a respite from a brutal father who sometimes shredded his schoolbooks. For Terman it was proof that here was another "gifted child"--a phrase he coined--and he added the youngster to the long list for his landmark research group. In newspaper stories across Depression-era America, they would be known as the "1,000 Gifted Children." To these kids--actually 1,528 of them, mostly Californians--Terman became both surrogate father and academic spy, monitoring their progress from afar, guiding their careers and, often enough, meddling in their lives. Neither he nor the children realized then that Terman would be part of their lives for decades, longer in some cases than jobs, parents, spouses.

Fig. 6.8

A Few of "Terman's Termites" Publicly Identified

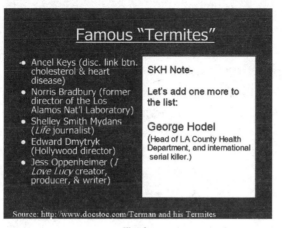

Fig. 6.9

Both George and Edward had a love for science and mathematics. They both attended Pasadena's prestigious California Institute of Technology (Cal Tech) around the same time in the mid-twenties. (It's not known if they were actual classmates, as it appears Dmytryk entered one or two years after George.) Both left Cal Tech after just one year to go their separate ways.

Dmytryk worked in the Hollywood studios and quickly rose from film editor to a working director.

When the HUAC (House Un-American Activities Committee) was established in the late forties to headhunt for communists, Dmytryk was identified as one of the "Hollywood Ten." After initially refusing to testify, he was sent to prison. But after several months behind bars, he decided to name names. Dmytryk identified some of his Hollywood friends and associates as communists and was released. However, now he found himself "blacklisted" by Hollywood, which had a significant impact on his future career.[22] A close acquaintance, also named and arrested with Dmytryk as one of the "Hollywood Ten," was screenwriter and film director Herbert Biberman. Biberman, active in Hollywood in the thirties and forties, married actress Gale Sondergaard in 1935. The following year, Gale would become the first woman to be nominated and win an Oscar for Best Supporting Actress in her debut role as Faith in *Anthony Adverse* (Warner Brothers, 1936).

Edward Dmytryk and Herbert Biberman (brother to artist Edward Biberman, a Hodel family friend) seen standing in front of courthouse in 1950

Fig. 6.10

In October 1949, I was just a few weeks short of my eighth birthday. Tamar, my fourteen-year-old half-sister (same father, different mothers) had been living with us during the summer and had run away from home. At the time we were living at the Sowden/Franklin house, a Mayan temple and historic Hollywood landmark built by Frank Lloyd Wright Jr., in 1926.

---

22   For those interested in gaining a deeper understanding of HUAC and the "Hollywood Ten" I highly recommend *Odd Man Out: A Memoir of the Hollywood Ten,* written by Edward Dmytryk. (Southern Illinois University Press, 1996)

My father was forced to file a missing person's report and after a three-day search, Tamar was found by the police, who had traced her to the home of Edward Biberman (Herbert's brother) in the Hollywood Hills. According to Tamar, she was good friends with the Biberman's daughter Sonia, and she was "hiding out" while Sonia's parents vacationed in Europe. Tamar had earlier revealed to Sonia that she was pregnant and she claimed her father, George Hodel, was the father.

Taken into police custody, Tamar then disclosed the fact that she ran away from home because she feared for herself, and because of the sexual relationship she had had with her father and other adults at our home. She also informed LAPD juvenile officers that her father had obtained an abortion for her from a Dr. Ballard in Beverly Hills the previous month.

On October 6, 1949, LAPD juvenile officers arrested Dr. George Hill Hodel for child molestation and incest. My father was defended by Jerry Giesler, the nation's top criminal defense attorney. Despite three adults testifying to being present during the sex acts, George Hodel was acquitted at a three-week trial that December. (Later, secret DA files not discovered until 2004, suggested there was a "payoff" to gain an acquittal.)

All of this information is detailed in my previous books, but what is important here is the George Hodel/Biberman connection as "family friends." It is very likely that, like the Bibermans, Edward Dmytryk knew and socialized with George Hodel. He probably frequented the Franklin house along with the many known screenwriters, directors, and actors who were regular partygoers between 1945 and 1950.

So, with Edward Dmytryk, the director of *The Sniper*, we have either direct or, at most, one degree of separation from George Hodel.

Director Edward Dmytryk's star at 6241 Hollywood Boulevard is located in front of the world famous Pantages Theatre. The Frolic Room, seen above immediately west of the theater, was a popular watering hole during the nineteen forties, and police reports document it was occasionally frequented by Elizabeth "Black Dahlia" Short.

Fig. 6.11

Harry Brown (1917-1986), The Screenwriter

BORN IN PORTLAND, MAINE, he attended Harvard and was an early writer for both *TIME* and *The New Yorker* magazines. In 1941, Charles Scribner's Sons published his epic poem, *The Poem of Bunker Hill*, which won high acclaim.

In 1944, Brown wrote the WWII novel *A Walk in the Sun*, which a year later was made into a feature film starring Dana Andrews, Richard Conte, and John Ireland.

Brown remained in Hollywood and his filmography shows thirty-five separate credits, including writing the screenplay for *The Sniper*.

Of particular interest to our investigation is the fact that three years before writing *The Sniper*, Harry Brown wrote the screenplay for *Arch of Triumph* (United Artists, 1948). The film starred Ingrid Bergman, Charles Boyer, and Charles Laughton.

The costume designer in *Arch of Triumph* was Marion Herwood Keyes.

Just a few years earlier (1943 to 1945), Marion had been working as the personal secretary to Dr. George Hill Hodel at his First Street Clinic in Downtown Los Angeles.

At that time, Ruth Spaulding, a close personal friend and coworker of Marion's, was also working for Dr. Hodel at his clinic. Miss Spaulding, while working there, was also romantically involved with George Hodel.

In May of 1945, George Hodel claimed he went to check on Miss Spaulding at her apartment and found her unconscious and comatose. After waiting several hours, he then ordered a cab and had her taken to a nearby emergency hospital where she died within one hour.

Though the Spaulding death was listed by the coroner's office as a "suicide by pills," LAPD suspected foul play and investigated the case as a possible homicide. Three months later, Dr. Hodel joined UNRRA (United Nations Relief and Rehabilitation Agency), and, by February 1946, had left the United States for China, effectively terminating LAPD's ongoing investigation.

After the unexpected death of her close friend, Marion Herwood Keyes quit her job as secretary to George Hodel and became a full-time Hollywood costume designer in some of Hollywood's greatest films of the forties. Her filmography credits her with fifteen films, which include *Gaslight, Mrs. Parkington, The Picture of Dorian Gray, The Clock, The Postman Always Rings Twice,* and more.

Black Dahlia Avenger II contains a complete summary of Marion Herwood Keyes' relationship with George Hodel, as well as my father's later admission to killing his secretary, Ruth Spaulding.

Marion and Harry Brown, through their work together on *Arch of Triumph,* would most certainly have known each other. Here again, we have documented just one degree of separation between George Hodel and the actual writer of *The Sniper* screenplay.[23]

George Anthiel (1900-1959), The Composer

GEORGE ANTHIEL COMPOSED THE music for *The Sniper.*

Anthiel was multitalented, and a superficial review of his biography reveals he was extremely complex. He was a musical genius, pianist, avant-garde composer, Dadaist, mystery writer, author, and inventor.

He traveled to Paris in the twenties and mixed with a number of the well-known artists, writers, and musicians including James Joyce, Ernest Hemmingway, Ezra Pound, Gertrude Stein, Salvador Dalí, and the surreal photographer/artist Man Ray.

Anthiel is perhaps best known for his early composition, *Ballet Mécanique,* first performed in Paris, France in 1926, followed by "an ill-fated concert at New York's Carnegie Hall in 1927."

---

23   The 1950 DA's secret Hodel/Black Dahlia files also revealed that a bit actress by the name of Ann Toth, a personal acquaintance and friend to Elizabeth "Black Dahlia" Short, had a small role in *Arch of Triumph.* In 1947, just weeks after the Dahlia murder, Toth was interviewed at length by detectives regarding what she knew about the victim or the crime.

In 1924, while living in Paris, Man Ray introduced Anthiel to a young American film producer, Dudley Murphy, who wanted to make a short, avant-garde film. They joined forces and Anthiel's *Ballet Mécanique* score was put to film.

Internet Movie Data Base lists *Ballet Mécanique* as a silent, black-and-white, 35mm film, produced in 1924, with a total running time of nineteen minutes. It credits George Anthiel as composer of the theme music, Dudley Murphy and Man Ray as cinematographers, and Dudley Murphy and Fernand Léger as codirectors.

Murphy would return to the United States and become one of Hollywood's most controversial film directors. In the forties, he and his wife Virginia became close personal friends of George and Dorothy Hodel, and he'd eventually reunite with his old friend Man Ray, who by then had become our family photographer, a regular visitor and partygoer at the Sowden/Franklin house.

Dudley Murphy's life is brilliantly captured in author Susan Delson's biography, *Dudley Murphy, Hollywood Wild Card*, (University of Minnesota Press, 2006). An excerpt from of her book cover:

> *Dudley Murphy (1897-1968) was one of Hollywood's most intriguing figures. Active from the 1920s through the 1940s, Murphy was one of the industry's first independents and a guiding intelligence behind some of the key films in early twentieth-century cinema.*
>
> ...
>
> *Delson pays close attention to Murphy's cinematic style, which favored visual play over narrative and character, and she offers provocative new insights into his two most important works,* Ballet Mécanique *and* The Emperor Jones.

By the mid-thirties, George Anthiel also found his way to Hollywood and began writing scores for dozens of films, working closely with independent filmmaker and screenwriter Ben Hecht. Anthiel is credited as composer in two Hecht-directed movies, *Angels Over Broadway* (1940) and *Specter of the Rose* (1946)

Those that have read *Black Dahlia Avenger* and *Black Dahlia Avenger II* will recognize the name Ben Hecht, who figures prominently in the life and times and criminal investigation of Dr. George Hodel.

Hecht's link to my father, Man Ray, and the surreal connections as revealed in the 1945 Hitchcock film, *Spellbound*, (Hecht wrote the screenplay) are all addressed in detail in the *BDA II* chapter, "A Surrealist Signature."

From 1925 to 1955 George Anthiel scored the music for twenty-nine separate Hollywood films. He died from a heart attack in New York in 1959.

Edward Dmytryk, Harry Brown, and George Anthiel were the three major creative forces in the making of *The Sniper*.

I suspect in the case of Dmytryk and Anthiel that no degree of separation existed and that they very likely both knew and socialized with George Hodel at the Sowden/Franklin house. Too many opportunities existed for there not to have been at least some casual meetings through their mutual Hollywood acquaintances, such as Dudley Murphy, John Huston, and Man Ray.

However, even if we assume that George Hodel never met any of the three men—which seems highly improbable—we can be certain that cinephile and self-proclaimed "master criminal" George Hodel most certainly saw *The Sniper* when it was released in 1952.

Like so many other examples of his criminal plagiarism from art, literature, music, and films, the 1968 to 1969 Zodiac crimes are most certainly George Hodel's remake of *The Sniper*, in which he performs as both actor and director.

I will close this chapter by adding another amazing investigative synchronicity. This fourth person had a minor role in the original movie but doesn't fall into the same category as the three others. His link to the film is not what I consider one of the "degrees of separation" from George Hodel.

Instead, I mention him here as an example of "happenstance." It's just an anecdote, but without question one of the strangest yet told.

Charles Wagenheim (1896-1979), Character Actor

CHARLES WAS A CHARACTER actor who performed on-screen for fifty years. He has over 250 credits to his name. His first film role was as a court stenographer in the 1929 film *The Trial of Mary Dugan*. In his last, in 1979, he played a "homeless bum" in the popular *All in the Family* television series. Wagenheim's best-known character part was that of an assassin in Alfred Hitchcock's 1940 thriller, *Foreign Correspondent*.

Charles Wagenhcim as the Assassin in Hitchcock's
Foreign Correspondent

Fig. 6.12

As previously mentioned, Charles Wagenheim had a small role in *The Sniper*, playing Eddie Miller's boss, who was obviously unaware that his delivery driver was the serial killer stalking the streets of San Francisco.

Clip from The Sniper. *Actor Charles Wagenheim (seated) as "Mr. Alpine" talking to detectives about his employee, deliveryman Eddie Miller.*

Fig. 6.13

In a bizarre twist of fate, the veteran actor Charles Wagenheim, at the advanced age of eighty-three, would himself become a murder victim.

On the afternoon of March 6, 1979, a caretaker for Wagenheim's wife Lillian, who was paralyzed from a stroke and was unable to communicate, returned from the laundry room to find the husband lying dead on the floor in the bedroom. She immediately called the police and an ambulance.

Paramedics pronounced the victim dead and LAPD Hollywood patrol officers called for homicide detectives.

At that time, I was the senior homicide detective II at Hollywood Detectives and became the lead detective on the case. My partner was Rick Papke.

Our only witness to the crime was the caregiver, Miss Stephanie Boone, who discovered the body.

My on-scene investigation revealed that there had been a violent struggle and that the victim had been assaulted and struck in the head. The next day, the coroner's autopsy confirmed the cause of death to be blunt force trauma. The bedroom window was wide open, suggesting the victim may have surprised a daytime burglar in the process of ransacking the house. No intruder had been seen or heard by any of the neighbors.

Three weeks later, Rick and I made our arrest and filed it with the district attorney. Stephanie Boone was charged with murder and forgery.

The facts revealed that Charles Wagenheim had suspected Boone of stealing and writing checks from his account. He confronted her in his apartment, an argument ensued, and she struck him in the head, resulting in his death.

Los Angeles Times May 26, 1979

Nurse Arrested in Slaying of Actor, 84

BY KRIS LINDGREN
Times Staff Writer

A 24-year-old practical nurse was arrested Friday afternoon in the bludgeoning death of veteran Hollywood character actor Charles Wagenheim, police reported.

Wagenheim, 84, who appeared in such television series as Gunsmoke, All in the Family and Baretta, was found on the bedroom floor of his Hollywood apartment March 0, severely beaten on the head.

After an intensive, three-month investigation, Hollywood detectives arrested Stephanie Boone, 24, of Lakewood at the Los Angeles County Animal Shelter in Downey, where she recently began working as a kennel attendant.

Homicide Det. Steve Hodel said Miss Boone had been employed by Wagenheim for nearly a year to nurse his invalid wife, Lillian, in their apartment.

Hodel said it was Miss Boone who notified authorities of Wagenheim's death. At that time, Miss Boone told investigators she found the victim lying face down on the bedroom floor upon her return from a brief trip to a nearby laundry room.

Lillian Wagenheim, 78, a former clinical psychologist, was in the living room when the slaying occurred. Left without speech by a stroke three years ago, Mrs. Wagenheim has been unable to relate anything she may have seen or heard to authorities.

Hodel said Miss Boone has been a

"prime suspect all along" but he declined to elaborate on a possible motive for the slaying.

Hodel said Miss Boone has been ruled out as a suspect in a similar slaying of another veteran character actor, Victor Kilian.

Kilian, 81, best known for his role as the "Fernwood Flasher" on the Mary Hartman, Mary Hartman television series, was found beaten to death in his Hollywood home five days after Wagenheim was slain.

The two elderly character actors had appeared together in a taping of All in the Family, just before Wagenheim's death. But investigators have ruled out any possible link between the murders.

Fig. 6.14

Stephanie Boone pleaded guilty to voluntary manslaughter and served eight years in prison for the murder of veteran character actor Charles Wagenheim.

LAPD Homicide Detective Steve Hodel accepting Award from the Hollywood Coordinating Council in appreciation for his and his partner Rick Papke's solving the Charles Wagenheim murder in 1979.

Fig. 6.15

How sad that after a long and magnificent film career, and after giving so much of himself to others, in the eighth decade of his life, Charles Wagenheim should fall victim to a brutal and senseless murder.

In a 1980 letter to my father, who was residing and working in Manila, Philippines, I mentioned being honored by the Hollywood Coordinating Council for solving the Wagenheim murder. I enclosed a newspaper article that summarized the investigation. (Of course, at that time, I had no idea of the victim's connection to, nor had I even heard of, *The Sniper* film.)

In June of 1980, my father responded with a very remarkable letter, which I have named "The Parable of the Sparrows Letter." That four-page typed letter, due to its relevance to the Dahlia and Zodiac investigations, was reproduced in its entirety in both *Black Dahlia Avenger* (2003) and *Most Evil* (2009). While some of those findings are on-point about surrealism, I am not going to reiterate those findings here, which are available for examination in those chapters. (I also present a separate analysis of what I believe was my father's unconscious reference to a Hollywood murder as it relates to surrealism. When he refers to the Wagenheim murder, he writes, "There must be an enigma inside a riddle there, too.")

Copy of closing page 4 of 1980 George Hodel letter to me,
in which he responds to my informing him of solving
the Charles Wagenheim murder.[24]

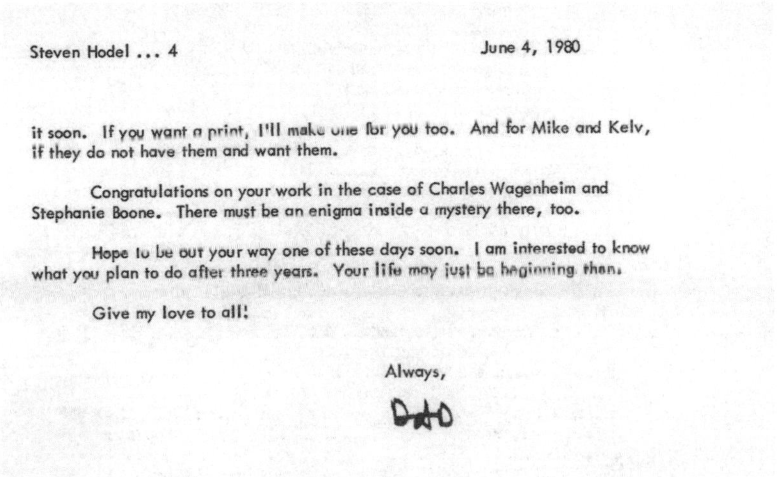

Steven Hodel ... 4   June 4, 1980

it soon. If you want a print, I'll make one for you too. And for Mike and Kelv, if they do not have them and want them.

Congratulations on your work in the case of Charles Wagenheim and Stephanie Boone. There must be an enigma inside a mystery there, too.

Hope to be out your way one of these days soon. I am interested to know what you plan to do after three years. Your life may just be beginning then.

Give my love to all!

Always,

Dad

Fig. 6.16

---

24   Earlier in this chapter I mentioned that film-noir historian Eddie "Czar of Noir" Muller provided an excellent running commentary in the bonus section of the DVD for *The Sniper*. Muller also narrated the DVD commentary for another 1951 film noir, also shot in San Francisco, *The House on Telegraph Hill*, in which Charles Wagenheim also had a bit part. In Muller's video narration, he mentions the Wagenheim murder but unfortunately gets it wrong and goes on to tell the audience that, "to this day, it remains one of Hollywood's unsolved murders." Note to Charles Wagenheim fans, and to my friend and fellow mystery writer Eddie Muller, the case was solved in three weeks and his killer speedily sent to prison.

Los Angeles Times
January 29, 1980

Nurse Sentenced to 8-Year Term in Slaying of Actor

A young practical nurse received an 8-year prison sentence Monday for the bludgeoning death of 82-year-old character actor Charles Wagenheim.

Superior Court Judge Robert Roberson Jr. imposed the sentence on Stephanie Tonette Boone, 24, of Lakewood, who had pleaded guilty to voluntary manslaughter.

Roberson sentenced her to six years on the manslaughter charge and added two years as the result of her prior armed robbery and escape convictions.

Wagenheim was found last March 6 sprawled in the bedroom of his Hollywood apartment, where Miss Boone was one of the nurses caring for him.

Investigators theorized she attacked Wagenheim with a table leg after he confronted her about stealing checks from him and converting them to her own use.

Wagenheim appeared in a variety of roles which included parts on such television series as "Gunsmoke," "Baretta," and "All In The Family."

Fig. 6.17

CHAPTER 7

Background

A QUICK REVIEW OF some basics.
Zodiac's primary signature found in almost all of his mailings was this symbol, a simple Celtic cross.

Simple Celtic

Fig. 7.0

In Ireland, it is a popular legend that the Celtic Christian cross was introduced by Saint Patrick or possibly Saint Declan during his time converting the pagan Irish, though there are no examples from this early period.... Some of these 'Celtic' crosses bear inscriptions in ogham.[25]

---

en.wikipedia.org/wiki/Celtic_cross

Architect Frank Lloyd Wright adopted the Celtic cross as his original business logo and placed it on his stationery and letterheads. Historians report this was partially out of respect for his Welsh family roots, as the cross was also known and popular in Wales.

Frank Lloyd Wright Logo

The logo is based on a Celtic cross inside a circle inside a square.

Fig. 7.1

Dr. George Hill Hodel was a huge fan of Frank Lloyd Wright, as well as a personal acquaintance of his son, Frank Lloyd Wright Jr. (aka Lloyd Wright).

George Hodel was such a great admirer of both men that, in 1945, he purchased the Sowden house in Hollywood, California, which had been designed and built by Lloyd Wright in 1926, with assistance and collaboration from his father, FLW. Dr. Hodel then hired Lloyd Wright to renovate the residence and prepare it for his return from China, expected to be "the spring of 1947." (In point of fact, he resigned his position with UNRRA "for personal reasons" and returned to Los Angeles in September of 1946.)

1946 Letter from George Hodel Posted from China to Lloyd Wright Found in UCLA Special Collections Library

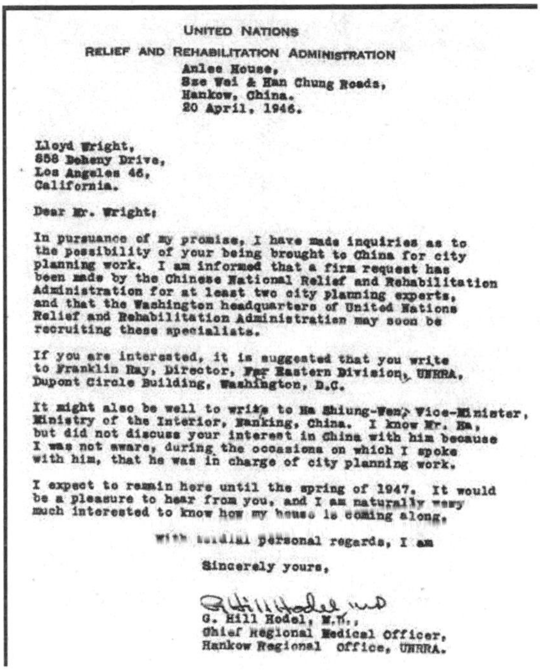

UNITED NATIONS

RELIEF AND REHABILITATION ADMINISTRATION
Anlee House,
Sze Wei & Han Chung Roads,
Hankow, China.
20 April, 1946.

Lloyd Wright,
858 Doheny Drive,
Los Angeles 46,
California.

Dear Mr. Wright:

In pursuance of my promise, I have made inquiries as to the possibility of your being brought to China for city planning work. I am informed that a firm request has been made by the Chinese National Relief and Rehabilitation Administration for at least two city planning experts, and that the Washington headquarters of United Nations Relief and Rehabilitation Administration may soon be recruiting these specialists.

If you are interested, it is suggested that you write to Franklin Ray, Director, Far Eastern Division, UNRRA, Dupont Circle Building, Washington, D.C.

It might also be well to write to Ma Shiung-Wen, Vice-Minister, Ministry of the Interior, Nanking, China. I know Mr. Ma, but did not discuss your interest in China with him because I was not aware, during the occasions on which I spoke with him, that he was in charge of city planning work.

I expect to remain here until the spring of 1947. It would be a pleasure to hear from you, and I am naturally very much interested to know how my house is coming along.

With cordial personal regards, I am

Sincerely yours,

G. Hill Hodel, M.D.,
Chief Regional Medical Officer,
Hankow Regional Office, UNRRA.

Fig. 7.2

Dr. Hodel, in apparent imitation of (or inspired by) FLW, also adopted, designed, and incorporated the Celtic cross into his own business stationery and letterhead.

The logo first appears in his market research firm logo for INRA-ASIA.

Then, again, it appeared as a logo for his overseas real estate company known as Land Growth International Ltd., which he formed in 1972, just a few years after the Zodiac murders in 1968 and 1969.

Dr. George Hodel's
Land Growth International LTD. Estab. early 1970s

Land Growth logo

Fig. 7.3

George Hodel adapted the logo a third time, after relocating to San Francisco and moving into his penthouse suite in the downtown business section. There, in 1990, he established a new company, International Travel Research Institute (INTRI), and again incorporated the simple Celtic cross (think: Zodiac) logo, this time "sitting on top of the world."

Dr. Hodel's International Travel Research Institute (INTRI) 1990 Letterhead

Fig. 7.4

In, 1974, Zodiac wrote a letter to the *San Francisco Chronicle*. In it, he mentioned an obscure reference to an "old Norse word." Here is the complete text of that letter, which Zodiac signed "a friend"[26]:

Dear Mr. Editor,

Did you know that the initials SLA, (Symbionese Liberation Army) spell "sla," an old Norse word meaning "kill."

—a friend

---

26   George Hodel, as the Black Dahlia Avenger, also signed one of his 1947 Los Angeles mailings to the press in this exact manner, including the lowercase "a" as shown in the below photos.

Mailed to *San Francisco Chronicle* Newspaper
by Zodiac in February 1974

Near Mr Editor,
 Did you know that the
initials SLA (Symbionese
Liberation Army) spell "isla"
an old Norse word
meaning "kill"
 a friend

Editor
San Francisco Chronicle
San Francisco, California

Feb 1974

Fig. 7.5

Mailed to Los Angeles Newspapers January 1947 by
Black Dahlia Avenger Signed "a friend"

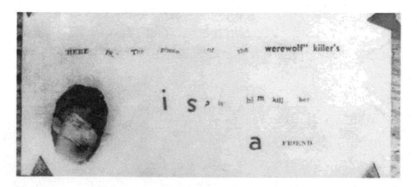

Fig. 7.6

CHAPTER 8

"I am crack proof."

—Zodiac

Excerpt from Zodiac Letter Mailed March 13, 1971, from Pleasanton, California, to the *Los Angeles Times*

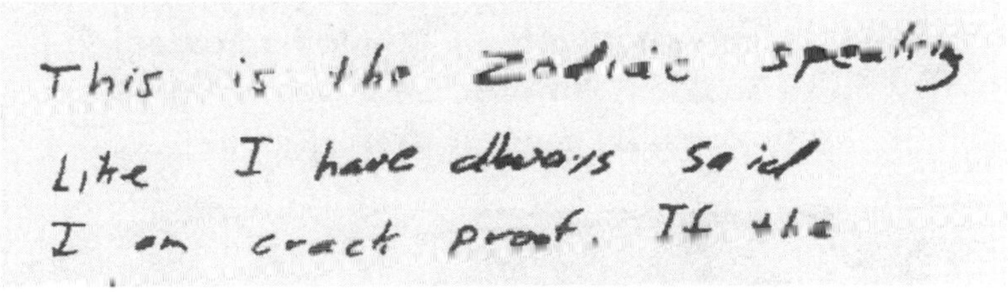
This is the Zodiac speaking
Like I have always said
I am crack proof. If the

Fig. 8.0

Zodiac 1970 Halloween Card Revisited

In Chapter 21 of *Black Dahlia Avenger II*, we examined the 1970 Halloween card mailed by Zodiac. The examination included its potential connections to the classic film *Spellbound* and screenwriter Ben Hecht, and to George Hodel's good friend, surrealist artist Man Ray.

I then asked, rhetorically, if my father was again paying homage to the surrealists Dalí and Man Ray in that 1970 Halloween card, as he had in the 1947 Black Dahlia murder.

Two years later, in my 2014 updated version of *BDA II*, I again referred to new potential links between George

Hodel and Zodiac's Halloween card. Zodiac wrote "By Rope, By Gun, By Knife, By Fire," displaying the words on the card to form what law enforcement speculated was a possible secret monogram for the letter "H."

In the new chapter, I was able to trace that exact phrase back to a 1952 comic book that I believe was connected directly to my father.

The comic book story linked directly to two of my father's acquaintances from that period: Tim Holt, the Western cowboy star and comic book hero known as Red Mask, and actress Carol Forman, known as Spider Lady. At the time, Forman was Holt's girlfriend and lived with us at my father's Lloyd Wright-built home in Hollywood.

1952 Tim Holt, Red Mask Comic Compared to Zodiac Halloween Card Message; "By Rope, By Gun, By Knife, By Fire"

In the late forties, actor Tim Holt was a friend and frequent guest of Dr. George Hill Hodel at his Hollywood mansion. Law enforcement speculated that Zodiac wrote the message in the shape of a letter "H" as a possible monogram of his real name.

Fig. 8.1

In this 1970 Zodiac Halloween card mailed to the *San Francisco Chronicle*, Zodiac used a number of mixed messages, as well as a direct threat to the life of the newspaper's star crime reporter, Paul Avery, who had "called Zodiac out" in a number of front-page articles. The card included a number of separate taunts and cryptic "clews," which might have helped Zodiac dramatically reintroduce himself back into the public spotlight.

In addition to drawing a "red mask" on the face of the skeleton, there is also the second connection to the comic book character "Lady Doom," in which Zodiac informs reporter Avery, "Peek-A-Boo, you are doomed."

Halloween Card and Liquid Paper

ON OCTOBER 25, 2014, I received the following email from my long-time friend and fellow true crime writer, Robert Sadler. Robert is also a private investigator, Vietnam veteran, former Dallas cop, novelist, essayist, poet, artist, photographer, and all-around good guy.

Robert "Dr. Watson" Sadler

Fig. 8.2

Over the years, Robert has familiarized himself with many of the details of my ongoing investigations in both *BDA* and *Most Evil*. His highly-qualified skills and powers of observation have been of great assistance to me, and I have welcomed him as my sometime partner—my own "Dr. Watson."

Here is just one example:

October 25, 2014
Dallas, Texas
Hi, Steve.

I don't know if you've discussed this, if so forgive me, I just noticed this.

In the last few days, being able to see available scans of the 'color' [Zodiac Halloween] card rather than the B&W had me wondering. What could Zodiac/ Hodel use to 'write' in white on the card? In 1970, there were only a small number of media that could be used to 'write' in white and leave brush marks. I can think of six products that would have been available in 1970: 1) perhaps the longest used would be artist's oil paint, i.e. Titanium White; 2) next might be white tempera paint; 3) watercolor paint; 4) acrylic paint; 5) model builders or hobby paint; and 6) Liquid Paper.

An artist, professional or amateur, might have oil, acrylic, watercolor, or tempera paint's [sic], but usually the artist usually tends to work in one media. Of these media only oil and acrylic paints would (generally) have the viscosity to leave the brush marks observed on the Halloween card. Tempera and watercolor paint sufficiently thick enough to show brush marks would tend [to] not adhere well to the paper and flake off fairly quickly, [especially if the card were flexed at any point]. Model paint would work, but most model paints at the time (as I recall) were glossy, not flat as the white 'writing [and decorations]' on the card appears in the available color scans. Liquid Paper, a typewriter correction fluid, was also applied with a short, thin brush.

My question then is, [which] of these six media did GHH have ready access to? Unless GHH was into painting or model building in 1969-70, I would rule out the painting media. He did type and type his own letters from time to time. So, given the ubiquity of Liquid Paper as the go-to typo corrector, I'm guessing GHH had access to Liquid Paper in his home and or home/office.

My observation of the color scans available of the October 1970 Halloween card and surmise is that the Zodiac writing [and decorations] was made by brushing and dabbing Liquid Paper onto the card surface. The viscosity [and opacity] of Liquid Paper would allow it to cover and cling to the surface, drying in-place fairly quickly and leaving the brush/dab marks.

In 1970 the idea of testing/analyzing the writing [and decoration] media used on the card may never have been considered. Even today, sophisticated testing could determine what the the [sic] white media is/was, Liquid Paper for example. It would be unlikely to be able to determine from what bottle it came frpm [unless the exact bottle were available for testing]. Thus, its investigative relevance in tying the writing [and decoration] media to an individual bottle of Liquid Paper or the owner thereof might be moot.

However, identifying the writing [and decorating] media could be another link in the chain.

—Robert

An hour later, I emailed him the following response:

October 25, 2014
Los Angeles, California
Robert:

Yes, I believe you are correct on the Liquid Paper. It was omnipresent in dad's office back before the computer. I recall seeing it in use when I visited him in Manila in the early seventies and in San Francisco much later in the nineties, as he continued to use a typewriter, while June had of course switched over to computer. I think I even have a photo of dad at his desk?

(Goes to his file cabinet, searches for twenty-five minutes, and returns.)

Unfreaking believable!

Found the photo of dad I took circa 1992 in San Francisco. There he is at his typewriter, and on the shelf behind him and off his left shoulder is the "prime suspect" LIQUID PAPER. (See photo.)

You make a hell of a WATSON!

—Steve[27]

Below is the photograph I found in my files, which I had taken circa 1992, just two years after George and June had relocated from Asia to their penthouse suite on Bush Street in Downtown San Francisco.

We see my father seated at his desk, still in his "old school mode," using his typewriter, with the ever-ready Liquid Paper at hand for any necessary typo corrections to his papers. (For those younger readers that may not be familiar with its use, Liquid Paper was the go-to product for correcting errors when using the typewriter. We dinosaurs simply opened the small bottle, dabbed on a little of the white liquid, let it dry, and corrected—typed over—the misspelled word. Bingo, back in business!)

---

27   The other misc. item that has always added to the circumstantial evidence for me has been the fact that Zodiac used a piece of *telex* paper to send at least one of his messages. (As you may recall, I mention this in *Most Evil.*) Dad, back then, was sending dozens of telex messages on a daily basis to his many offices throughout Asia. For *him*, its use was almost as common as using regular paper, but it's use was very rare for others, especially for serial killers to use and/or send in to a newspaper.

George Hodel "At Work" In His San Francisco Home Office, Circa 1992

(Left) George Hodel seated at home office desk with typewriter and Liquid Paper on shelf behind him in San Francisco penthouse, circa 1997.

(Right) White Arrows indicate Zodiac's use of Liquid Paper to draw words, letters, and symbols on 1970 Halloween Card.

Fig. 8.3

Interior of 1970 Zodiac Halloween Card

Bottom photo (enlarged) shows bottle of Liquid Paper clearly visible on the shelf behind him.

Fig. 8.4

Without viewing the original card, currently booked in evidence at SFPD, it is impossible to identify all of the "add-ins" written on the card by Zodiac. However, I believe the following objects were written by Zodiac using Liquid Paper:

1. All of the white crescent shapes used in the eyes

2. "Peek-A-Boo—You are doomed!"

3. 4-TEEN

4. BOO!

5. Zodiac cipher

6. Z

7. Zodiac Circle and Cross

8. Spider Web upper right corner (Unknown if added by Zodiac)

I believe the importance of Robert Sadler's Liquid Paper observation, coupled with my subsequent locating of the 1992 office photograph, is valuable in that it moves us from the generic to the specific. It adds one more link in the long chain of circumstantial evidence we have presented.

Yes, Liquid Paper was a standard item, found in every office and many homes back when Zodiac used it in 1970. However, it was an item commonly used by secretaries, not serial killers.

Fast forward to 1992. We are well into the computer age. Except for a few of us dinosaurs (I continued using a typewriter until 1995), Liquid Paper has all but evaporated.

But not so with George Hodel! As the photo reveals, Liquid Paper, like the telex paper from a roll off a UP Model 15 Teletype machine that Zodiac used to mail several of his notes, was an item kept at arm's reach and used by him on a daily basis.

In the sixties and seventies, George Hodel maintained Teletype machines in each of his fifteen INRA-ASIA offices, which also included one in his private penthouse suite,

(General MacArthur's old headquarters) on the bayfront, in Manila, Philippines.

George Hodel 1978 Telex Sent To Me From Dad's INRA-ASIA Office in Australia

Zodiac used this identical telex paper (blank) to send several of his 1970 mailings.

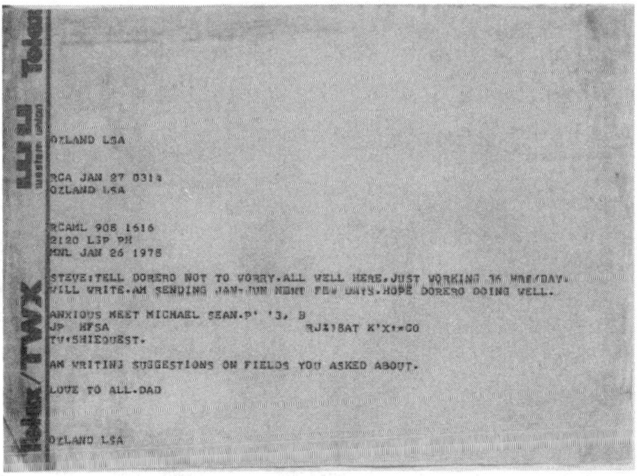

OZLAND LSA

RCA JAN 27 0314
OZLAND LSA

RCAML 908 1616
2120 LIP PH
MNL JAN 26 1978

STEVE:TELL DORERO NOT TO WORRY.ALL WELL HERE.JUST WORKING 16 HRS/DAY.
WILL WRITE.AM SENDING JAN-JUN NEXT FEW DAYS.HOPE DORERO DOING WELL.

ANXIOUS MEET MICHAEL SEAN.P' '3, B
UP HFSA RJ%1BAT K'X*-GO
TV*SHIEQUEST.

AM WRITING SUGGESTIONS ON FIELDS YOU ASKED ABOUT.

LOVE TO ALL.DAD

OZLAND LSA

Fig. 8.5

George Hodel received and sent dozens of telexes a day. Before we had fax and emails, this Teletype machine was the communication instrument of choice. It was his lifeline, connecting him to all of his market research offices.

Several of the Zodiac letters, (Bates "Confession Letter" and one of the early July 31, 1969, three-part cryptograms) were sent to the police and press purportedly written on telex paper cut from a roll of a UP Model 15 Teletype machine. This is the very same model Teletype machine used by Dr. George Hill Hodel to send his international telexes with their yellow telex paper on a daily basis—as frequently as we send out our emails today!

Cracking the Zodiac Signature Cipher

> *CIPHER—A cipher (pronounced SAI-fuhr) is any method of encrypting text (concealing its readability and meaning). It is also sometimes used to refer to the encrypted text message itself. In addition to the cryptographic meaning, cipher also means (1) a combination of symbolic letters as in an entwined weaving of letters for a monogram.*[28]

Below is the front of Zodiac's 1970 Halloween card, in which Zodiac promises to give a clue to his name.

Fig. 8.6

"...You ache to know my name, And so I'll clue you in..."

When addressing the Halloween card in *BDA II* Chapter 21, I also wrote:

> *"...In addition to writing his signatory circle and cross, Zodiac included a strange symbol at the bottom of the card, as well as drawing a set of thirteen eyes, with a threatening message to the* Chronicle *reporter Avery that read, "peek-a-boo, you are doomed."*

This "strange symbol" followed his message, as a signatory at the bottom of the card, as well as in the envelope's "return address" space, as if to reemphasize it as a clue to his identity.

Zodiac's 1970 Halloween Card
Arrows Point to "Mysterious Symbol"

The below pictured "sorry no cipher" message was also included on the back of the card.

Fig. 8.7

Fig. 8.8

Over the past forty years, there has been much speculation about this mysterious symbol, but no real answer has been forthcoming. To this day, the symbol remains an enigma.

Astonishingly, Zodiac was so overly confident in his ability to be esoteric and "crack-proof" that his megalomaniacal ego demanded he actually sign his real name. But he would conceal it in little-known, long-forgotten arcana. Like Poe's purloined letter, he would place it in plain sight, but bury it so deep that it would never be deciphered. He was wrong.

CHAPTER 9

*"There was a painter named Copley who never would
miss a good lay and to make his paintings erotic instead
of brushes, he simply used his prick."*

—Marcel Duchamp

*"He [Copley] is absolutely sincere in his pursuit of joy and
of liberty, in his love of life and his refusal of cliché. He
is the wisest of us all carefully hiding his sophistication
under the guise of a simple man."*

—Man Ray

Surrealist Enigmas—Riddles Wrapped in Mysteries

IN 1935, GEORGE HODEL's family photographer and close
friend, surrealist artist Man Ray, cleverly secreted
his own name in one of his artworks (*Space Writing
Self-Portrait,* 1935). Using a penlight to draw the abstract
loops, the artist signed his name but then reversed the
print, intending to conceal his signature forever from his
bourgeois public as a mischievous "inside joke."

But it didn't last forever.

In 2009, keen-eyed Hartford Art School professor Ellen
Carey discovered the artist's seventy-four-year-old secret
signature after holding the abstract photograph up to a
mirror, which then revealed his hidden signage.

Man Ray's *Space Writings* (1935)

Right: Photo retraced by author to emphasize professor Carey's discovery of hidden Man Ray signature.

Fig. 9.0

The following is an excerpt from an online article in the *Smithsonian* magazine, titled "Man Ray's Signature Work: Artist Man Ray mischievously scribbled his name in a famous photograph, but it took decades for the gesture to be discovered."

The article by Abby Callard appeared on November 10, 2009:

> *...In 1935, the avant-garde photographer Man Ray opened his shutter, sat down in front of his camera, and used a penlight to create a series of swirls and loops. Because of his movements with the penlight, his face was blurred in the resulting photograph. As a self-portrait— titled* Space Writings—*it seemed fairly abstract.*
>
> *But now, Ellen Carey, a photographer whose working method is similar to Man Ray's, has discovered something that has been hidden in plain sight in Space Writings for the past seventy-four years: the artist's signature, signed with the penlight amid the swirls and loops.*

"I knew instantly when I saw it—it's a very famous self-portrait—that his signature was in it," says Carey, a photography professor at the University of Hartford. "I just got this flash of intuition." Her intuition was to look at the penlight writing from Man Ray's point of view—which is to say, the reverse of how it appears to anyone looking at the photograph. "I knew that if I held it up to a mirror, it would be there," Carey says. She did, and it was.

Following in His Guru's Footsteps?

ANOTHER CLOSE FRIEND AND Hollywood confidant to Man Ray in the forties was surrealist artist/gallerist William Copley. So close were the two men that in 1951 Copley closed his Beverly Hills art gallery, packed up his personal possessions and his new girlfriend, artist Gloria de Herrera, and took the same ship with Man Ray and his wife Juliet to Paris, where he would live and paint alongside his fellow surrealist for the next decade.

Copley completed the drawing below in 1961, some eleven years after Dr. Hodel fled Los Angeles and the United States to avoid arrest for murder.

His painting depicts a nude woman lying supine on what appear to be bathroom tiles. The tiles in his drawing are identical in appearance to those found in George Hodel's master bathroom at his private residence, which my earlier investigation has shown was the actual crime scene location of the 1947 Black Dahlia murder.

In Copley's painting, we see "the doctor" holding his black bag. Oversized surgical tools have been laid out near the supine and unconscious victim, suggesting an "operation" is about to be performed at the witching hour of midnight.

It is Midnight Dr. _____

Bill Copley and Man Ray and Marcel Duchamp were the closest of friends. Copley in 1951 closed his Beverly Hills Art Gallery and left Los Angeles to live and work with Man Ray in Paris

Fig. 9.1

Was Bill Copley revealing his knowledge of Dr. Hodel's 1947 Black Dahlia Murder in his artwork? Did Copley conceal and actually spell out the name of the doctor-killer in his cryptic placement of the surgical tools to represent hidden letters in his 1961 drawing, *It is Midnight Dr. _____?*

Master Bathroom Tiles in Hodel Residence Compared to Those Seen in Copley's *It is Midnight Dr. ____*

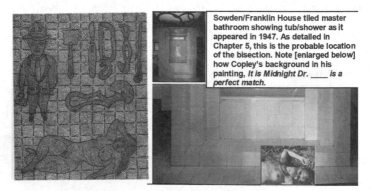

Sowden/Franklin House tiled master bathroom showing tub/shower as it appeared in 1947. As detailed in Chapter 5, this is the probable location of the bisection. Note [enlarged below] how Copley's background in his painting, *It is Midnight Dr. ____* is a perfect match.

Fig. 9.2

Étant Donnés 1947-1967 by Marcel Duchamp

"The strangest work of art any museum has ever had in it."
—Jasper Johns

SURREALIST ARTIST MARCEL DUCHAMP's creation, *Étant Donnés*, is believed by many to be copied from the original 1947 Black Dahlia crime scene photographs. The press photos (obtained both before and after LAPD arrived at the location) were readily obtainable and in circulation by many of Hollywood's "inner circle" including numerous newspaper reporters and screenwriters closely connected to George Hodel and to the original investigation as documented in *Black Dahlia Avenger II*.

Duchamp's Étant Donnes *(left) is here compared to an actual Elizabeth "Black Dahlia" Short 1947 crime scene photograph.*

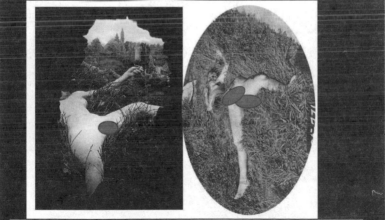

Duchamp's *Étant donnés* (begun in 1947 and worked on * for twenty years in secret before being first shown to his close friend William Copley), made public only after his death and here compared to Elizabeth Short crime scene. Both show knife cuts to victim's private parts.

*Some sources claim 1946

Fig. 9.3

Surreal artist Marcel Duchamp's two closest friends were William Copley and Man Ray. Here, we see a photograph of one of Duchamp's most famous works, the *Étant Donnés*, which has been on display at the Philadelphia Museum of Art since 1969, just two years after Duchamp's death. The artwork was gifted to the museum and William Copley oversaw its assembly, per Duchamp's specific and extremely detailed instructions.

Author Visiting Marcel Duchamp's *Étant Donnés* at the Philadelphia Museum of Art in November 2014.[29]

The viewer (or witness) must approach the door inside the museum's small room and peek through the two holes set at eye level to observe the hidden "crime scene."

(Above photographs courtesy of photographer and friend, Robert Juckett)

Fig. 9.4

29   During my short trip to the museum, I noted that more than half of the visitors that entered the room simply glanced at the door and left, without realizing or viewing Duchamp's artwork.

Aboard the *S.S. De Grasse* About to Depart the United States for Paris, France on March 12, 1951[30]

(Left to Right): William Copley, Juliet Man Ray, Man Ray, Gloria de Herrera, and Marcel Duchamp

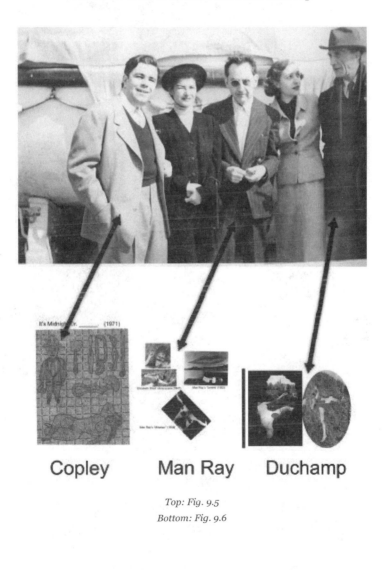

Top: Fig. 9.5
Bottom: Fig. 9.6

---

30   Photographer unknown.

L'Équivoque (1943) by Man Ray

Fig. 9.7

Fig. 9.8

As summarized in detail in *Black Dahlia Avenger II*, Elizabeth "Black Dahlia" Short may have been the original model for Man Ray's 1943 painting *L'Équivoque*.

Newspaper accounts and a 1947 interview with a local Hollywood artist independently established that Short posed for at least two different oil paintings in Hollywood in the summer of 1944. Additional investigation has established that Short knew George Hodel prior to her murder. Elizabeth could very likely have been introduced by Dr. Hodel to Man Ray, and agreed to do the modeling for the painting at Man Ray's home studio located just two miles from the Hodel residence.

Shown below is the strange crosshatch symbol carved into victim Elizabeth Short's right hip by surgeon/killer George Hodel in 1947. The incision is identical in every respect to his good friend's *L'Équivoque* artwork, painted in Hollywood just three years prior to the murder. Two other Man Ray artworks have been previously connected to this specific crime. (Man Ray's *Minotaur* and *Lover's Lips*.) *L'Équivoque* appears to be the third. The crosshatch is another inside joke and additional homage to George Hodel's surrealist guru Man Ray.

For a complete summary of the L'Équivoque *linkage,*
I refer the reader to BDA II, Chapter 26, pages 433-439,
"Murder As a Fine Art: The Hodel/Man Ray Nexus"

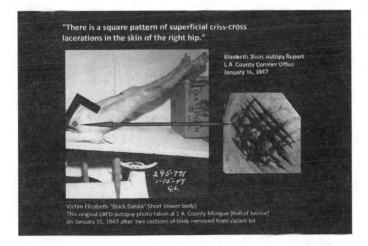

Fig. 9.9

MAN RAY The Equivoque 1943 Tempera on cardboard
35x28cm Courtesy of the Marconi Foundation

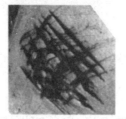

Cuttings surgically carved into right hip of victim
Elizabeth "Black Dahlia" Short by her killer in 1947

Fig. 9.10   *Fig. 9.10.1*

An Unexpected Partner

EIGHT WEEKS INTO MY reexamination of the Zodiac Halloween
card, on September 6, 2014, I received an email from England.

It was from a previously unknown reader, a Ms. Susan
Wilshire, who was just finishing my newly updated *Black
Dahlia Avenger II*. Here is a reproduction of that first
contact:

Hi Steve:

*I've nearly finished reading your BDA II book.
Always been interested in this case and saw you on a
documentary. Been looking at some Man Ray stuff. In a
1948 publication,* Alphabet for Adults *album of drawings
(Copley Galleries, Beverly Hills) I found some interesting
quotes/drawings online.*

Man Ray quotes of this book/series of drawings:

"A letter always suggests a word, and a word always suggests a book. There are words that are for everyday use, and there are words reserved for the more special occasions, for poetry. One may glean from the former those disinherited symbols which by an inadequate association can be divested of their prosaic meaning and finally projected into the domain of greater emotional exclamations. To make a new alphabet of the discarded props of a conversation can lead only to fresh discoveries in language. Concentration is the desired end, as in an anagram whose density is the measure of its destiny."

Just thought aspects of this were interesting given the date of publication and in all likeliness the fact that Man Ray may have produced the latter images during 1947/post-BD case.

More interestingly, if you seek out the image he has drawn which relates to the letter Q, which he denotes as "quarrel," the drawing, albeit simple, depicts two people face-to face and looks like a view of the courtyard, looking South, toward the living room of Sowden house. Some other images I also think are interesting.

Man Ray had a second edition of this book published, but this was much later when he had returned to France. I can't find all of the alphabet images online. Sorry if this is duplication of something you're already aware of, but thought you might be interested. I can't attach an image so you'll have to look on the web yourself.

Warmest Regards,
—Sue
P.S.: Fascinating, truly fascinating.

In fact, I had never heard of or seen Man Ray's 1948 *Alphabet for Adults* publication and immediately responded to Ms. Wilshire's email :

September 6, 2014
Hi Sue:

Thank you for the email on "Alphabet for Adults."
I was not aware of this book and find the quote from Man Ray fascinating, all things considered. Really shows his mindset on this.
Can you email or direct me to the Q image location (link) online you refer to? Haven't found it online and looks like the book purchase starts at around 1,500.00 dollars (ouch!). Are other letters shown online?

Most Appreciatively Yours,
—Steve Hodel
Los Angeles

Within hours of my request, Ms. Wilshire forwarded the information and related images along with her astute insights and observations.

This resulted in an exchange of emails and thoughts on the subject which have now been synthesized and are here presented as what I believe to be strong corroboration and support of the Man Ray Nexus as discussed throughout *Black Dahlia Avenger II*, and how it is germane and relates directly to the present Zodiac Halloween card analysis.

I cannot overstate Ms. Wilshire's contribution to my ongoing criminal investigation.

Subsequent to our exchange of emails and ideas, I complimented Sue for her "keen eye and objective thinking." Her casual and exceptionally modest response caught me completely off guard:

> *...not only my thoughts having read your book, but I was trained as a designer and went to art school, and now am a Detective Chief Inspector in the UK!*

A detective chief inspector in the UK! As it turns out, DCI Wilshire is an active, serving police inspector. No wonder she had a "keen eye"—her day job is that of a real-life DCI Jane Tennison! (Actress Helen Mirren played the role of DCI Tennison in the popular British police procedural miniseries *Prime Suspect*.)

Detective Chief Inspector Susan Wilshire

Fig. 9.11

Alphabet for Adults

Abecedaire-ABC Book, a primer (after the first four letters of the Latin alphabet: A, B, C, D) is a visual medium (paper, poster, embroidery) with all the symbols of the alphabet, almost always listed in the alphabetical order. The primers were a medium of instruction for children.[31]

---

31   fr.wikipedia.org/wiki/Ab%C3%A9c%C3%A9daire

Photo shows cover and front matter page introduction to
Alphabet for Adults.

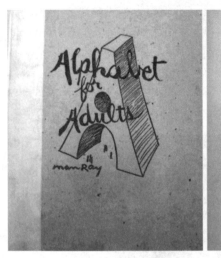

ALPHABET FOR ADULTS

A letter always suggests a word, and a word always suggests a book. There are words that are for every day use and there are words reserved for the more special occasions, for poetry. One may glean from the former those disinherited symbols which by an inadequate association can be divested of their prosaic meaning and finally projected into the domain of greater emotional exclamations. To make a new alphabet of the discarded props of a conversation can lead only to fresh discoveries in language. Concentration is the desired end, as in an anagram whose density is the measure of its destiny.   MAN RAY

This first hardcover edition was published by Man Ray's close friend and gallerist William Copley in Beverly Hills in 1948. It was a limited edition of 500 copies. The book contained eighty pages and included thirty-nine Man Ray drawings with captions from A (anchor) to Z (zinc). A later edition, Alphabet pour Adults, *was published in France in 1970, some six years before Man Ray's death in 1976.*

Fig. 9.12

In this 1948 *Alphabet for Adults*, Man Ray speaks of creating "a new alphabet of the discarded props which can lead to fresh discoveries in language" and "concentration being the desired end, as in an anagram..."

In the photograph below we see three samples from Man Ray's adult alphabet: "A" for anchor, "E" for Elephant, and "K" for kimono, with each drawing containing the shape of the letter concealed within the object; the anchor, the elephant, and the kimono. He is whimsically playing with the letters as words.

Our earlier review and analysis of the separate artwork contributions of Man Ray, William Copley, and Marcel Duchamp (post-Black Dahlia) were without benefit of this new information.

As we add this new knowledge to the former, let us consider the fact that *Alphabet for Adults* was a 1948 Man Ray/William Copley collaboration created and published by the two surrealists in Hollywood less than one year after the Black Dahlia murder (January 15, 1947). The book was first offered for sale at the Copley Gallery in Beverly Hills in a limited edition of 500 copies.

Was this collaborative book of whimsical anagrams and word play the inspiration for William Copley's 1961 drawing, *It is Midnight Dr.* _____? Did Copley, as we have previously speculated, disguise the letters H, O, D, E, L as surgical tools and place them in his drawing as a variation on the theme that he and Man Ray presented some thirteen years earlier?

Another Word Play?

A   E   K

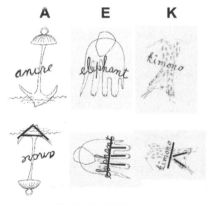
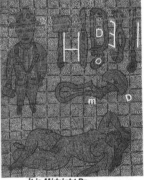

Alphabet For Adults
Man Ray (artist) and William Copley (publisher) 1948

It is Midnight Dr._____.
William Copley (artist) 1961

Fig. 9.13

Man Ray's Letter "Q" for Querelle (Quarrel)

Fig. 9.14

Detective Chief Inspector Susan Wilshire, in her initial September 2014 email to me, observed:

> *...More interestingly, if you seek out the image he [Man Ray] has drawn which relates to the letter Q, which he denotes as "quarrel," the drawing, albeit simple, depicts two people face-to-face and looks like a view of the courtyard, looking South, toward the living room of the Sowden house. Some other images I also think are interesting.*

As I viewed the "Q" drawing she had sent me, I quickly recognized an object that gave instant validation to her suggestion that the location depicted was the Frank Lloyd Wright Jr. built Sowden house, our family home in Hollywood throughout the forties.

Objet de mon affection—L'Oculiste 1944-1948

L'Oculiste *sculpture signed by Man Ray in 1944, gifted to Dr. George Hill Hodel in Hollywood, California in 1948.*

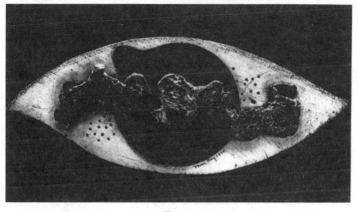

Fig. 9.15

Man Ray created the sculpture *Object of my affection—L'Oculiste* in 1944, during the ten-year period he resided in Hollywood (1940 to 1950). His "object of my affection" was made out of "fragments of lead and a rubber sink stopper on a curved piece of wood mounted on board." The sculpture was first exhibited at Hollywood's Circle Gallery, 7623 Sunset Boulevard, from September 3 to September 30, 1946, then later displayed at the Julien Levy Gallery in New York.

Man Ray gifted *L'Oculiste* to his good friend George Hodel in 1948.

The sculpture remained in my father's personal possession for the next fifty years. In the photograph below, we see it proudly displayed in my father's penthouse office on Manila Bay, Philippines, circa 1985.

George Hodel (wearing glasses) circa 1985, is seen displaying his sculptured artwork at his residence office in Manila, Philippines.

In this photograph, mailed to me sometime in the eighties, my father has handwritten in green ink "Man Ray," and drawn an arrow pointing to the original sculpture, framed and mounted on his wall. (Other individuals in photo not identified.)

Fig. 9.16

After being based in Manila and traveling the world for more than forty years, my father and his wife June relocated back to the United States. In 1990, they leased a thirty-ninth floor penthouse in downtown San Francisco, where Dr. George Hill Hodel would spend the final decade of his life.

On May 16, 1999, at the advanced age of ninety-one, my father died in his San Francisco residence. The official cause of death, as listed on the death certificate was, "congestive heart disease." (Since my father's personal physician had attended and was treating him on a regular basis in the weeks preceding his death, and was willing to sign the death certificate, by California law no autopsy was required.) Based on information presented to me some months later, it is my belief that the actual cause of death was "suicide by pills" (Seconal).

In the months immediately preceding his death, my father had arranged to sell a number of personal items, all of which were connected to his decade of friendship with Man Ray in the forties. The items included a self-portrait of Man Ray along with a number of individual Hodel family photographs taken by Man Ray including George Hodel, Dorothy Hodel ("Dorero"), posed photographs of Dorothy and Juliet Man Ray, and a photograph he took of my two brothers and me in 1944. Also offered for sale was a prized piece of artwork from George Hodel's collection: Man Ray's sculpture *L'Oculiste*.

The items were to be sold by Butterfield & Butterfield in two separate auctions. The first was to be on May 27, 1999. The second, which included Man Ray's *L'Oculiste*, was to follow five months later, in an October 27 sale. The suggested catalog bid price for my father's Man Ray sculpture was $30,000 to $50,000.

As part of his sale conditions, George Hodel arranged with the auction house that he was to remain anonymous. His name was not to be revealed or included in any of the promotional materials or the sales brochure. Butterfield & Butterfield agreed and consequently the sale was titled: "PROPERTY OF A GENTLEMAN."

Because of Man Ray's recognition as a high-profile artist and the rarity of the items, the auction house decided to present the "Property of a Gentleman" collection as the cover piece for their upcoming sales catalog.

Butterfield & Butterfield's May 27 Sales Catalog (left)
Butterfield & Butterfield's October 27 Sales Catalog (right)

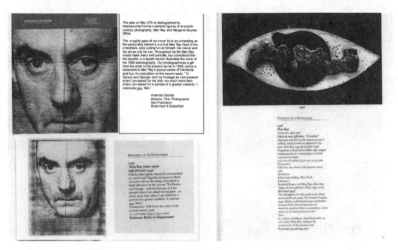

Fig. 9.17

As seen in the photograph, the Butterfield & Butterfield catalog contained the 1946 Man Ray self-portrait, which Man Ray had also used as his book cover on the first edition of his *Man Ray: Self-Portrait* (Little, Brown and Co., 1963).

This photograph was gifted to George and Dorothy Hodel in 1946, some two years before the *L'Oculiste* sculpture.

In 1999, Ms. Amanda Doenitz, Butterfield & Butterfield's Director of Fine Photographs, introduced the upcoming sales catalog and cover art writing in the description as follows:

> *The sale on May 27 is distinguished by masterworks from two seminal figures of twentieth-century photography, Man Ray and Margaret Bourke-White.*
>
> *The weighty gaze of our cover lot is as compelling as the personality behind it; we find Man Ray fixed in the crosshairs, slyly poking fun at himself, his viewer, and his art as only he can. Throughout his life, Man Ray would make many self-portraits, but considered this his favorite; a cropped version illustrates the cover of his*

*1963 autobiography. Our photograph was a gift from
the artist to the present owner in 1946 and is a testament
to Man Ray's joyous series of friendship and fun. An
inscription on the mount reads, "To Dorero and George—
and my homage as I am pleased when I am asked for my
phiz—so much more than when I am asked for a portrait
of a greater celebrity. I celebrate you. Man."*[32]

Two Man Ray Family Photos

*"Dorero," photographed circa 1944, and Dr. George Hill Hodel, shown
wearing his UNRRA overcoat and posed holding the Tibetan god
Yamantaka. The god is shown in the "Yab-Yum" position, having sexual
intercourse with his consort. Photo taken in September/October 1946.*

Fig. 9.18

Let us return to the subject at hand—Man Ray's 1948
drawing of the letter "Q"—querelle, quarrel.

Now with the necessary background information, you,
my readers, can see what I saw when I first viewed the "Q"

---

32   As told in *The Black Dahlia Avenger*, "Dorero" was my father's pet name for my mother,
Dorothy. He would confide with his friends that he created the name out of two separate words: "Dor"
meaning, "a gift of" and "Eros," the word representing sexual desire. Hence, Dorero, a gift of sexual
desire. All of my mother's intimate friends and partygoers from that period knew and referred to her as
Dorero.

letter—*L'Oculiste*! Man Ray's 1948 gift to George Hodel has been placed right in the center, as witness to "the quarrel."

Fig. 9.19

So in one year, 1948, Man Ray first drew and then immediately gifted the oculist—the "object of my affection," the eye and representative witness to the quarrel—*to George Hodel*.

With this added information, the connections now become obvious, and I believe that DCI Susan Wilshire is correct!

We have strong corroborative evidence that the drawing does, in fact, depict the Sowden house. The view of the quarreling couple is looking south viewing the two figures standing in the courtyard. Man Ray has even included the concrete block columns, the roof-line, above their heads as shown in the comparison photograph.

I believe the most reasonable assumption is that the couple represented in Man Ray's picture are George and Dorothy Hodel arguing inside their home.

However, based on the timing of the publication of *Alphabet for Adults* and the simultaneous gift of the sculpture to George, both following just one year after the Black Dahlia murder, there will be those that question, "Could the woman in the Man Ray drawing be Elizabeth Short?" Or, "Could Man Ray have witnessed an argument between Elizabeth and George the previous year and secretly documented it in his book as 'Q' for quarrel?"

The question is legitimate for several reasons:

1. The fact that Elizabeth "Black Dahlia" Short is now known to have been murdered at the Sowden house.

2. The new evidence suggesting that she may likely have modeled for two Man Ray paintings in the years preceding her murder. (See *BDA II* chapter on *L'Équivoque* for evidence.)

3. George Hodel was known and identified by law enforcement to have been one of Elizabeth's "former suitors."

4. In January of 1947 Elizabeth was known to be running from a man that had "threatened to kill her," and had argued and fought with him, and bore scratch marks on her arms as a result of an altercation with this "former suitor."

Indeed, a case can be made that the woman in the Man Ray drawing could be Elizabeth Short—but, absent any new findings or documentation that must, at least for now, remain purely speculative.

What is most important in this new discovery is the fact that we are able to make a compelling case that the "word play" and surreal images suspected to be "anagrams," or ciphers, in Copley's, 1961 *It is Midnight Dr.* _____ are here connected to his and Man Ray's past. It was Copley and Man Ray's artistic MO, drawn and presented to the public by these two artists from Hollywood in 1948.

Further, within the same pages of their 1948 letter games book, these artists have provided us with a direct link to George Hodel, the Sowden/Franklin house, and publicly documented his violent nature. (Albeit, in this case, verbal.)

For foundational reasons, I have had to juggle my investigative timeline a bit.

As previously indicated, it was September 6, 2014, when I was first contacted by DCI Susan Wilshire and presented with the valuable information contained in Man Ray's, *Alphabet for Adults*.

However, the big bang, and what I consider to be a Zodiac investigative tsunami, came two months earlier, also from across the pond—this time from France!

CHAPTER 10

Rosetta Stone

Fig. 10.0

ROSETTA STONE.—An inscribed stone found near Rosetta (now called Rashid) in Egypt in 1799. Its text is written in three scripts: hieroglyphic, demotic, and Greek. The deciphering of the hieroglyphs by Jean-Francois Champollion in 1822 led to the interpretation of many other early records of Egyptian civilization.

(as noun) A key to some previously undecipherable mystery or unattainable knowledge.[33]

The Zodiac Rosetta Stone—Cracking the Cipher

"For tis the sport to have the enginer / Hoist with his owne petar."

—*Shakespeare*, Hamlet, *ACT III Scene iv.*

IT WAS WEDNESDAY, JULY 2, 2014; I had just begun preparing for a relaxing four-day holiday. No travel. No fighting traffic to and from the airport. Just some quiet time, at home, with the anticipation of watching three or four good classic films, along with my July 4 traditional favorite, *Yankee Doodle Dandy*, starring James Cagney and Walter Huston. A welcome respite from writing and research. (Or so I thought.)

Just as I was closing down my computer, it happened. The sound of an incoming email. I glanced at my inbox and noted it was from France. I clicked on the new message:

Dear Sir,

Have you ever noticed that Zodiac's signature was a compound of two ogham "letters"? The letter on the left side is for "H" and the letter on the right side is for "L." The Irish name of the first "letter" is "beithe," that means "flash," "flame," and the other is called "uath," the old-Irish word for "scare." The dots remain mysterious.

I read your first book shortly after it was published, and it deeply changed my mind upon the real meaning of XXth century (namely, in the fields of ideology and culture).

Best regards from France.
—Y. P.

I responded with a few questions to "Y. P." and several follow-up emails arrived in quick succession from this anonymous Frenchman:

Encore-Ogham alphabet:
I'm back from my Celtic languages handbook: according to certain forms of writings (or engravings) the dots are for the vowels. Two dots = "O"; four dots = "E."

I refer to the signature that is drawn on the Halloween postcard and its envelope. (An inverted "L" on the left side, an inverted "F" on the right side and the four dots in the middle of the signature.) The inverted "L" is the Irish "letter" for "H"; the inverted "F" is the Irish "letter" for "L." There would be no "translation" into Irish, just a cryptic game from an alphabet to another one.)

A few of Y. P.'s words seemingly jumped off the page:

Zodiac's signature a compound of two Ogham letters, "H" on the left and "L" on the right? Celtic languages? Ogham Alphabet? Cryptic game from an alphabet to another?

I spent the next several days researching Y. P.'s references, analyzing the material, and putting together a chart that, I believe, "cracks the code" to Zodiac's mysterious Halloween card symbol. The key to the symbol is just as "Y. P.," my newfound *ami français,* had speculated. And, with this key—the ancient Ogham alphabet—we can now, for the first time, unlock, decipher, and read the signatory name of Zodiac.

See for yourself:

Ogham—The Key

Halloween Card   Halloween Envelope

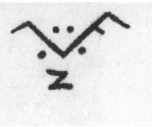

Fig. 10.1   Fig. 10.2

OGHAM /ˈɒɡəm/—[1] (Modern Irish [ˈoːm] or[ˈoːəm]; Old Irish: ogam [ˈɔɣam]) is an Early Medieval alphabet used primarily to write the early Irish language (in the so-called "orthodox" inscriptions, 4th to 6th centuries), and later the Old Irish language (so-called scholastic ogham, 6th to 9th centuries).

...

In Scotland, a number of inscriptions using the ogham writing system are known, but their language is still the subject of debate. It has been argued by Richard Cox in The Language of Ogham Inscriptions in Scotland *(1999) that the language of these is* **Old Norse**[34][35]

Ogham Writing on Standing Stone

Photo Courtesy of Jessica Spengler

Fig. 10.3

34   Author's note: Emphasis mine

35   en.wikipedia.org/wiki/Ogham

The Ogham

The Celtic "Tree Alphabet" is a secret cypher of the Celtic bards and Druids, meant to make magical inscriptions on monuments. (Chart from McManus. *A Guide To Ogham*)

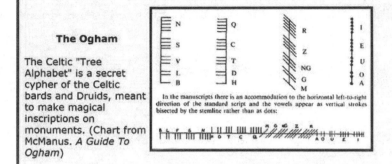

In the manuscripts there is an accommodation to the horizontal left-to-right direction of the standard script and the vowels appear as vertical strokes bisected by the stemline rather than as dots:

Fig. 10.4

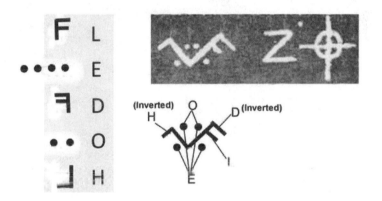

Fig. 10.5

Fig. 10.6

Below is shown a slightly more detailed rendering of the solution. (Courtesy of the artistry of my good friend, Robert "Dr. Watson" Sadler.):

Ogham Cypher Symbol	Equivalent English Letter	Zodiac Placed Symbol	
F	L	⌃	~⋰⌃
••••	E	⋰•	~⋱
⌐	D	⌃ (reversed)	~⋰
••	O	••	~⋱•
L	H	⌃ (inverted)	~⋰•

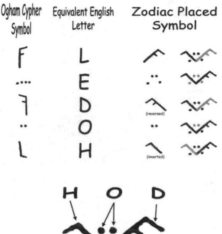

Spells HODEL

Fig. 10.7

The decryption is perfect. Zodiac's signature reads **H O D E L.** Nothing is missing. No additional letters have been added or omitted.

Based on this decryption, it is my belief that Dr. George Hill Hodel, thoroughly convinced that he was a "master criminal" and that his high-genius insulated him from detection—confident that his cleverness insured his cipher was "crack-proof"—wrote, as promised, on the front of his Halloween card, "...you ache to know my name, and so I'll clue you in." George Hodel threw all caution to the wind and signed his real name to the card.

Zodiac Halloween Card Deciphered

Fig. 10.8

The credit for this remarkable discovery must go to "Y. P." in Paris, France. I recently wrote and asked him if I might have permission to credit and use his real name, which he has just granted. "Y. P." is M. Yves Person, and to add a further ironic twist to our ongoing investigation, he teaches literature at a high school in the suburbs of Paris.[36]

M. Yves Person, Paris, France 2015

Fig 10.9

---

36   Many readers will recall that after the US military and intelligence experts were unable to solve Zodiac's original 1969 three-part cryptogram, a married couple, Donald and Bettye Harden, "cracked the code" after studying it for just one weekend. Their solution was confirmed by the Vallejo Police Department and published in the San Francisco newspapers. Donald Harden, like Yves Person, was also a high school teacher. Harden taught history and economics at North Salinas High School in Salinas, California.

Ogham & Surrealism

YVES PERSON'S "CRACKING OF the code," and his mention of the "Ogham," was the first time I had heard the word.

My research not only brought me full circle but has also identified what I believe was the original source my father, as Zodiac, used to create his 1970 Halloween card cipher.

Incredibly, this inspiration for George Hodel's "code" did not come from some obscure book of Druid mysteries hidden on a dust-covered shelf in a cobblestone bookstore in Dublin.

Instead, like many of George Hodel's signature clues, it sprang full-born, again, from his love of modernism and twentieth-century art. More specifically, from the avant-garde movement known as Surrealism.

The secret clue embedded in his serial murders, possibly his most significant and most dangerous? His real name hidden in a five-letter cipher.

George Hodel, the supreme Dadaist, was playing the role of his childhood hero, the arch-villain Fantomas. Or, maybe it was George Hodel playing the master criminal Moriarty, outwitting all and leaving his riddle wrapped in a real-life murder mystery—risking all, for a wink and a nod to his fellow surrealists.

Once again, we find zero degrees of separation between George Hodel and our family photographer, Man Ray, and from Ray to his fellow Dadaist Marcel Duchamp, and the Irish artist/author Brian O'Doherty (aka Patrick Ireland).

Artist Brian O'Doherty—Connecting the Dots (and Lines)

Excerpt from Brian O'Doherty, "Self, Sign, Scenario," a Galerie Thomas Fischer Exhibit, open from September 20 to November 8, 2004.

...*Brian O'Doherty—Born in 1928 in County Roscommon, Ireland, Brian O'Doherty worked as an artist from 1972 until 2008 under the pseudonym Patrick Ireland.*

Exhibitions have been held at the Smithsonian American Art Museum, Washington, DC, at P.S.1, New York, at the National Gallery of Ireland, Dublin and he has also been featured at documenta 6 and the Biennale in Venice (1980).

After studying medicine in Dublin, O'Doherty emigrated in 1957 to the US, where he conducted research for a time at Harvard before he resumed his artistic career.

He was also the editor of Art in America *and later became the part-time director of the Visual Arts Program, and subsequently of the Film and Media Arts Program of the National Endowment for the Arts.*

In 1976 his essay "Inside the White Cube" appeared in Artforum.

For his novel, The Strange Case of Mademoiselle P., *O'Doherty received the award of the British Society of Authors.*

In 2000 The Deposition of Father McGreevy *was short-listed for the Booker Prize.*

His works are in numerous collections including the Museum of Modern Art and the National Gallery in Washington.

Brian O'Doherty has lived in New York since 1960 and is married to the art historian Barbara Novak.

In 2014 Brian O'Doherty's new novel, titled The Crossdresser's Secret *was published (in English) by Sternberg Press.*

...

His interest in identity and spatial logic was always accompanied by his interest in "signs": systems, grids, labyrinths, notations, and letters. In 1967 he had found a way, in his own words, to "fuse minimalism, serialism, and language," by deploying an ancient Gaelic letter system called "Ogham."

Ogham is found on the rim of a couple of hundred Irish Ogham stones, dating from the 5th century. Its letters form a certain number of vertical or diagonal lines in relation to a horizontal line (see [figure 10.10]). On the ancient Ogham stones, the line of reference is simply the rim of the stone. O'Doherty transformed this principle by creating aluminum-covered, contemporary versions of the archaeological stones. Inscribed is one of the three words ONE, HERE or NOW, which appear quite often in O'Doherty's/Ireland's Ogham works.

The Ogham Alphabet Transcribed by Brian O'Doherty

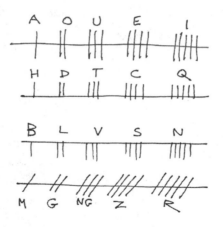

Fig. 10.10

In the reflective sculpture ONE (1970), the visitor's physical reflection is constantly accompanied by this logical reflection about the self in a certain time and space. In his Ogham drawings, with which Patrick Ireland even participated in documenta 6 in 1977, and in the paintings that are based on the Ogham principle, the rhythmical, structuring lines provide both form and content (One drawing, 1969, or Vaughan's Circle, 2004/5) and can literally be read with the help of the transcription.

There is more to the Ogham lines than first meets the eye: The large format painting Ogham on Broadway *(2003) is a reflection on the grid—and an ode to Piet Mondrian's* Broadway Boogie Woogie, *a piece the Dutch artist had done shortly after his arrival in New York in 1942/3, just a couple of years before O'Doherty's own immigration.*

...

Stefanie Gerke

—*Galerie Thomas Fischer*
Potsdamer Str. 77-87, Haus H
10785 Berlin +49 30 74 78 03 85
mail@galeriethomasfischer.de

And this excerpt from *The New York Times*, April 25, 2007:

Outside the Box: Rethinking All Geometric Limits of Form and Frame, Floor and Ceiling

By Bridget L. Goodbody

Mr. O'Doherty—Patrick Ireland is the politically influenced name he signs on some works—has spent his life promoting the arts, though he was trained as a doctor, not as an artist, in his native Ireland. He has worked as an editor and a critic but in contemporary art circles he's best known for his 1976 essays Inside the White Cube. *These review the history behind postmodernism's break from modernism, when art became part of the gallery because artists started using the space around the work— literally, the wall, floor, and ceiling—as part of their art.*

...

Much of Mr. O'Doherty's early work shows a clear debt to Marcel Duchamp, whose art often exposed the art world's underpinnings and prejudices. In 1966 he invited Mr. Duchamp to dinner and persuaded him to let him administer an electrocardiogram and make a portrait from it. Two light boxes here depict Mr. Duchamp's heartbeat: one is literal, showing it at a state of rest; the other, an artistic representation, shows it at an even slower rate. In other words, one is a stand-in for Mr. Duchamp, while the other is more a reference to the Duchampian idea.

Like Mr. Duchamp (and John Cage, Max Ernst, and Man Ray, among others), Mr. O'Doherty found inspiration in chess. Unlike him, Mr. O'Doherty used it to explore minimalism's grid. He started by making drawings, some on view here, that turned the grammar of the chess pieces' moves into linear fretworks.

Because he saw the movement of the pieces as labyrinthine, he started to make actual, human-sized labyrinths, a form also cherished by his contemporaries Alice Aycock, Robert Morris, Tony Smith, and Robert Smithson, among others.

Conceptually, it's not a big leap from the chessboards and labyrinths (some took the form of a St. Brigid's Cross) to Mr. O'Doherty's sculptural series based on the Ogham script, an ancient Celtic notational language system. Made from reflecting metal or plexiglass and inscribed with the script, these sculptures marry minimalism's reductivism to ancient architectural forms like the obelisk, ziggurat, and pyramid.

In spring 1963, Brian O'Doherty wrote several back-to-back articles on Man Ray, who had just arrived in New York for the opening of his one-man exhibition. The first article appeared in the *New York Times* on May 3, 1963, titled *Art: Man Ray the Forgotten Prophet*, which announced the upcoming Man Ray exhibition at the Cordier & Warren Gallery, 978 Madison Avenue at 76th Street.

In that first article, O'Doherty writes:

...Man Ray, an original Dadaist, a founder of surrealism, and thus, indirectly, a partial granddaddy of Pop. Now about as French as an American can get, he lives in Paris. America, deserted, is the less.

...He [Man Ray] still has the Dada disrespect for the artist's media. Painting is a vehicle for ideas not for just painting.

The ideas of course are those that contradict the possible whenever possible. Ambiguities, anagrams, puns (those double-faced liars) turn up again and again.

The second, much longer piece, *Light On An Individual: Man Ray*, appeared in the *New York Times* two days later, after O'Doherty had met and interviewed Man Ray at the gallery.

The New York Times, May 5, 1963
Man Ray Interview by Brian O'Doherty

Fig. 10.11

Comparing the O'Doherty and Hodel Ogham Decryptions

HERE, I HAVE SCANNED artist Brian O'Doherty's five individually hand-drawn Ogham alphabet for the letters H, O, D, E, L and compared them to the Ogham alphabet letters used by Zodiac.

Keeping in mind that Ogham vowels were represented either as line drawings or dots, we see that O'Doherty's alphabet is identical to the traditional Ogham (shown earlier in this chapter as the *Chart from McManus, A Guide to Ogham*) and both match the letters incorporated into the cipher symbol drawn by Zodiac.

O'Doherty's Ogham first appeared publicly in 1967-1970. I believe my father saw the artist's works at that time, during one of his many international business trips to New York. (One of his INRA-ASIA Market Research offices was actively operating in New York at that time.)

After seeing O'Doherty's use of this ancient and obscure alphabet represented as modern art, I believe my father decided to also include the Ogham letters in his 1970 Zodiac Halloween card, combining and concealing the letters in a cipher. (It's another example of his lack of originality and his need to pick and plagiarize from real artists.)

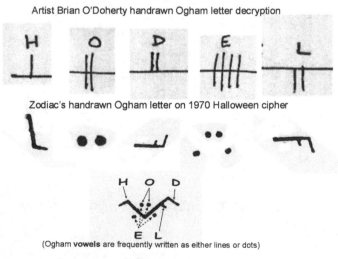

Artist Brian O'Doherty handrawn Ogham letter decryption

Zodiac's handrawn Ogham letter on 1970 Halloween cipher

(Ogham **vowels** are frequently written as either lines or dots)

Fig. 10.12

In 1972, O'Doherty created his *I-Drawing*, a new Ogham-lettered artwork comprised of 225 symbols (fifteen across and fifteen down).

In 1974, Zodiac mailed another of his taunting letters to the *San Francisco Chronicle*. This one became known as "The Exorcist Letter." He mentioned having recently seen director William Friedkin's horror film. At the bottom of that letter, Zodiac included a mysterious hand-drawn symbol (shown below), which remains undeciphered to this day.

Was this also inspired by O'Doherty and plagiarized by George Hodel, a second rip off (this time from the artist's newer work, his 1972 *I-Drawing*)?

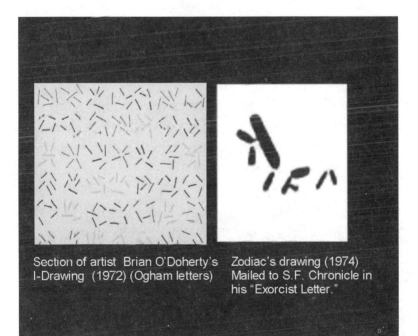

Section of artist Brian O'Doherty's I-Drawing (1972) (Ogham letters)   Zodiac's drawing (1974) Mailed to S.F. Chronicle in his "Exorcist Letter."

Fig. 10.13

Betty Parsons Gallery—Brian O'Doherty 1970

...In 1967, O'Doherty first introduced the ancient Celtic language of Ogham (c 5th-7th century AD, pronounced 'oh-um'), into contemporary art. Ogham, originally found on standing stones which may have been grave or boundary markers, transcribed twenty letters of the Roman alphabet into a series of vertical or slanting lines on or across the edge of the stone. Unlike any other conceptualist, O'Doherty's use of a "silent" language system shows that, like visual forms, languages are ultimately artefacts belonging to a particular culture.

Irish Arts Review, *Spring 2003*

Ms. Betty Parsons (1900-1982) was an American painter, art dealer, and gallerist.

Betty Parsons Gallery was located on 57th Street in New York from the mid-forties until its closing in 1983, one year after her death. For more than forty years, Parsons promoted contemporary American artists and was a staunch supporter of abstract expressionists.

In my research of the artist, Brian O'Doherty, I discovered that Ms. Parsons exhibited some of O'Doherty's early Ogham works at her New York art gallery in *1970*.

This led me to Ms. Parson's personal studio records and papers (1946-1983) which, fortunately, have been scanned and made available for review at the Archives of American Art.

From these original archival documents we are able to confirm that Brian O'Doherty's one man show did open at the Betty Parsons Gallery, 24 West 57th Street, New York, and we further discover the actual dates of his exhibit, which were: *September 22-October 10, 1970*.

BETTY PARSONS GALLERY

24 WEST 57 STREET, NEW YORK, N. Y. 10019/CI 7-7480

SCHEDULE OF EXHIBITIONS - 1970-71

FALL 1970

Sept. 22 - Oct. 10	Brian O'Doherty	Sculpture
Oct. 13 - Oct. 31	Thomas George	Paintings
Nov. 3 - Nov. 21	Ruth Vollmer	Sculpture
Nov. 24 - Dec. 12	(V.V. Rankine (Dorothy Sturm	Sculpture Enamels and Drawings
Dec. 15 - Jan. 9, 1971	Group Show	Sculpture

Fig. 10.14

Ironically, the O'Doherty exhibit closed on October 10—George Hodel's sixty-third birthday.

This information provides us with a dramatic time link between the artist O'Doherty's one-man show and George Hodel's cipher, signing and mailing the Halloween card as Zodiac.

If I am correct that the source of my father's use and inclusion of the Ogham alphabet came from O'Doherty's modern art, then it appears the act (Zodiac's mailing of the Halloween card) followed almost immediately after his "inspiration."

The card addressed to "Paul Averly," received by the *San Francisco Chronicle,* was postmarked October 27, 1970— *just seventeen days after the closing of O'Doherty's New York Exhibit.*

As I've indicated previously, Dr. George Hill Hodel, as president of INRA-ASIA, made multiple trips each year to the United States.

His itinerary, generally speaking, during the sixties through the eighties, was from Asia, to San Francisco, Los Angeles, and on to New York, then reversing back to Los Angeles and San Francisco, then on to Manila, Philippines. His expenses (First Class travel and five-star hotel lodgings) were all "gratis," as the lion's share of his international market-research surveys were conducted for and on behalf of the airline and hotel industries.

Dr. Hodel's office in New York, International Research Associates (INRA-USA), was located at the Americas Building, 1270 Avenue of the Americas. He would have visited that office multiple times during the year 1970, and, while in New York, would have visited many art galleries, as was his passion.

Below, we see that in 1970, at the time the O'Doherty Ogham artwork was on display, the distance from Dr. George Hodel's office to the Betty Parson's Gallery was *only seven city blocks*.

George Hodel New York INRA Office to Betty Parson's Gallery

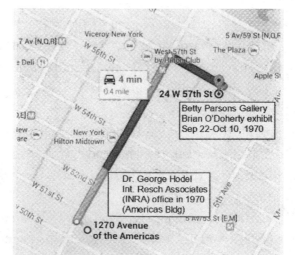

Fig. 10.15

These facts hugely underscore the very real possibility that George Hodel attended the New York exhibit in the fall of 1970, was inspired by the artist's use of the secret Ogham language, and within a few weeks of seeing the exhibit, on his return stop in the Bay Area, included his own variation of the theme and mailed the taunting Halloween card on October 27 to the *San Francisco Chronicle*.

Virginia Dwan Gallery—Earthworks 1968

THIS 2015 PARSONS/O'DOHERTY ART connection is all the more remarkable based on related information originally presented in *Most Evil* in 2009.

Here are some excerpts referencing the independent observations of Gareth Penn, an author and early Zodiac researcher, that Zodiac, in his Bay Area killings, based on his use of maps and his mention of "radians," might very well have been creating his own *artwork*!

Most Evil, Chapter 18, pages 210-211:

> ...*The map with its obscure notations was first brought to public attention in a November 1981 article published in* California *magazine, titled "Portrait of the Artist as a Mass Murderer." Author Gareth Penn, who wrote under the pen name George Oaks, is the son of an Army cryptographer who was a former employee of the California Attorney General's Office. Gareth is a member of Mensa—the most famous high-IQ society in the world.*
>
> *In his* California *magazine article, Penn theorized that Zodiac had used his crimes to create a form of land art. Land Art, also known as Earthworks, is a movement said to have been launched in October 1968 with the group exhibition "Earthworks" at the Dwan Gallery in New York. Zodiac's first Bay Area murder occurred just one month*

later, in December 1968. If Zodiac was influenced by the Earthworks movement, it might mean he had carefully selected his murder sites and positioned his victims to create his own masterpiece. If George Hodel was Zodiac, working his crimes into a piece of art only he could fully understand would continue the tradition he began when he posed Elizabeth Short as his surreal masterpiece.

As Penn (Oakes) states in the article:

"Seen from the perspective of outer space, the Zodiac murders make a certain kind of sense. They show, in fact, a degree of precision and consistency of design that, combined with the savagery and viciousness of the crimes, is downright blood-chilling."

Today, some six years later, armed with the new Parsons/ O'Doherty linkage, we are forced to ask the obvious: "In 1968, where exactly was the Virginia Dwan Gallery located?"

The answer: 29 West 57th Street, New York, NY. *Directly across the street from the Betty Parsons Gallery; both only seven blocks from Dr. George Hill Hodel's UNRA-US office.*

24 and 29 West 57th Street, New York: Buildings that in 1968 and 1970 housed the Betty Parsons and Virginia Dwan art galleries.

Fig. 10.16

It is my belief that in October of 1968, my father, while conducting one of his numerous business trips to his New York office, attended the Dwan Art Gallery "Earthworks" exhibition and was inspired.

He then formulated a plan to continue his earlier version of "Murder as a Fine Art," (the 1947 posing of victim Elizabeth "Black Dahlia" Short in imitation of several well-known artworks by his close friend, surrealist Man Ray). However, this time he would use multiple murder victims to "map out" a larger canvas on a much grander scale.

Then, just ten weeks after visiting the Earthworks exhibit, on his return trip to Manila, making his usual stop in San Francisco, he created the first brush strokes of his land map, by lying in wait at his preselected coordinates (the north leg of his radian) until the victims (any victims) moved into place.

Sadly, on December 20, 1968, this happened to be two teenagers, Betty Jensen and David Faraday, out on their "first date," who had decided to park in a lover's lane just off Lake Herman Road, near Vallejo.

Young Betty and David would be the first two victims of George Hodel's Land Art, which would require another year and five more "positionings" before it could be considered a "finished work."

As referenced earlier in this chapter, it is my further belief that George Hodel, in October of 1970, walked down the street and around the corner from his INRA office, this time deciding to visit the Betty Parsons Gallery, where he was again inspired by a new piece of modern art.

Three weeks later, on his usual layover in San Francisco, rather than killing another victim he decided to send another message. A "You're aching to know my name" Halloween greeting to his "Secret Pal," *San Francisco Chronicle* newspaper reporter Paul Avery.

A new Zodiac taunt. But, in addition to signing with his now infamous cross-and-circle, he would add a unique and most daring touch.

This time, George as Zodiac decided to follow in the footsteps of his good friend and Dadaist guru Man Ray, who, for thirty-five years and counting, had concealed his own signature and name from the public by using a penlight to hide it in swirls and loops in his self-portrait *Space Writings* (1935).[37]

Inspired by his recent visit to Brian O'Doherty's exhibit at the Dwan Gallery, he would sign his Halloween card with a mysterious symbol, knowing it and he were "crack proof."

---

37   As mentioned previously, Man Ray's hidden signature was not discovered and "cracked" until 2009, remaining undiscovered for some seventy-four years. George Hodel's cipher-signature only fared half as well, being cracked by my friend, M. Yves Person, in 2014 after a mere forty-four years.

AFTERWORD

"This is the Zodiac speaking. Like I have allways said I am crack proof....I do have to give them credit for stumbling across my riverside activity, but they are only finding the easy ones, there are a hell of a lot more down there. (Southern California)
SFPD—0 Zodiac—17+

—*ZODIAC*

(*Letter mailed from Pleasanton, CA,*
to the Los Angeles Times *March 13, 1971*)

"Me- 37
SFPD-0"

—*ZODIAC*
(*Letter mailed to* San Francisco Chronicle
January 29, 1974, claiming 37 kills)

AY 16, 2015, IS the sixteenth-year anniversary of my father's death.

Bizarrely, May 16 is also the date I began my investigation into the life and crimes of one of the world's most horrifying and sadistic serial killers.

Sadly, they were one and the same man—my father, Dr. George Hill Hodel

To date, the evidence amassed in establishing the guilt of just this one man's crimes is staggering. It includes:

1. Four published books, containing over eighty separate chapters with more than seven hundred separate photographic exhibits.

2. A total of forty-four separate cold case murder investigations, spanning more than twenty-five years (1943 to 1969.) Based on my findings, I believe the evidence supports that George Hodel committed, at minimum, twenty-three of those homicides, along with two additional attempted murders.

3. Seven separate US counties, eleven different law enforcement agencies, and one out-of-country murder in the Philippines were involved in the separate investigations. (To my knowledge, none of the cold case crimes that I include as "Category I" [definites] have ever been solved by law enforcement.)

In March of 1971, Zodiac, in a letter to the *Los Angeles Times*, claimed he had murdered seventeen separate victims, and three years later, in a letter to the *San Francisco Chronicle* (George Hodel's old employer), he bragged that his murder count totaled "37." Zodiac went on to say that the police in the Los Angeles area "were only finding the easy ones" (murders) and that there were "a hell of a lot more down there."

In that communique, I am convinced that Zodiac was specifically referencing his serial killings twenty years earlier as the Black Dahlia Avenger. I believe the eleven Lone Woman Murder victims, slain by him between 1943 and 1949, and actively investigated with George Hodel named as the "prime suspect," were the "hell of a lot mores" that Zodiac claimed credit for in 1974.

In August of 2002, some six months prior to the publication of *Black Dahlia Avenger*, Los Angeles County Head Deputy District Attorney Stephen Kay reviewed and rendered his legal opinion that two of those homicides were "solved."

Kay advised me that, based on the evidence, were the witnesses available and George Hodel still alive, he would have filed first-degree felony murder counts on both the Elizabeth Short/"Black Dahlia" and the Jeanne French/"Red Lipstick" murders. He further informed me that he would have requested the death penalty and believed he would have won a conviction on both counts.

I advised Kay that I wanted to fully brief LAPD on the investigation so that any DNA tests and forensic follow-up by their crime lab could be completed well in advance of the public being notified. The book's tentative publication was scheduled for April of the following year (2003).

Kay offered to contact the "powers that be" both within his office (LADA) and the LAPD, and to set up a time and place for the two of us to provide them with a detailed overview of the investigation and evidence.

During the next six months, Kay's attempts to schedule a meeting with LAPD were continually delayed. A September date was put off for two months, then, in November, a second cancellation. Despite our best efforts, it became clear that the LAPD had no desire to hear what we had to say, and finally, in early 2003, they "passed" with a simple, "Not able to meet in the foreseeable future."

April 2003 arrived and with it came my book launch and the publication of *Black Dahlia Avenger* on April 15, 2003. My publisher, Arcade, had scheduled a press conference at the Hollywood Roosevelt Hotel, where I presented the "breaking news" and, for the first time, publicly named my father as the killer of Elizabeth "Black Dahlia" Short. (Two weeks prior I had given *Los Angeles Times* reporter Steve Lopez a heads up print exclusive and provided him with most of the details of my investigation along with an advance copy of the book.)

Lopez's article ran in his "Points West" weekly column on April 11, 2003, headlined "A Startling Take on Black Dahlia Case."

As it turned out, his reputation, press pass, and dogged determination as an investigative journalist opened doors that remained closed to my "fuzz that was" status.

LADA Steve Cooley not only spoke with Lopez, but also granted him access to the original 1950 DA investigative files, which had been secreted in a DA vault and had remained unexamined (including by DA Cooley) for more than fifty years!

Lopez's news scoop was ground-shaking, even in LA, where we are accustomed to it. (I'd rate Lopez's discovery at about a 6.5 on the Richter Scale)

On April 13, 2003, he ran a follow-up article, headlined "Another Dance With LA's Black Dahlia Case."

All of Lopez's findings were "new information" discovered by him, post-publication of *Black Dahlia Avenger*. The importance of his discovery of the Hodel DA Files cannot be overstated, as these secret documents provided independent confirmation and corroboration to my separate investigation. Listed below are just a few of the highlights Lopez found inside the *LADA Hodel/Black Dahlia Secret Files* which were publicly revealed by him in his two companion articles.

- George Hodel in 1950 was the prime suspect on the Black Dahlia murder and suspected of other crimes, including the murder of his personal secretary.

- A DA and LAPD detective task force secretly installed electronic surveillance at the Hodel residence and "bugged" conversations 24/7 for forty days (February 15 through March 27, 1950).

- Tape-recorded police transcripts recorded George Hodel admitting to the murder of Elizabeth Short and the killing of his personal secretary (forced overdose by pills), as well as to his performing abortions and making "payoffs to law enforcement."

- The tape-recorded assault (using a pipe) and probable murder of an unidentified woman in the Hodel residence basement by George Hodel and a second male with a German accent (later identified by me as Baron Ernst von Harringa).

- Confirmation from LAPD that they had investigated George Hodel in the suspected murder of his personal secretary (later identified by me as Ruth Spaulding), and statements from an "unidentified source" that "something was buried at the Hodel house."

My follow-up investigation revealed additional DA reports that showed detectives in February 1950, while the stakeout was ongoing, interviewed a witness, a plumber called to the Hodel residence to conduct repairs.

In that report, the detectives asked the witness if he saw any "signs of digging" while working in the basement. (In 2014, analysis of soil samples from the rear of the property by forensic anthropologist Dr. Arpad Vass "showed numerous markers for a decompositional event, and these markers were human-specific and indicated that human remains were, or are, present in the vicinity of where the soil was collected.")

In the months following my publication and Lopez's reportage a number of the network television channels produced one-hour shows featuring my investigation (*Dateline, 48-Hours, Court TV*).

As a result of the massive publicity, LAPD finally agreed to a meeting in which Head DDA Steve Kay and I would present a joint briefing to the brass, and the captain and his detectives, from the Robbery/Homicide, Major Crimes, and Cold Case Units. That briefing occurred on August 13, 2003.

Following the presentation, and after reviewing my entire investigation, Assistant Chief James McMurray, Commander of LAPD's Detective Bureau, gave the following order to his Robbery/Homicide detectives:

> *"Unless you can find a major hole in Hodel's investigation, go ahead and clear the Black Dahlia Murder."*

The briefing also revealed that today's LAPD was totally unaware of the fact that Dr. George Hill Hodel had ever been named or investigated as the "prime suspect" in the Dahlia investigation. Neither were they aware that the secret Hodel/Black Dahlia Files had been turned over to LAPD by Lt. Jemison in 1950 and subsequently "disappeared" from the LAPD Homicide Unit, along with all of the original Black Dahlia evidence.

The hundreds of investigative documents linking George Hodel to the crimes, including all the witness statements implicating him as the killer, had been selectively removed from LAPD files. The only police reports still in existence were the DA originals which had been secretly locked away by DA Bureau of Investigation OIC, Lt. Frank Jemison.

Had this "second set of books" not been accidentally found and publicly revealed by *LA Times*' Steve Lopez, we would never have obtained the independent confirmation that George Hill Hodel killed and confessed on tape to both the Elizabeth "Black Dahlia" Short torture/murder and the forced overdose of his personal secretary, Ruth Spaulding.

During the August 2003 meeting, Chief McMurray, upon learning of the existence of the DA Hodel/Black Dahlia Files, ordered his Robbery/Homicide detectives, to "immediately conduct a follow-up to the DA's office and obtain and review the secret files."[38]

More than eleven years have now passed since Head DDA Steve Kay provided his legal opinion that "the Black Dahlia and Red Lipstick Murders are solved" and LAPD Assistant Chief James McMurray gave his order to "clear the case." To date, LAPD has taken no action other than to claim they are "too busy with current investigations."

In November of 2004, then-LAPD Chief William Bratton, when queried about any follow-up on the Hodel/Dahlia investigation, made the following jaw-dropping statement that literally left his audience in stunned silence:

> *"I just told our cold case squad guys to give [the Dahlia investigation] up. I'm more concerned about the nine murders we had last week than one going back that many years.... I know that is problematic for some people who would like to see it solved. But what would you have to write about if it was solved? Better it go unsolved. There are more and more books being written about it all the time."*

Chief Bratton quickly changed his tune in May of 2009, when DNA linked a local serial killer to several thirty-five-year-old rape/murders. The suspect, John Floyd Thomas Jr., was charged after his DNA profile was matched through the Combined DNA Index System (CODIS), the FBI's national DNA database.

LAPD informed the press that they suspected Thomas was responsible for as many as thirty-five separate crimes dating back to the seventies.

---

38   Claiming a "heavy caseload," detectives ignored the order and would not respond to the DA's Office and copy the files until the following spring, some seven months later. It is also doubtful that they have ever read or reviewed the actual documents, again due to "time restraints."

At a press conference, Chief Bratton proudly announced that LAPD's Robbery Homicide Cold Case Unit's motto as relates to murder investigations is:

"No Case is Too Old or Too Cold."

LAPD Chief William Bratton at a press conference in May of 2009, announcing the arrest of a suspect in a thirty-five-year-old murder case linked to the crime through the DNA computer database. Chief Bratton informed the press of LAPD Robbery/Homicide Division's motto: "No case is too old or too cold." May 2009.

Fig. 11.0

In November of 2009, Chief Bratton retired and Los Angeles Mayor Antonio Villaraigosa selected the new chief from within the department ranks. Charlie Beck, a thirty-two-year veteran of LAPD, would now take command.

By 2010, I was able to obtain a full DNA profile on my father, Dr. George Hill Hodel, and was optimistic that a comparison to either the Los Angeles Black Dahlia and Lone Woman Murder serial crimes, or the San Francisco Bay Area's Zodiac murders, would be forthcoming.

In 2012, after establishing new evidence indicating that LAPD was unknowingly in possession of potential DNA evidence related to the 1947 Black Dahlia investigation, (several newly-discovered letters believed to be mailed in by the suspect) I wrote a letter to Chief Beck and the newly-appointed Commander of Robbery-Homicide Division, Captain William Hayes.

In that letter, I requested a meeting with Robbery-Homicide detectives so that I might present my new findings, which I believed would result in the obtaining of DNA from evidence currently in their possession. In my letter, I updated the new linkage and indicated that I expected that our meeting would only require about two hours of their time.

Several months later, Chief Beck responded with a letter which included a polite decline to have his detectives attend a two-hour meeting, using the same excuse as his predecessor, Chief Bratton. Chief Beck's operative sentence: "I believe that Robbery-Homicide Division Detectives should expend their valuable skills on more contemporary investigations." (So much for their new motto, of "No case is too old or too cold.")

Below is a copy of Chief Beck's response—received by me on August 2, 2012:

LOS ANGELES POLICE DEPARTMENT

CHARLIE BECK
Chief of Police

ANTONIO R. VILLARAIGOSA
Mayor

P. O. Box 30158
Los Angeles, Calif. 90030
Telephone: (213) 486-6850
TDD: (877) 275-5273
Ref #: 8.6

July 30, 2012

Mr. Steve Hodel

Sherman Oaks, California 91423

Re: Black Dahlia Investigation

Dear Mr. Hodel:

I have received your correspondence regarding your theories concerning the Black Dahlia murder investigation and the suspect responsible for the crime. I am also aware of your request to be allowed to present those theories in a meeting with myself and other Detective Bureau Staff Officers. Unfortunately, I must respectfully decline that request. Given the fiscal constraints facing the City, and the impact on investigations assigned to my command, I do not believe it prudent that we pursue the Back Dahlia investigation at this time. I realize this is not the response you would have liked to receive, but given my responsibilities to the citizens of this City, I believe that Robbery-Homicide Division Detectives should expend their valuable skills on more contemporary investigations.

I appreciate your interest in the Black Dahlia murder investigation and wish you the best in your quest to solve this notable crime.

Should you have any further questions, please contact Captain Hayes, Commanding Officer, Robbery-Homicide Division, at (213) 486-6850.

Very truly yours,

CHARLIE BECK
Chief of Police

WILLIAM HAYES, Captain
Commanding Officer

Fig. 11.1

History Repeats Itself

IN MID-NOVEMBER 2014, I wrote to the Cold Case Homicide Units of all four San Francisco Bay Area law enforcement agencies responsible for the investigation of the 1968 to

1969 unsolved Zodiac murders (San Francisco and Vallejo police, and Solano and Napa counties' sheriffs).

In my letter, I requested a meeting so that I might brief them, either collectively or individually, on my overall investigation and present the further linkage, along with what I believe to be the solution to the Zodiac cipher, in which the killer has identified and named himself as Zodiac.

As I had with LAPD a decade earlier, I wanted to be able to present my investigation to the Northern California authorities well in advance of any public release of the new evidence. Especially as it related to the solving of the 1970 Zodiac cipher, in which the killer provides his real identity.

Below is that letter in its entirety:

November 14, 2014

CONFIDENTIAL

To:

San Francisco Police Department-Homicide Unit
Solano Sheriff's Homicide Unit
Napa Sheriff's Homicide Unit
Vallejo Police Department-Homicide Detail

Subject: 1968-1969 "Zodiac" Cold Cases investigations of crime victims:

- *Betty Jensen and David Faraday (Solano Sheriff's) December, 1968*

- *Darlene Ferrin and Michael Mageau (Vallejo PD) July, 1969*

- *Cecelia Shepard and Bryan Hartnell (Napa Sheriff's) September, 1969*

- *Paul Stine (San Francisco PD) October, 1969*

From: Steve Hodel, LAPD Homicide Detective Supervisor (ret.)/True crime author

Dear Sir or Madam:

I am writing to request a meeting with the currently-assigned Cold Case Homicide detectives from your department responsible for the above named, unsolved murder and attempted murder victims' investigations.

The purpose of my meeting would be to provide a PowerPoint presentation summarizing my updated investigative findings as relates to the "Zodiac Murders." After hearing all of the evidence presented, I believe your officers will find that a strong and compelling circumstantial case has been made to support the named suspect.

In addition to the PowerPoint exhibits and evidence, I will also be presenting a solution to a forty-five-year-old, currently unsolved known Zodiac Cipher, in which Zodiac identifies and names himself as the killer.

As an LAPD homicide detective, I've experienced firsthand how the release to the public of newfound evidence and/or information on high-profile active or cold cases can bring with it a flurry or even a firestorm of publicity. It is my desire to meet privately with your detectives and discuss my findings with them for the sole purpose of assisting them in their ongoing pursuit to clear these five cold case homicides and the two cold case attempted murders prior to any release of information to the public.

I remain confident that once you have heard and seen the compelling evidence, along with the suspect actually naming himself in a known, authentic Zodiac cipher—your own department's investigative follow-up can and will solve the case by way of DNA.

Background & Expertise

I am a retired LAPD Detective III (the highest attainable rank within detective bureau). I was on the department for twenty-four years, 1963 to 1986. I was assigned to homicide for seventeen of those years, handling over three hundred separate murders in the Hollywood Division. After retirement, I obtained my P. I. License and have been actively conducting criminal investigations up to and including the present time. My experience as a criminal investigator spans the past fifty years.

I am also a true crime writer and have published five books (see attached bio). My first book, Black Dahlia Avenger, *was a* New York Times *bestseller and my second,* Most Evil, *was a* Los Angeles Times *bestseller. My investigations into these crimes have been featured as full one-hour shows on* 24 Hours, Dateline, *Bill Kurtis'* Cold Case Files, Court TV, *Discovery Channel, and throughout Europe.*

For the past fifteen years my investigation has focused on my father, Dr. George Hill Hodel, as a serial killer.

My first book summarized my investigation of his crimes in nineteen-forties Los Angeles as the Black Dahlia Avenger and presents a series of nine separate Lone Woman Murders that he committed in that city from 1943 to 1949.

Based on the evidence both then-active Head Deputy District Attorney Steve Kay and active LAPD Chief of Detectives James McMurray, after a review of my book and hearing my presentation of the evidence at a police briefing of "the brass" and Robbery/Homicide detectives, opined that the "Black Dahlia and Red Lipstick Murders were solved."

My second book, Most Evil, *published in 2009, examined the possibility that George Hodel may have also committed additional crimes in Riverside (Cheri Jo Bates murder); Chicago; Manila, Philippines; and the previously-named seven crimes in your San Francisco Bay area, possibly reinventing himself as Zodiac some twenty years after committing his serial crimes in Los Angeles as the Black Dahlia Avenger.*

Much new "Zodiac linkage" has been developed since the publication of Most Evil *that has not been publicly released, which, as new evidence, I will be presenting to your detectives, if and when we meet.*

I am residing in Los Angeles and am willing to come north to provide you with the information, on my own time and expense.

I anticipate that my investigative summary of all of the evidence will require approximately 2 ½ hours to present, not including any Q&A follow-up by your detectives.

While I could make separate presentations to your departments/agencies, obviously, the ideal would be for us to attempt to arrange a mutual date and time in which I could make a single presentation. (If that is not possible, I would be willing to make separate individual presentations.)

I am sending this letter to the Homicide Unit assigned to each of your four jurisdictions (San Francisco PD, Solano Sheriffs, Napa Sheriffs, and Vallejo PD) and would request that the supervisor from each detail contact and advise me if your department desires to attend and hear the presentation.

Once I determine which agencies and individuals want to be involved, I can then contact you individually and try to coordinate a date and time mutually convenient to all of us.

I would also ask that you let me know either by phone or email within two weeks of receipt of this letter if your department/agency is or is not interested in hearing the presentation and new evidence.

My contact numbers are as follows:

Steve Hodel
Mail: ███████████████, Sherman Oaks, CA 91423
Tel: 818. ██████████
Email: steve@stevehodel.com

Should you have any additional questions, feel free to contact me at any time.

Most Sincerely and Fraternally Yours,
LAPD Detective III Steve Hodel 11394 (ret.)
Los Angeles, California

As indicated, I requested a response from the separate law enforcement agencies within two weeks of their receipt of the letter. It is now August 2015. Nada. Not one of the four agencies even bothered to reply with a "thanks, but no thanks." I'm not surprised. In fact, I fully expected it.

> *TERRITORIALITY—(noun) The behavior of animals or people that try to keep others away from an area that they use or control.*[39]

This one word, *territoriality*, is the main reason that police and sheriff's departments murder solve and clearance rates remain so low—generally around fifty to sixty percent.

The simple fact is that law enforcement agencies from the smallest hamlet to the largest metropolis simply refuse to share their crime information and work together to solve crime—especially when it comes to murder.

Most detectives are dedicated to keeping control and use of their own unsolved murders to themselves. They might consider sharing information with their lieutenant or captain, but that's it.

---

[39]   www.merriam-webster.com/dictionary/territoriality

Potential leads and new information are tightly guarded and kept inside the assigned unit and, frequently, not even shared with other precincts or divisions within their own department. While claiming the old WWII adage, "Loose lips sink ships," and claims of confidentiality, what they are really doing is jealously guarding and protecting what they consider to be their territory. Their real attitude is, "This is our crime, our murder, and nobody outside of us is going to solve it."

This territorial attitude is the real reason why the LAPD detectives assigned to the Dahlia investigation refused to look at and acknowledge the solution which their superiors, "the brass" (who were not personally invested in the case), acknowledged was "solved."

This is the reason that, in more recent years, LAPD has been too busy to find two hours of time to hear about the "new evidence," with the "touch DNA" potentials to definitively link George Hodel to the science.

This is the reason that all four Northern California law enforcement agencies (San Francisco, Napa, Solano, and Vallejo) did not respond or make themselves available for a two-hour briefing to hear the evidence and be presented with the Zodiac cipher solution.

How was it that LAPD Chief William Bratton put it to his LA audience when questioned about Hodel's investigation back in 2004?

Oh yes,

> ..."I just told our cold case squad guys to give it up. (Dahlia investigation)... Better it go unsolved. There are more and more books being written about it all the time."

The Avenger/Zodiac Victims

ZODIAC IN 1971 FIRST took credit for "17" murders, then, three years later, in 1974, claimed he had killed "37," informing police and press that they were "missing a hell of a lot more of them down there [in Southern California]."

In my investigation to date, I am crediting my father, George Hill Hodel, with twenty-three murders, spanning the period of some twenty-five years (1943 to 1969).

These crimes I have previously classified as "Category I" murders—definites.

In *Black Dahlia Avenger*, I originally included some additional cold case murders (Category II's [probables] and Category III's [possibles]) which would add another twelve or so, bringing his total kill count to approximately "37."

I am not including those additional crimes in this summary and am only listing the names of the Category I victims that I am confident were slain by George Hodel, as Avenger/Zodiac.

Here are those twenty-five victims, along with the dates of their murders and the law enforcement agency currently responsible for the cold case investigation. I have included a photograph of each victim, when available.[40]

---

40   In nearly every listed murder the cause of death, be it "By Rope" (strangulation), "By Gun" (gunshot wound), or "By Knife" (stab wound), also included some form of blunt force trauma to the face and or body—suggesting a frenzied and vicious overkill.

Ora Murray
July 27, 1943
By Rope
LASD

No Photo Available
Ruth Spaulding
May 9, 1945
By Pills
(forced overdose)
LAPD

Josephine Ross
June 6, 1945
By Knife
Chicago PD

Georgette Bauerdorf
October 11, 1944
Asphyxiation By Cloth
(forced into the airway)
LASD

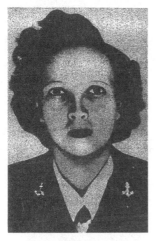

Frances Brown
December 10, 1945
By Knife-By Gun
Chicago PD

Elizabeth Short
January 15, 1947
By Rope-By Knife
LAPD

Jeanne French
February 10, 1947
By Stomping
(blunt force trauma, rib
pierced heart)
LAPD

Suzanne Degnan
January 6, 1946
By Rope-By Knife
Chicago PD
(classified as "solved")

Laura Trelstad
May 11, 1947
By Rope
(ligature strangulation-
cloth from man's pajamas)
LBPD

No Photo Available
Lillian Dominguez
October 2, 1947
By Knife
SMPD

Gladys Kern
February 14, 1948
By Knife
LAPD

Marian Newton
July 16, 1947
By Rope
SDPD

Louise Springer
June 13, 1949
By Rope
LAPD

Mimi Boomhower
August 18, 1949
Unknown—Body Never
Found
LAPD

No Photo Available
Jane Doe Franklin House
February 18, 1950
Unknown- Body Never
Found
LAPD
(September, 1950 George
Hodel Flees United States
to avoid arrest by DA
investigators.)

Jean Spangler
October 7, 1949
Unknown—Body Never
Found
LAPD

Cheri Jo Bates
October 30, 1966
By Knife
Riverside PD

Lucila Lalu
May 28, 1967
By Rope-By Knife
Manila Metropolitan PD

David Faraday
December 20, 1968
By Gun
Vallejo PD

Betty Jensen
December 20, 1968
By Gun
Vallejo PD

Darlene Ferrin
July 4, 1969
By Gun
Solano County SD

Michael Mageau
July 4, 1969
By Gun
(survived attack)
Solano County SD

Bryan Hartnell
September 27, 1969
By Rope-By Knife
(survived attack)
Napa County SD

Cecelia Shepard
September 27, 1969
By Rope-By Knife
Napa County SD

Paul Stine
October 11, 1969
By Gun
SFPD

Avenger/Zodiac Victims 1943 to 1969

Here, again, I appeal to law enforcement to simply test the evidence for DNA. The science is there. Evidence is just waiting to be scraped off a piece of rope, or a victim's clothing, or a stamp, an envelope, or the Paul Stine gloves, worn by his killer.

In the name of the above twenty-five victims and their families, I repeat my "Bottom Line" from *BDA II* Chapter 22, "touch DNA," pages 368-9:

Bottom Line

- I believe that the potential for obtaining the suspect's DNA on many of the forties unsolved Los Angeles Lone Woman Murders exists.

- I believe that the analysis of those samples will prove linkage like they did in the Grim Sleeper Murders.

- Once DNA is obtained, cold case detectives can enter the samples into state and federal CODIS data banks and very possibly identify a suspect and clear many of the cases.

- At the very least, detectives should make the attempt to obtain DNA from the Los Angeles-area Zodiac letters booked in evidence at LAPD and Riverside to see if they can be linked to a killer already entered in CODIS.

- With the recent advancement of "touch DNA," I am extremely confident that the forty-year-old unsolved Zodiac serial murders can be solved.

- All that it requires is just one dedicated cold case investigator in any of the many jurisdictions to take the initiative and make a first step forward! That detective might now be assigned to any of the following: Riverside PD, LASD Homicide, LAPD Homicide CCU, Long Beach PD, San Diego PD and or Sheriffs, San Francisco PD, Napa or Solano Sheriff, or Vallejo PD.

- The solution is there, just a simple phone call away. As an old time homicide detective who has been there and done that, I strongly urge that detective to pick up the telephone and make the call to his or her crime lab.

"The only thing necessary for the triumph of evil is for good men to do nothing."

—*Edmund Burke*

George Hill Hodel—1940's Black Dahlia Avenger

George Hodel 1949 LAPD Booking Photo for Incest/Child Molestation

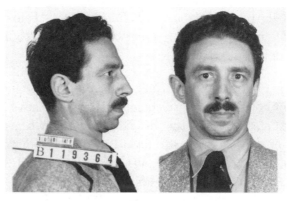

Fig. 11.2

GHH 1962–age 55

George Hodel full DNA profile on file and available for comparison

In 2010, Bode Technologies (one of the world's most respected DNA laboratories) obtained George Hill Hodel's full DNA profile from saliva they obtained off the inside flap of the pictured envelope (above). My father had mailed me the letter from his home base in Manila in 1971, some forty years earlier

Fig. 11.3

George Hodel 1962 **George Hodel 1974**

SFPD sketch   Joe Barros SFPD sketch   Neal Adams SFPD sketch

Fig. 11.4

Fig. 11.5

Dr. George Hill Hodel circa 1997/1998 in his San Francisco Penthouse suite one year prior to his death

Fig. 11.6

George and June Hodel Residence, 333 Bush St. West, Downtown San Francisco

Fig. 11.7

2015 Chris Matthews "Hardball" Show Broadcast from San Francisco

Shows George Hodel's former penthouse suite in background

Fig. 11.8

Final Resting Places of George Hodel, Paul Avery, and Elizabeth Short

Map (I have used Zodiac's original 1969 Phillips map mailed to *San Francisco Chronicle)* marks gravesites of George Hodel, Paul Avery and Elizabeth "Black Dahlia" Short. Both Hodel and Avery's ashes buried at sea in San Francisco Bay. Short was buried at Mountain View Cemetery in Oakland, just a few miles east.

Fig. 11.9

Per the instructions in George Hodel's Last Will and Testament, his ashes were buried at sea, in the San Francisco Bay. His widow, June Hodel, scattered them in Bonita Bay, just a few hundred feet off Point Bonita, in sight of the Golden Gate Bridge

George Hodel's Funeral and Burial Instructions

TO WHOM IT MAY CONCERN:

I do not wish to have funeral services of any kind. There is to be no meeting or speeches or music and no gravestone or tablet.

I direct that my physical remains be cremated and that my ashes be scattered over the ocean. There are several crematories in San Francisco which provide these services.

If I die in a foreign country, cremation and scattering of my ashes may be carried out in that country, or the ashes may be shipped to San Francisco for disposition, with the choice to be made by my wife JUNE, or if she is unavailable, the executor of my will shall decide.

Signed: George Hill Hodel
Dated: June 16, 1993

The burial occurred on June 2, 1999, which, by happenstance, is the birthday of one of George Hodel's most admired writer's—the infamous Marquis de Sade, who brought us the word—Sadism.

SADISM—*Etymology*[41]
From French sadism. Named after the Marquis de Sade, famed for his libertine writings depicting the pleasure of inflicting pain to others. The word for "sadism" (sadisme) was coined or acknowledged in the 1834 posthumous reprint of French lexicographer Boiste's Dictionnaire universel del a langue francaise.

SADISM—*noun*
- *(chiefly psychiatry) The enjoyment of inflicting pain without pity*
- *Achievement of sexual gratification by inflicting pain on others*
- *Gaining sexual excitement and satisfaction by watching pain inflicted by others on their victims*
- *A morbid form of enjoyment achieved by acting cruelly to another, or others*

As I did in *Most Evil*, I will again let my father have the last word. The following is a poem he wrote and published in his 1925 literary magazine *Fantasia* under the pseudonym

41   en.wiktionary.org/wiki/sadism

Vernon Morel. He was seventeen. Keep in mind as you read it that these are the earliest recorded words of the man who horrified Los Angeles in 1947 as the Black Dahlia Avenger, and then, twenty years later, spread his evil through the San Francisco Bay Area as Zodiac.

Inference

I was conceived
In sin
On a mad night
Carnal
And incarnadine

Then was the incense rising
Poisonously
In the temple of Cybele curling
Dolorously
And in phantasmal wraiths writhing
Languorously

Then the night waned
Gloomily
And the thin spectral moon paled
Pallidly
And the lurid somber skies darkened
Dismally
And I was born

EPILOGUE

IN 2009, UPON PUBLICATION of *Most Evil*, I told readers that, while I believed I had made a compelling case, more evidence was required. I challenged law enforcement to obtain confirmed Zodiac DNA. (Six years later, that hasn't happened.)

While I believe my father committed the crimes in Chicago, Manila, Riverside, and those attributed to Zodiac in the San Francisco Bay Area, I recognized more proof was needed. A preponderance of evidence existed, but not enough to convict beyond a reasonable doubt.

In 2009, I was in the same position as fictional detective Charlie Chan. In the 1939 film *Charlie Chan at Treasure Island* (Twentieth Century Fox), when Chan is hot on the trail of a phony psychic named "Zodiac," he is asked if Zodiac is guilty of various crimes.

"I'd say yes," the detective responds in his inscrutable way, "but facts say maybe."

I believed my father was Zodiac, but I also knew that without DNA, a jury would acquit.

However, six years later, with Zodiac's own enigmatic signed confession and new supporting evidence, I can now update my opinion. Was my father the killer known as Zodiac? I'd say yes, and the facts say yes.

Maybe the most difficult question—even for me, at first—is related to George Hodel's age.

According to witnesses, Zodiac was thirty-five to forty-five years old. At the time of the San Francisco murders, George Hodel was sixty-one. The knee-jerk response was, "no way." *If the age don't fit, you must acquit.* Seemingly, Dr. Hodel was much too old.

But once I hit the streets, examined the original police reports versus the loosey-goosey tabloids and Internet myths, and started separating fact from fiction, the truth became apparent.

According to SFPD's best eyewitness, Patrol Officer Donald Fouke, Zodiac "was at the high-end of the [thirty-five to forty-five] description." Fouke told the media that "Zodiac was closer to forty-five years."

Obviously, when a witness claims a suspect was "approximately forty-five years," his observation allows for leeway in either direction. At the time of his formal statement, if we asked Officer Fouke, "Could Zodiac have been slightly older, maybe forty-eight or forty-nine years?" his answer would have been, "Yes, possibly."

We also now know that the artist/illustrator Neal Adams based his Zodiac likeness on the original police composite, as well as the 1971 Zodiac drawing by the *Denver Post* fellow illustrator Joe Barros [Chapter 2]. Both drawings show an older suspect, whose age appears to be anywhere from a low of forty-five to a man possibly into his fifties.

As we have seen in his photographs, George Hodel at sixty could easily pass for a much younger man of, say, forty-five to fifty.

To my mind, these corrected facts explain and fully address any age discrepancies. Chapter 9, "Surrealist

Enigmas—Riddles Wrapped in Mysteries," is essential to understanding George Hodel's mental set.

It reveals that in his heart of hearts, George, like his close confidants Man Ray, William Copley, and Marcel Duchamp, was very much a devoted Dadaist.[42]

Included in Chapter 9 we have Detective Chief Inspector Susan Wilshire's discovery and significant contribution of the 1948 Man Ray/Copley *Alphabet for Adults* book.

Man Ray's book adds much to our understanding of the surrealists' love for and need to play their letter games. This included inserting within the book's drawings (albeit disguised) George Hodel, his private Hollywood residence, the Sowden house, and my father's personal "quarrels"— making George Hodel and his house a part of "The Game." More riddles wrapped in mysteries inside enigmas.

Chapter 10 is, of course, the crème de la crème, our Rosetta Stone, M. Yves Person's solution to the Zodiac cipher.

Two short sentences from a Frenchman in the City of Light, writing somewhat haltingly, communicating to me by way of his second language:

> *"Dear Sir, Have you ever noticed that Zodiac's signature was a compound of two Ogham letters? The letter on the left side is for "H" and the letter on the right side is for 'L.'"*

This, followed by our immediate exchange of emails, and within hours the solution to Zodiac's mysterious forty-five-year-old cipher.

Add to this my discoveries in that same chapter that my father's inspiration and the likely source for his 1970 cipher

---

42   ***Noun* 1. dadaism**—a nihilistic art movement (especially in painting) that flourished in Europe early in the twentieth century; based on irrationality and negation of the accepted laws of beauty.

did not come from some obscure textbook on the Druid mysteries. But, rather, in my opinion, connects directly to the contemporary (sixties) modern Ogham works of artist Brian O'Doherty, acquaintance to both surrealists Man Ray and Marcel Duchamp. (This unexpected connection dramatically underscores and supports George Hodel's thematic, *Murder as a Fine Art*, crime signature which is present in all four of my investigative texts: *Black Dahlia Avenger, Most Evil, Black Dahlia Avenger II*, and now here in *Most Evil II*.)

Yves' solution independently confirmed my theory that Los Angeles' Black Dahlia Avenger and Lone Woman Murders serial killer from the forties and San Francisco's Zodiac were one and the same—Dr. George Hill Hodel, MD.

Add to this Zodiac's thirty signature MOs matching the Black Dahlia Avenger's, his voice and handwriting, the street names, and Zodiac's hand-drawn map with his taunting clues informing us, "Mt. Diablo Code Set to Mag. N. Concern's Radians & # inches along the radians."

There's also Zodiac's mathematical alignment of victims and his assassination of the San Francisco cabdriver, Paul Stine, after instructing the unsuspecting victim to drive to the coordinate location that put him in exact alignment with Elizabeth "Black Dahlia" Short's gravesite.

This, followed by Zodiac's further taunts to the press and police with his enclosure of the *Phillip's 66* map of the Bay Area, with written instructions :

"The map coupled with this code will tell you where the bomb is set.

...With the Mt. Diablo code. ...Set the zero to Mag. [Magnetic] North.

...Concerns Radians & # inches along the radians."

(As diagrammed and explained in *Most Evil*, by following his instructions some forty years later I was able to ascertain the exact alignment of Elizabeth Short's burial site with the Paul Stine murder location.)

These and Zodiac's "Red Mask" ties to George Hodel and the past, along with the surrealist word games, should be enough for most. Case solved.

Others will continue to deny the proofs, claiming they are too subjective and open to interpretation.

In the end, I still hope law enforcement will eventually process and test the existing and as-yet-untested evidence that's available in the property rooms of the LAPD (Zodiac's letter to the *LA Times*), SFPD (the Stine gloves), and DOJ (Cheri Jo Bates and other letters).

In addition, we have the John Walsh (*America's Most Wanted*) Scorpion Letters sent to Walsh as death threats in 1990. (The very year my father permanently relocated to the United States.) These remain in FBI custody and should be tested and compared to George Hodel's DNA to rule him in or out.

All that is required is a five-minute phone call by detectives to ask their lab to test the evidence. Once the DNA is obtained, another three minutes to compare the profile to the full DNA profile of George Hill Hodel, already obtained by Bode Laboratories and now in my possession.

> Steve Hodel
> Los Angeles, California
> August, 2015

AUTHOR'S NOTE

IN THE SPRING OF 2014, HarperCollins published a true crime book titled *The Most Dangerous Animal of All: Searching for My Father and Finding The Zodiac Killer*. The book purported to have identified and solved the San Francisco Bay area crimes committed by Zodiac and was coauthored by Gary Stewart and Susan Mustafa.

Stewart, a Louisiana computer technician, was abandoned by his parents shortly after his birth and was then adopted. Stewart would not meet his biological mother, Judy Chandler, until adulthood and discovered that, after divorcing his father, she had married Rotea Gilford, a former SFPD homicide detective. Stewart began his search for Zodiac after seeing a photo of his birth father, which he believed resembled the 1969 Zodiac police composite. The father, Earl Van Best Jr., whom the son suspected was Zodiac, died in Mexico in 1984, at age fifty. The two never met in life.

I quote from the HarperCollins book cover:

> ...*including forensic evidence—that conclusively identifies [Gary Stewart's] father as the Zodiac Killer*
>
> ...
>
> *For decades, the Zodiac Killer has captivated America's imagination. His ability to evade capture while taunting authorities made him infamous. The*

vicious specificity of his crimes terrified Californians before the Manson murders and after, and shocked a culture enamored with the ideals of the dawning Age of Aquarius. To this day, his ciphers have baffled detectives and amateur sleuths, and his identity remains one of the twentieth century's great unsolved mysteries.

The Most Dangerous Animal of All reveals the name of the Zodiac Killer for the very first time...

On the same day as the HarperCollins Stewart/Mustafa book launch, a 130-page, companion book, *The End of the Zodiac Mystery: How Forensic Science Helped Solve One of the Most Infamous Serial Killer Cases of the Century*, was published by Michael Wakshull, Stewart and Mustafa's handwriting expert and a court-certified Questioned Document Examiner.

In the weeks following the publication of the two books with their claims that "the Zodiac Killer was identified and the case was solved," I received numerous emails from my readers, asking my opinion. "Was it true?" Did the forensic handwriting evidence hold up?

Short answer is an unequivocal: *No.*

In fact, now, nine months post publication of their books, the "handwriting evidence" which their expert, Mr. Wakshull, initially proclaimed "made their case" and proved that Earl Van Best Jr. (the author's father) was Zodiac, has become the very same evidence that exonerates him.

In a most embarrassing twist, the document (a marriage certificate) initially claimed by the son to have been written by his father and analyzed by the handwriting expert, Michael Wakshull, who opined he was "virtually certain was Zodiac hand printing"—was not written by the father.

After the document's authenticity had been called into question, it was later determined that the marriage certificate had actually been written by Reverend Edward Fliger, the Reno, Nevada minister who performed the father's marriage ceremony.

This left QDE Wakshull in the awkward position of either admitting his "virtually certain Zodiac handwriting identification" was incorrect, or standing fast and suggesting that the Reverend Fliger was Zodiac.

Unfortunately, Wakshull chose the latter stating,

> "Earl Van Best [the author Stewart's father] and the priest may have been in cahoots, or possibly the priest was Zodiac."

Here are a few excerpts from a May 22, 2014, newspaper article discussing Stewart's theory, written by *San Francisco Chronicle* reporter Kevin Fagan (the current San Francisco go-to-guy on all things Zodiac), titled "Zodiac Killer Suspect's Sex Scandal Shocks Cops:"

> There are Zodiac Killer theories and books by the trainload, but few have generated as much heat and noise as The Most Dangerous Animal of All, *published last week –or spun a tale with as much twisted extra value. That value is a sleazy sex scandal involving the latest suspect. Several such scandals, actually.*
>
> ...
>
> *And another oddity: Judy Chandler, the "barely teen-aged paramour" as* The Chronicle *called her, [Stewart's biological mother] went on years later to marry San Francisco Police Officer Rotea Gilford, who was the first black inspector in the SFPD and worked on—you guessed it—the Zodiac case. Gilford eventually became a*

deputy mayor, working in the administrations of several mayors including now-Senator Dianne Feinstein. He died in 1998...

Reporter Fagan's article went on to claim that the son admitted his mother, Judy Chandler, "didn't quite agree with my theory," and that in a number of postings on Zodiac websites, the author's mother adamantly denied that her ex-husband was the Zodiac Killer.

I refer readers to my blog site[43] for the details of my original follow-up investigation as posted in May and October of 2014.

Blog 1: One Week After Purporting the "Zodiac Case Solved," Handwriting Expert Appears to Have Inadvertently Accused a Baptist Minister of Being the Zodiac Killer[44]

Blog 2: Questioned Document Expert Wakshull Confirms Alleged Zodiac Handwriting is Not Earl Van Best Jr.— Misidentification Causes Expert to Question If Marrying Minister Might Be Zodiac?[45]

Steve Hodel
August 2015

43   stevehodel.com/blog
44   stevehodel.com/2014/05/one-week-purporting-zodiac-case-solved-handwriting-expert-appears-inadvertently-accused-baptist-minister-zodiac-killer/
45   stevehodel.com/2014/10/questioned-document-expert-wakshull-confirms-alleged-zodiac-handwriting-priest/

ADDENDA

ADDENDUM I

Essay and Analysis of Zodiac Cryptogram: Scratching the Surface of the Zodiac Ciphers

by Robert J. Sadler

L IKE UNTOLD OTHERS HAVE discovered, codes or ciphers are quizzical mind twisters and are often frustrating time wasters. I make no claims to any code-breaking skill. I do have a rudimentary skill with language and thus a common sense approach to looking at the various Zodiac ciphers.

I find it fascinating that 'experts' such as naval cryptographers and perhaps others knowledgeable in code breaking have not gotten anywhere close to solving the Zodiac's various ciphers. Does this mean that those experts only took a cursory look at the ciphers and threw up their hands? Did they employ the latest code breaking techniques then available in the seventies? Does that mean that no one has subjected these ciphers, even as an academic exercise, to any computer analysis available since? Unfortunately, I do not have the answers to those questions. But, shouldn't someone?

We know Zodiac publicly took credit/responsibility via his letters and ciphers for a number of murders in and around San Francisco. Recently Will Kane, of *Ratter*, interviewed San Francisco Inspector Gianrico C. Pierucci who is now in charge (for the past year) of the San Francisco cold case involving Paul Stine's murder in 1969 by the self-proclaimed Zodiac. According to *RatterSF* "the interview has been condensed and edited for clarity." That said, perhaps these lines from the interview provide a partial, if non-definitive, answer to my question.

> Ratter–*"Do you even bother with the cyphers anymore? The Feds have tried, everyone has tried to crack them."*

> Pierucci–*"So far the cyphers, they have been looked at by a multitude of professionals—every amateur sleuth is looking at these."*

Whether the "professionals" currently have any ongoing interest in solving Zodiac ciphers is unknown; obviously, the public is still engaged.

There are a number of Zodiac ciphers. The cipher I want to focus on is the one contained in the letter postmarked November 8, 1969, sent to the "S. F. Chronicle" and displayed as "Fig. 12.4" on page 141 of Steve Hodel's *Most Evil*, some refer to it as the "340 Code." Here it will be designated as: Fig. 12.4 and it's variants: Figs. 12.4a, 12.4b, 12.4c-4d, 12.4e, 12.4f, 12.4g, and 12.4h. Being a visual person, I made graphics so my eyes could help my brain process what is a hodgepodge of letters/symbols/graphemes (LSGs).

The assumption is that Zodiac's ciphers, once solved, contain a message in English. To understand the world of English words and their constituent elements, some explanation is helpful. For example, the English language alphabet consists of 26 LSGs. The English alphabet is based on letters contained in the Latin alphabet, as are most

European languages. These twenty-six letters are the most widely used by approximately seventy percent of our globe's populous.

The collating of various combinations of these twenty-six letters to form words creates inherent letter frequencies. Studies and books written are available to list the common English language letter frequencies and common letter pairs, as well as other comparables. With this knowledge, the novice and expert can attempt to solve various ciphers.

Opinion and Observations

GIVEN THE BASIS OF an English language alphabet of twenty-six letters whose frequency of use can be summarized or standardized (by known equivalents), it is evident that a person creating a message using the standard letter frequency might also create its concealing cipher (whose basis would contain or utilize letters adhering to the standard frequency), and whose solution could thus be deciphered by determining the cipher's LSGs.

Also, as seems evident from the information above that the randomized or intentional subterfuge of the cipher maker might obscure and make extremely difficult the solving of such deviously coded messages. One of the most successful codes is one that has as its basis a key; if one does not possess the key one has little hope of decoding the message.

Thus, The Questions I Have Regarding George Hill Hodel Are:

1. Did GHH have a key from which he encoded the Zodiac ciphers?

2. Did GHH have a written key, or given his genius, could he have memorized the sixty-six icons used in the Zodiac cipher

Figure 12.4 that represented the twenty-six letters of the alphabet and then used them 'out-of-hand,' 'off-the-top-of-his-head,' like someone writing in a learned foreign language?

3. Given the approximately forty additional LSGs (over and above the standard twenty-six letters of the English alphabet), [do some] refer to the same letter or have the same letter value, or are they simply red herrings or spacefillers?

4. What is the value of duplicated icons and their reverse?

5. Is the entire cipher the entire "message," or are there only words interspersed here and there that make up a composite message?

It is my opinion that the Zodiac cipher in Figure 12.4, page 141, of *Most Evil* may not be "crackable" given all the potentially "false flag" icons I believe are inherent in the cipher. I also believe that Zodiac may have written all or part of the message in reverse or in mirror image. Additionally, the decrypting of Figure 12.4 may revolve around directionality of the letter sequences (words) rather than the linear structure of the "normal" English language sentence.

To amplify these questions/opinions I have created several graphics to illustrate the number and type of the cipher's letters/symbols/graphemes.

Here is the Zodiac cipher in question from page 141 (Fig. 12.4) of *Most Evil*. A cursory glance makes the head swim. There are recognizable letters, their reverse, and a multiplicity of symbols in both variation and their reverse.

Fig. 12.4

In this graphic the Zodiac cipher (Fig. 12.4a) contains seventeen columns that I have lettered "A" through "Q" and twenty rows numbered one through twenty. The total number of LSGs per row is indicated on the left, the total number being 340.

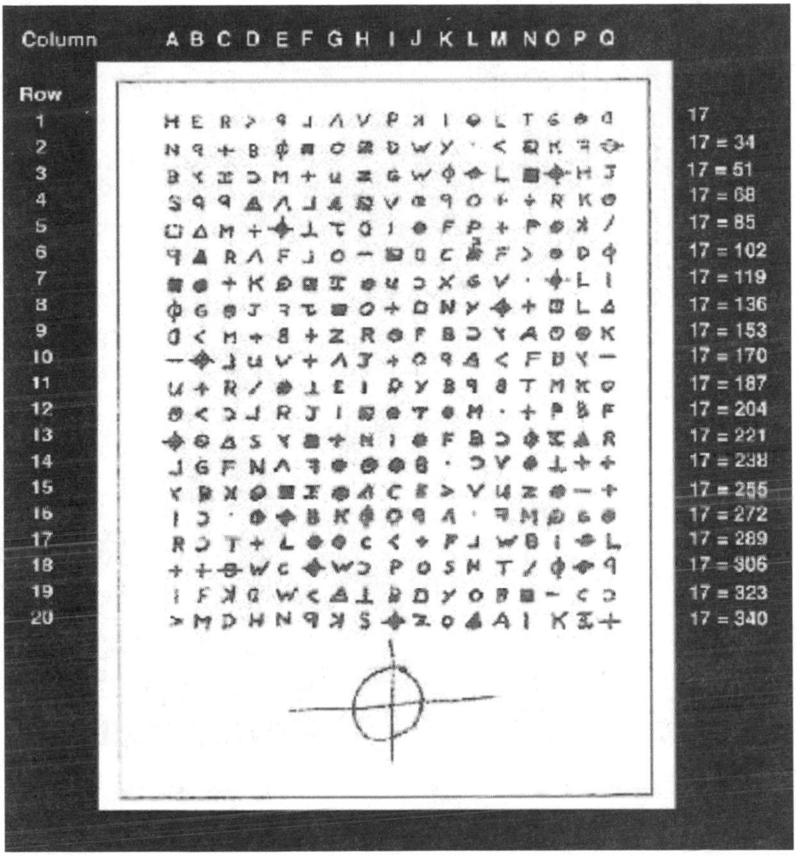

Fig. 12.4a

Next, the Zodiac cipher is shown twice in Fig. 12.4b. In the upper portion is a display of each letter/symbol/grapheme cut from the cipher and pasted in lines with correspondingly similar LSGs. I will not quibble with someone if they say this or that symbol is misplaced or dissimilar. Not having the original document from which to work, I had to subjectively choose whether individual LSGs were similar or not. By my count, there were (top graphic) sixty-six individually identified LSGs.

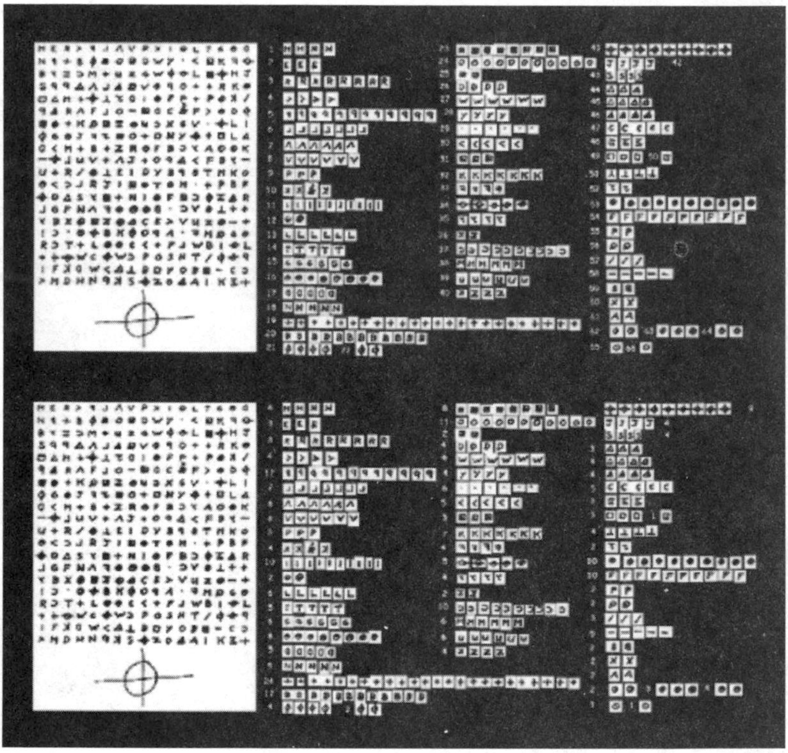

Fig. 12.4b

The bottom portion of Fig. 12.4b shows the number of individual LSGs used; for example, there were twenty-four "+" cross or plus symbols used. While eleven LSGs (22, 25, 36, 52, 55, 56, 59, 60, 61, 62, & 64) were used twice and three LSGs (50, 65, & 66) were used once.

Here is the cipher (top left), as it regularly appears reading left to right, top to bottom:

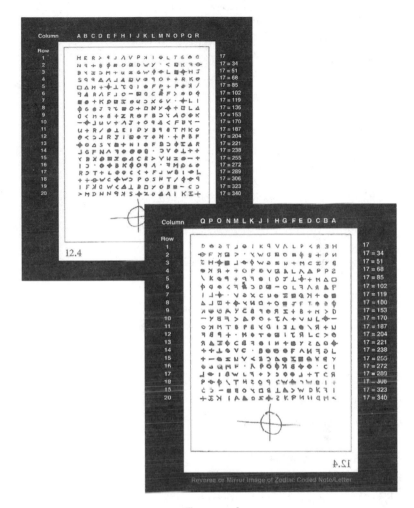

Fig. 12.4c-4d

And here the cipher (bottom right) is reversed, as if seen in its mirror image. The row numbers remain the same (top to bottom) but the columns are shown in reverse beginning on the left with column "Q" thru "A" on the right.

In addition to the cipher potentially having been intended to be read (either in whole or in part) in reverse, via its mirror image, there are other possibilities of which word game fans are familiar. Thus, we may have as many as nine directional memes with which to work:

- in line left to right

- in line right to left

- in line top to bottom

- in line bottom to top

- diagonally upper left to bottom right

- diagonally upper right to bottom left

- diagonally bottom right to upper left

- diagonally bottom left to upper right

- crossing patters which utilize at least one of the same LSGs

Using one or multiple of these memes (see Fig. 12.4e), whole words can be hidden within a variety of negative or space occupying LSGs where the words, once decoded, can then be assembled into a coherent message.

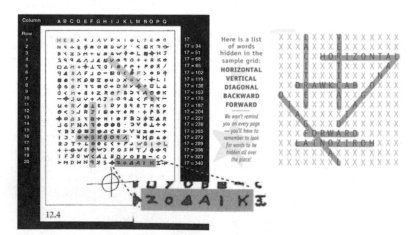

Fig. 12.4e

Looking closely at the bottom line of Fig. 12.4e (highlighted below), does this line, as it appears to indicate, actually "say": "Z," "O," "Delta" for "D," "A," "I," and "K" for "C" to make "ZODIAK" as in ZODIAC?

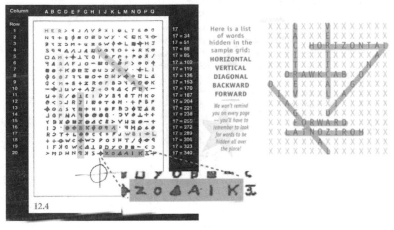

Fig. 12.4e

Is There a Mistake?

Perhaps the most critical LSG is the one Zodiac "corrected"! (See Fig 12.4f, the "reverse K" on row six, column "L.")

This "reverse K," written above the original LSG on row six, column "L," that was marked out may be very important. If it was a "mistake" that the cipher maker caught and then corrected, my assumption would be that the cipher's writer did indeed proofread his message/cipher to see if what he said in LSGs was what he meant to say in English. This would tend to bolster the expectation that there really is a message hidden in the cipher and it is not just a random jumble of LSGs meant to confuse, trick, or humble anyone attempting to solve the Zodiac ciphers.

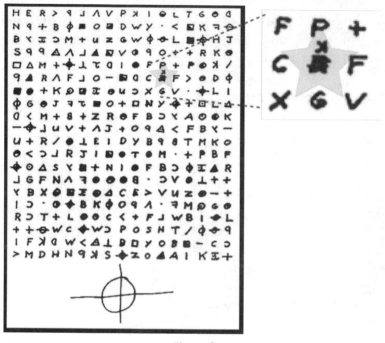

Fig. 12.4f

"340 Cipher Solution?"

RECENTLY APPEARING ON THE zodiackiller.com message board was a post titled: "340 Cipher Solution?"[46]

In this post a user, "Haley25," posted a solution to the Zodiac cipher, referred to here as "Fig. 12.4," which appears on page 141 of Steve Hodel's book, *Most Evil.*

This blog-poster gleaned from this Zodiac cipher that it had 340 characters (LSGs), which I agree is correct. Then, from the multi-page, handwritten letter (from the November 8, 1969 postmarked envelope) comprised of several thousands of individual LSGs, Haley25 finds and selects a portion of the letter containing 340 letters. Then, omitting punctuation, Haley25 appears to have superimposed these 340 letters over the Zodiac cipher. The Haley25 "340 Code" solution is a restating of the 340 LSGs portion of the multipage Zodiac letter.

Thus, it would seem, in the Haley25 assessment or "solution," none of the Zodiac's multiplicity of LSGs mean anything; none have an alphabetical equivalent value. I am not privy to Haley25's methodology, but it appears there was no attempt to correlate, for example, all the "i's" in the handwritten Zodiac letter with the LSGs of the cipher itself, which, when compared are, in my opinion, at odds with each other.

Bottom line: I do not believe the Zodiac cipher, referred to as the "340 Cipher" or Fig 12.4 on page 141 of *Most Evil,* has been solved.

Perhaps my musing and graphics will allow someone else to move forward in solving this Zodiac cipher containing his apparently oblique message.

Of course, at this point decrypting the message will be an exercise in futility in terms of its being of benefit in capturing the [long dead GHH, in my opinion] Zodiac. However, if the Zodiac's ego propelled him to name or identify himself either directly or by inference in this cipher, then time taken to solve its enigma is worth it; i.e. the Zodiac's "Halloween card" and its symbol as signature.

Cracking of the Zodiac Symbol and Halloween Card

Fig. 12.4g

Turning to the strange symbol (Fig. 12.4g) drawn on the bottom of the Halloween card sent to Paul Avery, many people have tried their hand at solving this enigmatic collection of lines and points. I refer to the lines and points as legs and dots.

One industrious person who has attempted to find answers to or relevance in this Zodiac symbol has found streets in San Francisco that he feels represent part of the Zodiac symbol and proceeded to mark those streets on a map (as recreated here).

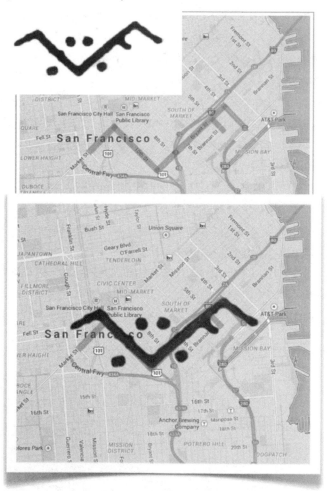

Fig. 12.4h

When the actual Zodiac symbol is enlarged and superimposed over the map and those marked streets, there is an approximate correspondence with part (what I call the legs) of the symbol. This "marked streets" application does not account for the four dots in the symbol.

Further, I submit there may well be other streets in San Francisco (or other cities) over which the legs of the symbol could be superimposed. But, unless there are meaningful structures or Zodiac-related events either on or near the streets themselves that include the symbol's dots, I do not see that this type of analysis aids in illuminating the Zodiac "mystery." The entirety of the symbol must be considered.

In all the suppositions about this Zodiac symbol, with which I am familiar, none answer all the questions as to its substance and meaning until the revelations you just read about in *Most Evil II*.

Steve Hodel's Cracking of the Zodiac Symbol and Halloween Card.

So compelling is Steve Hodel's revelation in *Most Evil II* of the Ogham language as the basis for the mysterious Zodiac symbol and his analysis of the Zodiac Halloween card, I can only conclude George Hill Hodel was Zodiac. Thus, no further search for Zodiac's identity in the cipher in Fig. 12.4, or any other ciphers, may be necessary.

–RJS

ADDENDUM II

Red Mask, Lady Doom, and "The Death Wheel": The Tim Holt-Zodiac Connections

(Originally published in Black Dahlia
Avenger II, *pages 454 to 461)*

IN THE SUMMER OF 1952, comic book Volume 30 was published featuring the well-known "RKO Western Star," Tim Holt. It was one in a long series of stories featuring Tim Holt as the hero "Red Mask." This volume was titled, *Red Mask Meets Lady Doom and the Death Wheel*.

On the cover below, we see Red Mask (Holt) bound with ropes as Lady Doom prepares to spin her death wheel, admonishing the gamblers to "place your bets gentlemen, you're playing for Red Mask." On the wheel behind him, we read the various potential manners of his death, to be determined by the spin: "By Rope, By Gun, By Knife, By Fire."

*The death wheel cover featuring RKO's Western
star Tim Holt as Red Mask with Lady Doom.*

Volume 30, published June/July 1952. "Manners of Death" on wheel read,
"By Rope, By Gun, By Knife, By Fire." (Published by Magazine Enterprises.)
Fig. 13.0

Here we are introduced to Lady Doom.

Fig. 13.1

Now let's reexamine the 1970 Halloween card mailed to
San Francisco reporter Paul Avery by Zodiac in light of this
new information. The envelope with the strange "Z" symbol as
a return address is postmarked "San Francisco on October 27,
1970" and addressed to "Paul Averly," a deliberate misspelling

of the actual reporter's name. Reporter Avery had just written an extensive article on Zodiac, which was published in the *San Francisco Chronicle* just two weeks prior, on October 12, 1970.

The Envelope

Fig. 13.2

On the front of the card, Zodiac promises a clue to his name. The only visible alteration to the card is the number "14" seen written in black on the skeleton's right hand.

Front of Zodiac's Halloween Card

Fig. 13.3

Full Interior of Card

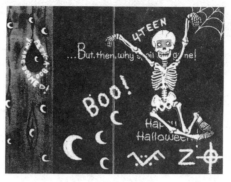

Fig. 13.4

Inside, Zodiac used a white marking pen and wrote mixed messages. On the left he wrote, "Peek-A-Boo, you are DOOMED!" He inserted the thirteen "Spellbound Eyes" that we examined in Chapter 21, "A Surrealist Signature." He repeated the "4-Teen" along with his signature Zodiac sign, the letter "Z," and repeated the strange symbol used as his return address on the envelope. (Also, note the spider web in the upper-right portion of the card. I am unaware if this was part of the original card or inserted by Zodiac, but either way, I will consider its potential relevance as "a clue" in subsequent pages.)

Back of Card with Promised "Clue"

By **P** By
F **A** G
i **R** U
R E N

SLAVES

B **D** By
y i R
K C O
N E P
I E E
F
E

Fig. 13.5

Full Zodiac Halloween Card Showing
Front, Interior, and Back

Front   Interior   Back

Fig. 13.6

Now let's reexamine the card based on the 2014 information we have from the Tim Holt/Red Mask comic book published in 1952.

- The card was mailed by Zodiac as a direct personal threat to crime reporter Paul Avery, informing him, "You are doomed." I believe this is Zodiac's singular use of that word in all of his several dozen mailings, and I would suggest that, when all the additional factors are considered, it is a subtle reference and "clue" dating back to its use in the original comic book and to Lady Doom.

- In the original Halloween card, Zodiac drew a mask on the skeleton using red ink. Enlarged below we see the red mask in comparison to Tim Holt as the original Red Mask comic book hero. Again, a direct reference to the original comic book.

Zodiac Red Mask Skeleton Compared to Tim Holt as Red Mask

Zodiac using red ink, drew and inserted "red mask" on his card.

Fig. 13.7

The "clues" left by Zodiac, to my mind, establish beyond any reasonable doubt that *the source and inspiration for Zodiac's 1970 threat came from this specific Tim Holt/Red Mask comic book.* The combination of his use of the red mask, "you are doomed," and the distinct phrase "By Rope, By Gun, By Knife, By Fire" seals the deal.

**Red Mask and Lady Doom Death Wheel
Reproduced on Zodiac card**

Fig. 13.8

George Hodel-Tim Holt—Zero Degrees of Separation

WHEN I INITIALLY INTRODUCED the fact that actress Carol Forman and her boyfriend, actor Tim Holt, were close friends of my father, and that Carol resided with us at the Franklin house in 1948 and 1949, I had no idea that Holt, a regular visitor to our home, would later be tied directly to evidence from the 1970 killer known as Zodiac.

Based on this new evidence, let's reread the original Tim Holt anecdote I presented in Chapter 10, originally published back in 2012.

Here it is:

Carol, Tim Holt, and my Bro

MY YOUNGER BROTHER, KELVIN "Kelly" Hodel, was born in October of 1942, just eleven months after the birth of my twin John and me. He would be Dorothy and George's fourth and final son. From an early age, Kelly "loved the girls" and, believe me, the girls loved him. This 1949 Franklin house anecdote is appropriate:

At the time, Carol was living with us at the Franklin house. She was dating film star Tim Holt. The two actors had worked together in a number of B-westerns, including the 1947 *Under the Tonto Rim* and again in 1948 on *Brothers in the Saddle*. Holt, who had just received huge critical acclaim for his role as the down-on-his-luck drifter Bob Curtin in John Huston's *The Treasure of the Sierra Madre*, naturally visited Carol at the house regularly.

Brother Kelly, then six or seven, had a terrible crush on Carol. And whenever Holt showed up to take her on a date, Kelly would object, informing him in no uncertain terms, "She's my girlfriend." Finally, Holt could take it no longer and took Kelly into the center courtyard, *mano a mano*, and made the following suggestion:

"Look, Kelly. You're too young to be with Carol now. I will date her only until you get old enough. And then you and Carol can get married. And I will get on my horse and ride off. Fair enough?"

Kelly agreed. Holt and Hodel shook hands, and the battle for Carol's heart was ended—without having to fire a shot to find out which was the fastest gun alive.

As we have learned, in the forties and early fifties Tim Holt was not just a top Western movie star, but was also featured in various comic book publications for many years preceding his introduction as Red Mask.

So, too, with Carol Forman, Holt's then-girlfriend, who lived for several years with us at the Sowden/Franklin house as "part of the family."

In addition to appearing in several Western films with Tim Holt, Carol also had her own independent career and was considered one of the top box office draws due to her multiple roles as a villainess. She starred as The Black Widow, Spider Woman, and in 1952 as the slinky foreign spy Laska in the comic book strip, *Blackhawk*, starring Kirk Alyn as "the Fearless Champion of Freedom." (Carol was also Alyn's costar in his *Superman* series on film and in comics in the late-forties and early-fifties.)

Here is Carol's short obituary from the *Los Angeles Times* in the summer of 1997.[47]

Carol Forman; Actress in Movies, TV Series

July 18, 1997

Carol Forman, seventy-eight, a movie and television actress. She joined RKO Pictures in 1946 and played opposite Raymond Burr in the film San Quentin. *She also played Burr's girlfriend in his first film,* Code of the West. *Other credits included* By the Light of the Silvery Moon *with Doris Day, as well as several Westerns with Tim Holt. She appeared in the* Charlie Chan *series, was the Spider Lady in the* Superman *series, and was perhaps best known as the lead in the* Black Widow *series. She is survived by three daughters, Lee Dennis, Suzy Dennis, and Debbie Geiger. In Burbank on July 9 of natural causes.*

---

47   articles.latimes.com/1997/jul/18

Seen below is a clip from a *Superman* serial in which Carol is playing the part of the villainess, Spider Lady, said to be "as cunning as Moriarty and as venomous as a spider." Here, I have compared it to Zodiac's spider web, inserted in the 1970 Halloween card. Was George Hodel, in his role as Zodiac, leaving us another clue to his past? This time, not just to his friend, Tim Holt, but also to Holt's girlfriend, Spider Lady?

Carol Forman (1948) as Spider Lady.

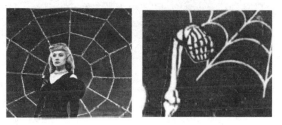

Fig. 13.9

This film was made at the same time she was living in residence with the Hodel family at the Hollywood Sowden house, which we now know was the original crime scene where Elizabeth "Black Dahlia" Short was murdered, just one year before Carol moved to the residence.

This latest Zodiac linkage has most of the hardcore Zodiac researchers and armchair detectives scratching their heads. While most recognize the 1952 Red Mask comic book connection is undeniable, they remain confused about the how and why of it. In their chat rooms, and on their blogs and message boards, they ask, "Why would Zodiac use a seemingly random 1952 cover of a Western comic book as the inspiration for, and a "clue" to solving, his serial murders some eighteen years later?"[48]

---

48   The existence of the original Red Mask/Tim Holt Comic book was originally made known and posted on Tom Voigt's zodiackiller.com website Message Board by a poster using the name "Tahoe27" in December 2013.

I believe the information contained in my foregoing overview has provided <u>the answer</u>.

With Zodiac, nothing is random. The link to Tim Holt and his Red Mask character has *zero degrees of separation.* It is direct and personal. As I've said many times, the key to understanding Dr. George Hill Hodel and his many crimes is revealed through a knowledge of his past.

ADDENDUM III

Handwriting Update

(Originally Published In Black Dahlia
Avenger II, *pages 274 to 290)*

I HIRED COURT-CERTIFIED DOCUMENT examiner Hannah McFarland to examine many of the 1947 Black Dahlia Avenger notes, as well as the lipstick handwriting on the body of Jeanne French in the Red Lipstick Murder.

In her expert opinion as a Questioned Document Examiner (or QDE), it was "highly probable" that Dr. George Hill Hodel wrote at least four of the Avenger notes, as well as the writing on the body of Jeanne French. [A finding of "highly probable" is the highest finding an expert can provide as to authorship without having the original documents in their possession. It is equivalent to the forensic term of being "virtually certain."]

In subsequent examinations of other Lone Woman-related handwritings, it was also McFarland's expert opinion that it was "highly probable" that George Hodel also printed notes found on the purse of murder victim Mimi Boomhower, kidnapped in August 1949.

In a later examination of the murder note on victim Gladys Kern, McFarland found that it was "probable" that the note mailed to the police was written by George Hill

Hodel. This finding is one degree below the other opinions and is defined as, "The evidence found in the handwriting points rather strongly toward the questioned and the known writings having been written by the same individual; however, it falls short of the 'virtually certain' degree of confidence."[49]

In a previous chapter, I mentioned CBS' hour-long *Black Dahlia Confidential* (2006), in which the network asked its own experts to revisit several aspects of my investigation. I noted that their medical expert, Dr. Mark Wallack, chief of surgery at New York's St. Vincent Hospital, reviewed the killer's skill at bisection and stated, "In my opinion, a doctor did it."

On that same program, CBS also asked independent document expert John Osborn to compare my father's known handwriting samples to the notes written by the Black Dahlia Avenger. His inconclusive opinion caused some viewers and critics to claim Osborn contradicted my expert, proving George Hodel did not write the Avenger notes.

John Osborn gave no such finding. Here is his verbatim, expert opinion, as stated on the program:

> *"There is simply not enough evidence to prove one way or the other whether his father is the writer, or is not the writer."*

Osborn was likely provided with only a very limited number of known samples of Dr. Hodel's handwriting, maybe only two or three documents. As is often the case with television, he was likely only given a short time to analyze and articulate his results to the network.

49   *Journal of Forensic Sciences*, Letter to the Editor, March 1991.

Ultimately, his examination was inconclusive.

For six months, my document expert Hannah McFarland studied a couple dozen documents known to be written by Dr. George Hill Hodel.

Osborn discussed a difference in handwriting styles between Dr. Hodel and the Black Dahlia Avenger, specifically pointing to the Avenger's printed block letter "N." He showed comparative samples of both writings and demonstrated that Dr. Hodel's letter "N," in his words, was "more classic in style, whereas the Avenger's writing was much narrower."

QDE John Osborn on CBS' *48 Hours*, "Black Dahlia Confidential," August 2006

Fig. 14.0

Here is a sample of the difference in the two writings of the letter "N" as pointed out by Osborn:

George Hodel

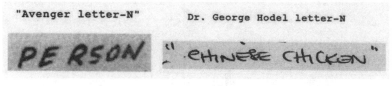

Fig. 14.1

Black Dahlia Avenger; Disguised Handwriting

Fig. 14.2

Below are additional samples of George Hodel's known handwriting that were not shown, and apparently not seen or used in Osborn's comparison (although these exact same samples were available and printed in my book).

Note in these samples how my father writes the letter "N," as compared to the Avenger's letter "N." Though known to be written by George Hodel, it is quite dissimilar to his "Classic N," as described by Osborn and quite similar to the Avenger's style of writing the letter "N." I am confident that had their expert seen these George Hodel handwriting documents, it would have altered or at least modified his opinion regarding George Hodel's handwriting of the letter "N."

"Avenger letter-N"   Dr. George Hodel letter-N

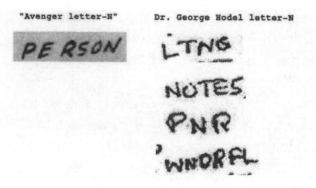

Fig. 14.3

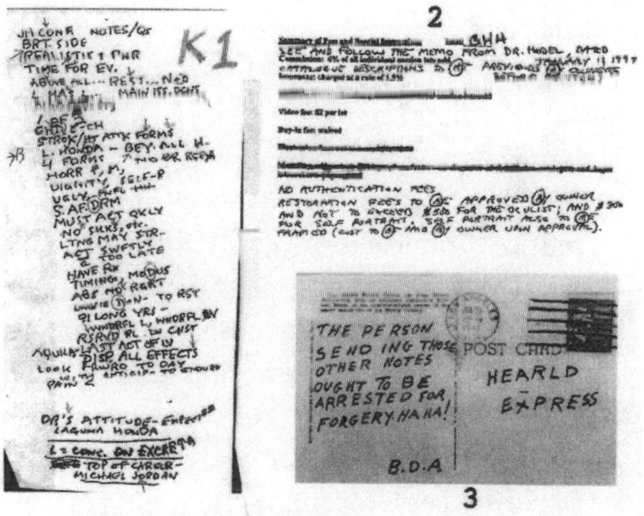

1 & 2-   **George Hodel known handwriting**
3-   **Black Dahlia Avenger handwriting**

Fig. 14.4

George Hill Hodel Handwriting

THOSE OF YOU THAT have read *BDA* and *Most Evil* know that I am not a huge fan of handwriting analysis. That is not to say that I totally discredit it—I do not. It has its place and can be a very effective tool in the investigative process as long as the QDE's findings are not elevated to an absolute.

For me, handwriting analysis remains an inexact half-science. Why?

Because of its subjectivity. Handwriting analysis is like the polygraph. It's a useful investigative tool, but it cannot and should not be relied on by itself. Two different QDE's of equal stature will and often do provide "expert testimony" that a specific questioned document "was" and "was not" written by a specific individual. Who to believe? Flip a coin. That's not science. The same is true with polygraph examiners' testimony. Examiner number one says, "He's lying." Examiner number two, "No, he's telling the truth and was not at the crime scene."

The same can be said of psychiatric experts. The prosecutor's doctors testified, "He's sane. He knew right from wrong when he stabbed her." The defense psychiatrist countered, "Psychotic and insane during the commission of the crime."

Because of this inherent subjectivity, one must use great caution when considering the results of any single QDE's findings. (That includes my own expert's opinions and reports as presented in *BDA* and *Most Evil*.)

With that disclaimer, let me add that as far as handwriting is concerned, I believe that in both its psychology and technical writing aspects, one cannot ignore the fact that each of us, in our handwriting, regularly and unconsciously displays some unique characteristics in both our cursive and printed writing.

Consider these somewhat akin to the "points" in a fingerprint. The more unique points one finds in a handwriting sample, the stronger the case becomes that he or she is "probably" the writer. But unlike fingerprints, where a "make," or positive match, can be scientifically verified to a certainty, handwriting cannot.

Bottom line: in my opinion, handwriting analysis and conclusions should be considered as a piece of the overall puzzle and circumstantially relevant, but these "expert findings" should never be overweighed to the point where they become the major consideration in determining an individual's guilt or innocence, especially when the handwriting is deliberately disguised.

Handwriting is such a large part of both the Avenger and Zodiac investigations that it demands major consideration. In the 1947 Avenger communications, we have about a dozen letters, and twenty years later, Zodiac's separate mailings include two dozen—over four thousand words! That's about ten times the amount of words written in Abraham Lincoln's "Gettysburg Address."

At the end of this chapter, I will provide twenty-five separate "known" samples of my father's handwriting, which include both letters and numbers. They span a seventy-three-year period from 1925 to 1998. I offer them for your individual consideration and analysis.

1948 Avenger Kern Letter and 1966 Zodiac-Bates Poem—Some Comparisons

GLADYS KERN WAS ONE of the Los Angeles Lone Woman Murder victims. She was a real estate agent who was stabbed multiple times in the back with a long-bladed knife in 1948. Her killer, posing as a prospective home-buyer, met her at her office and requested that she take him to view a vacant Hollywood house that was for sale. Witnesses later observed two men leaving the house, but no description was made public on the second suspect.

The Hollywood murder occurred in the Los Feliz district of Hollywood, less than two miles from the Franklin house. The victim's office was just one mile from George Hodel's residence.

1948 Witness Composite Drawing of the Gladys Kern Killer

1948 composite drawing of Kern murder suspect [center] Since no moustache was included in original drawing I have airbrushed out my father's from the two photographs

Daily News

KERN MURDER SUSPE

George Hodel circa 1946   Kern Murder Suspect 1948   George Hodel 1952

Fig. 14.5

Body Found Inside the Vacant Residence
Two Days After the Murder

Fig. 14.6

Immediately after the murder, Kern's killer mailed a long, rambling, handprinted letter to police at a downtown mailbox. It was at Fifth and Olive, just three blocks from George Hodel's medical office. *The mailbox was the same one used by the Black Dahlia Avenger in 1947.* The police received the killer's letter before the victim's body was discovered at the vacant house two days later.

Los Angeles 1948, Gladys Kern Letter
Her Killer's Handwriting

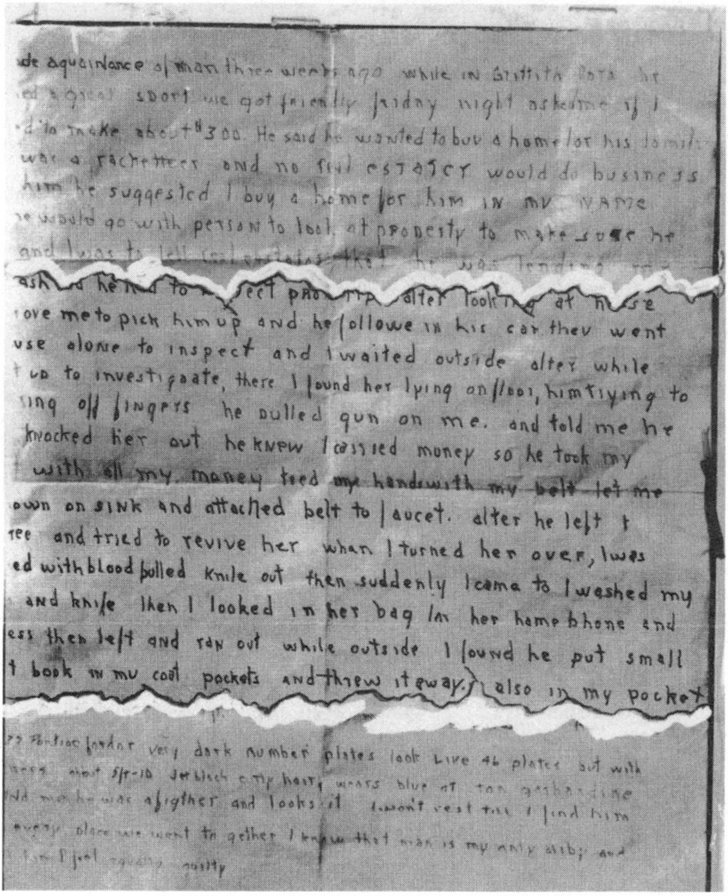

Fig. 14.7

Riverside, Cheri Jo Bates Notes—1966

IN 1966, IN WHAT the San Francisco Police Department now believes was likely a Zodiac-connected murder, college student Cheri Jo Bates was brutally attacked in the dark of night after she left the Riverside Community College Library.

It was a savage attack. As in the Gladys Kern murder, Bates died of multiple stab wounds .

As in the 1947 Black Dahlia Avenger crimes, the killer taunted both police and press by telephone, and later mailed in several handwritten letters, promising "There will be more."

The investigation revealed that Bates' killer was likely "lying in wait" and wrote the sadistic "poem" below on a desktop while waiting for his victim to leave the library. The message was discovered only after the attack.

On April 30, 1967, the sixth month "anniversary" of his killing, he mailed in more sadistic notes to the Riverside police and the victim's father. One was a lengthy, typewritten letter, and the second was scribbled in his distinctive block printing. It read: "Bates had to die. There will be more—signed, 'Z.'"

1966 Bates Desktop Poem

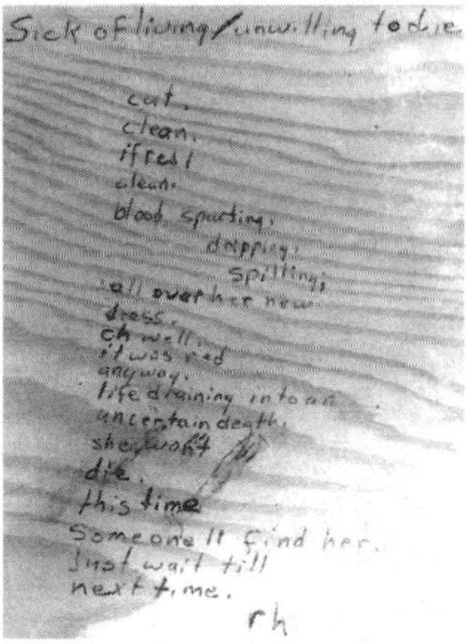

Fig. 14.8

Bates Killer's Typed and Handprinted Letters
Mailed April 30, 1967

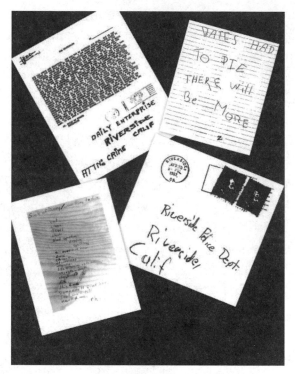

Fig. 14.9

Fig. 14.10

In the exhibit below I have taken each letter of the alphabet and created a side-by-side comparison of the 1948 Kern killer's handwriting to the 1966 Riverside Bates/Zodiac's handwriting. Keeping in mind that twenty years elapsed between the two authors' notes, what is the likelihood that so many of the letters would be identical? I count twenty-one—what is your count?

Same Author?

Lowercase letter comparisons of 1948 Kern letter to 1966 Bates poem

1948 Avenger - 1966 Zodiac HW letter comparisons

Fig. 14.11

In the exhibit below I am comparing not just letters, but complete words found in both the Kern and Bates writings. The Kern words are found inside the boxes with a line connecting them to their Bates counterparts. Note the highly distinctive and uncommon use of the word "till" in both letters. The Kern killer proclaims, "I won't rest *till* I find him." The Bates killer warns, "Just wait *till* next time."[50]

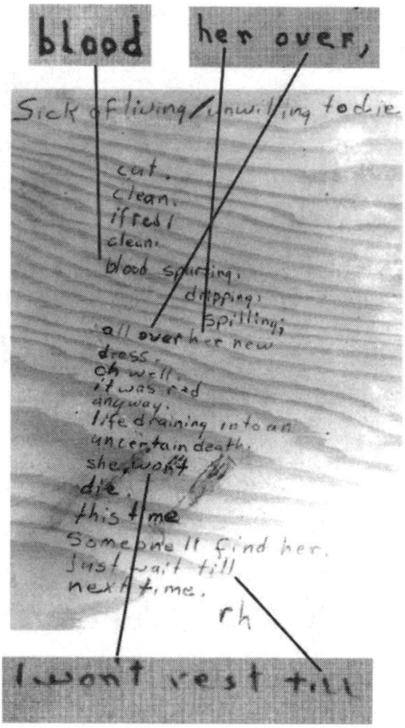

Fig. 14.12

In reviewing the Kern/Bates writings, I noticed one of the most distinctive handwriting "anomalies" yet discovered. Look at the unusual letter "h" written by the killer in the 1948 Kern letter. It is found in the word "attached" and only appears once in the entire letter.

---

50   Author's note: Emphasis mine.

Now compare it to the letter "h" written by Zodiac in the words: "hell-hole" and "Chronicle" in his 1974 "Red Phantom" letter.

Unusual letter "h" in Avenger-Kern Note compared to Zodiac "h" in Red Phantom letter

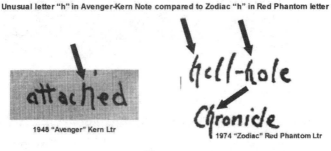

1948 "Avenger" Kern Ltr   1974 "Zodiac" Red Phantom Ltr

Fig. 14.13

Some additional Kern Letter idiosyncrasies:

Note the writing variations on the letter "M" within the same sentence.

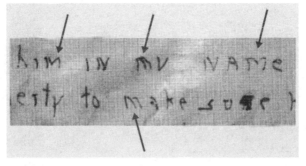

Fig. 14.14

Note the stylistic writing variations of the letter "a" (tail up then tail down) and in the letter "n" (upper and lowercase ["aNd" vs. "and"]) all within the same sentence.

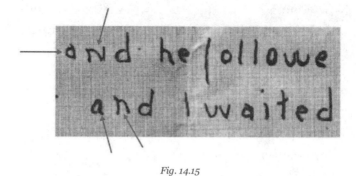

Fig. 14.15

More samples of the writer's fluidity as we see a switch in the same sentence from "aNd" to "And" deviating from the previous use of "and." Most notably, in the below sentence, he has written a backward or "mirrored" letter "r." My guess is that this was not intentional on his part, but just "came out" as he wrote it—simply an unconscious writing anomaly.

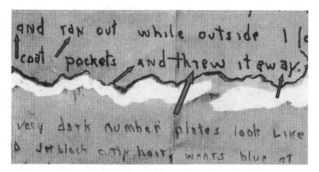

Fig. 14.16

Below we see the killer changing his style of writing the letter "r" from upper case to lower—again within the same sentence and within a word.

Fig. 14.17

Are these unusual writing characteristics exhibited in the 1948 Kern letter indicative of someone with high intelligence, who is simply wired differently than most of us?

We cannot know for certain, but in closing this chapter, let me offer some observations originally made in 2002 by my document expert Hannah McFarland.

After positively identifying George Hodel's handwriting as being the same as the Black Dahlia Avenger and providing her expert opinion that "it was highly probable that he authored at least four of the 1947 'Black Dahlia Avenger' notes," QDE McFarland went on to describe one of my father's unique and highly unusual handwriting characteristics.

I quote from *BDA I,* my chapter on "Handwriting Analysis" pages 289 to 290:

> *... In the sample below, I have enlarged my name, "STEVEN." During her character analysis of the known writing, Ms. McFarland noted a handwriting phenomenon so exceptionally rare that in her examination of documents over many years she had never come across it. This rarity related to the manner in which the three letters "TEV" in "STEVEN" were written. As Ms. McFarland explained:*

It appears that all three letters were highly connected. The T bar connects directly to the top of the E. Most people lift the pen at this point to complete the E. But instead, the printer keeps going in order to form the V, and then goes back to complete the E.

She advised me that to find two connected letters was not particularly rare, but three connected was unheard of, and would indicate the type of exceptionally high intelligence and forethought that might be found in a master chess champion such as a Boris Spassky or a Bobby Fischer. Confirmation of her observation was possible because I possessed the original drawing and was therefore able to verify the three unbroken letters. Thus, in this particular instance, because we were able to view the original document, her analysis of the three connected letters was "positive" instead of highly probable.

Section of George Hodel's Handwriting from April 1949

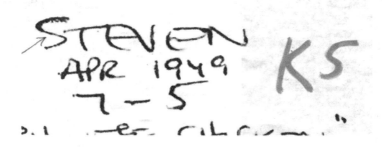

Fig. 14.18

Above is the sample K-5, with an enlargement of the name "STEVEN" demonstrating the printed "TEV" connected and unbroken.

I suspect that some of these other Kern handwriting characteristics we have seen and noted above would fall into a similar classification or category—handwriting authored by a mind that works quickly and functions somewhat out of the norm.

The final exhibit compares what might also be an unconscious handwriting habit. Note that the Bates killer has used a slashmark [arrow] to divide two separate thoughts at the heading of his "poem": "Sick of living/unwilling to die." Likewise, George Hodel at the heading of his conference notes for June Hodel has also used a slashmark to divide his thoughts: "Notes/Qs" [Questions].

Coincidence or Characteristic?

Left: Bates Killer Desk Poem Heading
Right: George Hodel Conference Notes Heading

Fig. 14.19

As promised, for those interested in pursuing additional handwriting comparisons, I have here provided an additional five exhibits that contain a total of twenty-five separate samples of George Hodel's handwriting, spanning some seventy-three years. As can be seen, he nearly always wrote using block printing. Most of his correspondence to me was typewritten. I am in possession of only one instant sample of his lowercase cursives.

Handwriting Samples of George Hill Hodel 1925 to 1997

Fig. 14.20

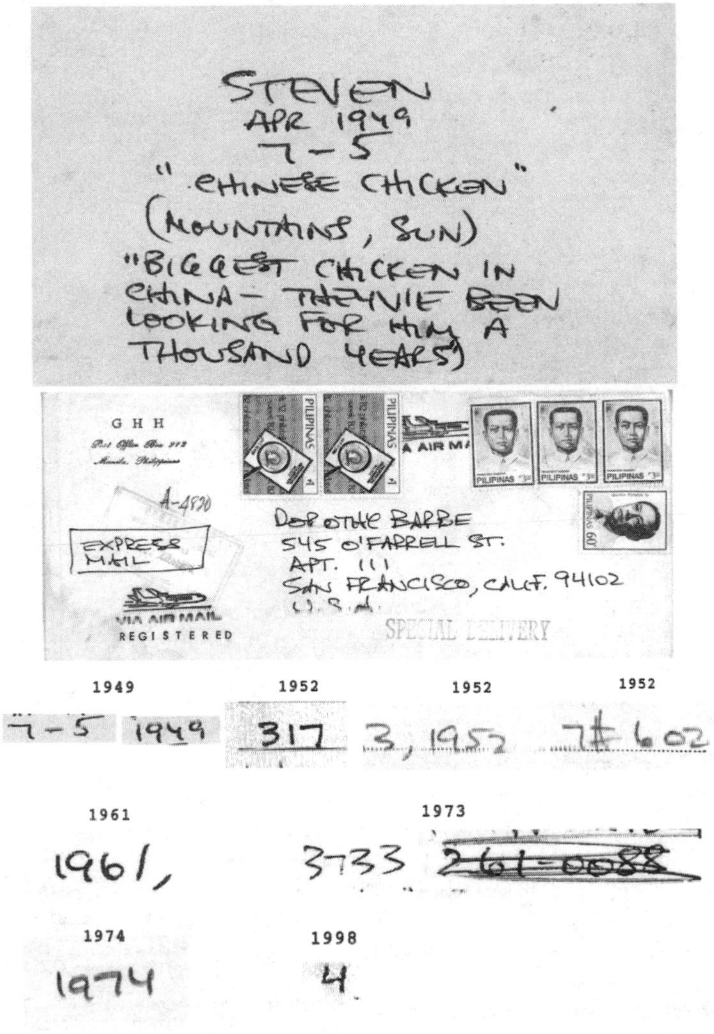

STEVEN
APR 1949
7 - 5
" CHINESE CHICKEN "
(MOUNTAINS, SUN)
"BIGGEST CHICKEN IN
CHINA — THEY'VE BEEN
LOOKING FOR HIM A
THOUSAND YEARS)

GHH
Post Office Box 212
Manila, Philippines

A-4820

EXPRESS
MAIL

VIA AIR MAIL
REGISTERED

DOROTHE BARBE
545 O'FARRELL ST.
APT. 111
SAN FRANCISCO, CALIF. 94102
U.S.A.

SPECIAL DELIVERY

1949	1952	1952	1952
7 - 5 1949	317	3, 1952	7± 602

1961	1973
1961,	3733 261-0088

1974	1998
1974	4

Fig. 14.21

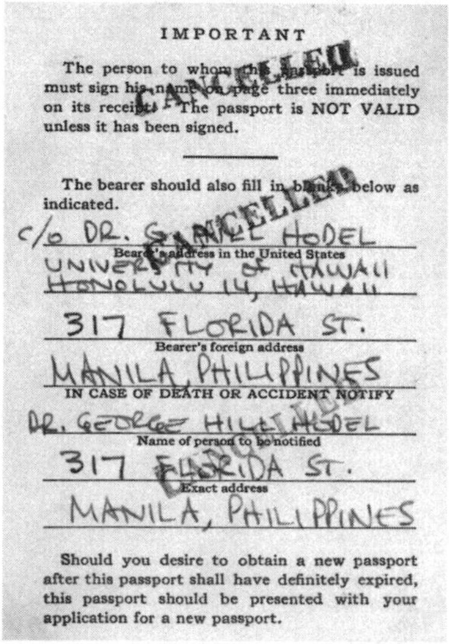

IMPORTANT

The person to whom this passport is issued must sign his name on page three immediately on its receipt. The passport is NOT VALID unless it has been signed.

The bearer should also fill in blanks below as indicated.

CANCELLED

c/o DR. GEORGE HILL HODEL
UNIVERSITY OF HAWAII
HONOLULU 14, HAWAII

Bearer's address in the United States

317 FLORIDA ST.

Bearer's foreign address

MANILA, PHILIPPINES

IN CASE OF DEATH OR ACCIDENT NOTIFY

DR. GEORGE HILL HODEL

Name of person to be notified

317 FLORIDA ST.

Exact address

MANILA, PHILIPPINES

Should you desire to obtain a new passport after this passport shall have definitely expired, this passport should be presented with your application for a new passport.

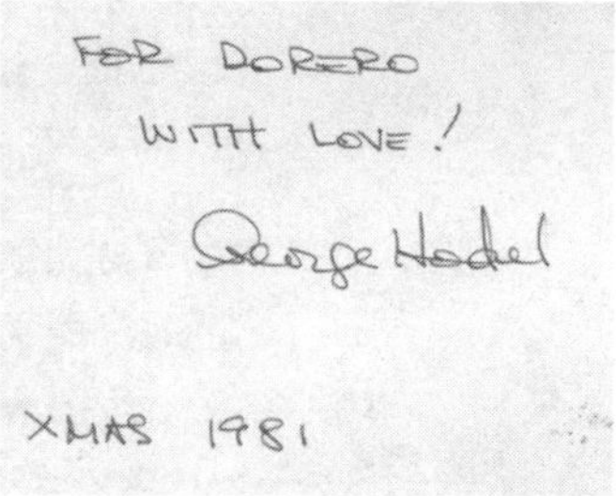

FOR DORERO
WITH LOVE!
George Hodel

XMAS 1981

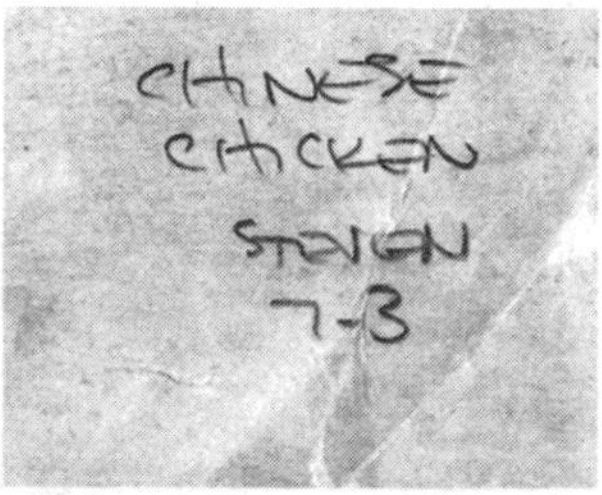

CHINESE
CHICKEN
STEVEN
7-3

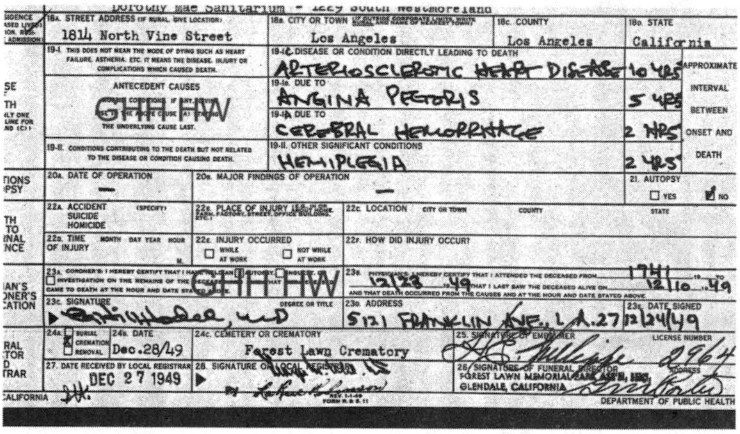

Dorothy Mae Sanitarium - 1229 South Westmoreland

18A. STREET ADDRESS (IF RURAL, GIVE LOCATION): 1814 North Vine Street
18B. CITY OR TOWN: Los Angeles
18C. COUNTY: Los Angeles
18D. STATE: California

19-I. THIS DOES NOT MEAN THE MODE OF DYING SUCH AS HEART FAILURE, ASTHENIA, ETC. IT MEANS THE DISEASE, INJURY OR COMPLICATIONS WHICH CAUSED DEATH.
19-Ia. DISEASE OR CONDITION DIRECTLY LEADING TO DEATH: ARTERIOSCLEROTIC HEART DISEASE — 10 YRS
ANTECEDENT CAUSES — GHH HW
19-Ib. DUE TO: ANGINA PECTORIS — 5 YRS
19-Ic. DUE TO: CEREBRAL HEMORRHAGE — 2 YRS
THE UNDERLYING CAUSE LAST.
19-II. CONDITIONS CONTRIBUTING TO THE DEATH BUT NOT RELATED TO THE DISEASE OR CONDITION CAUSING DEATH.
19-II. OTHER SIGNIFICANT CONDITIONS: HEMIPLEGIA — 2 YRS
APPROXIMATE INTERVAL BETWEEN ONSET AND DEATH

20A. DATE OF OPERATION: —
20B. MAJOR FINDINGS OF OPERATION: —
21. AUTOPSY: ☐ YES ☑ NO

22A. ACCIDENT SUICIDE HOMICIDE (SPECIFY)
22B. PLACE OF INJURY
22C. LOCATION — CITY OR TOWN — COUNTY — STATE
22D. TIME OF INJURY — MONTH DAY YEAR HOUR M.
22E. INJURY OCCURRED ☐ WHILE AT WORK ☐ NOT WHILE AT WORK
22F. HOW DID INJURY OCCUR?

23A. CORONER'S: GHH HW
23B. PHYSICIAN'S: I HEREBY CERTIFY THAT I ATTENDED THE DECEASED FROM 1941 TO 12/23 49 THAT I LAST SAW THE DECEASED ALIVE ON 12/10 49 AND THAT DEATH OCCURRED FROM THE CAUSES AND AT THE HOUR AND DATE STATED ABOVE.
23C. SIGNATURE: George Hodel, MD — DEGREE OR TITLE
23D. ADDRESS: 5121 FRANKLIN AVE., L.A. 27
23E. DATE SIGNED: 12/24/49

24A. ☐ BURIAL ☒ CREMATION ☐ REMOVAL
24B. DATE: Dec. 28/49
24C. CEMETERY OR CREMATORY: Forest Lawn Crematory
25. SIGNATURE OF EMBALMER — LICENSE NUMBER 2964
26. SIGNATURE OF FUNERAL DIRECTOR — FOREST LAWN MEMORIAL PARK ASS'N, INC. GLENDALE, CALIFORNIA
27. DATE RECEIVED BY LOCAL REGISTRAR: DEC 27 1949
28. SIGNATURE OF LOCAL REGISTRAR

CALIFORNIA — DEPARTMENT OF PUBLIC HEALTH

Fig. 14.22

JH CONF. NOTES/QS
BRT. SIDE
REALISTIC: PNR
TIME FOR EV.
ABOVE ALL... REST... N+D
L HAS L...   MAIN ISS, DENS
NEGS, POSTS

K1

1 OF 2
GHD E-CH
STROK/HT ATTK FORMS
→B   L. HONDA — BEY. ALL H-
4 FORMS   NO BR RFEM
HORR P, M,
DIGNITY, SELF-R
UGLY, PNFL
S. AF. DRM
MUST ACT QKLY
NO SILKS, etc.
LTNG MAY STR..
ACT SWFTLY
TOO LATE
HAVE RX
TIMING, MODUS
ABS NO R&R?
LNGNG (D)+N- TO RST
21 LONG YRS-
WNDRFL L, WNDRFL EV
RSRVD RL ON CHST
AQUILA LAST ACT OF LV
LOOK FLWRD TO DAY
WITH ANTICIP- TO ENDURE
PAIN 2   DISP ALL EFFECTS

DR'S ATTITUDE- EXPECTED
LAGUNA HONDA

L = CONC. ON EXCRETA
TOP OF CAREER-
MICHAEL JORDAN

Fig. 14.23

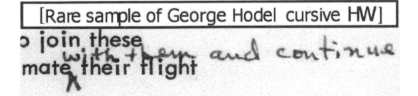

[Rare sample of George Hodel cursive HW]

o join these
with them and continue
mate their flight

Fig. 14.24

ADDENDUM IV

"Touch DNA"

(Originally Published in Black Dahlia
Avenger II, *pages 343 to 369)*

*"The family of JonBenét Ramsey has been formally
cleared of any role in the six-year-old's 1996 murder,
a Colorado prosecutor announced Wednesday, citing
newly discovered DNA evidence."*

—USA Today *April 16, 2009*

THE 2009 *USA TODAY* article went on to state:

Boulder, Colorado—District Attorney Mary Lacy said in
a statement on Wednesday that DNA evidence recovered
from the child's clothing [pajamas] pointed to an
"unexplained third party." Lacy apologized to the family
for the suspicions that made their lives "an ongoing
living hell."

...

The new evidence, described as "irrefutable" in clearing
the Ramseys, would be checked against other profiles in the
national DNA database managed by the FBI.

The new physical evidence was obtained by technicians
from Bode Technology, in Lorton, Virginia. Bode is

considered to be one of the top forensic laboratories in the United States and is frequently the lab of choice used by the FBI and law enforcement agencies across the nation.

The relatively new procedure used by Bode Labs in extracting the suspect's DNA in the Ramsey investigation is called "touch DNA."

"Touch DNA" is the collection of skin cells which have been transferred from an individual's skin to the surface of items it has come in contact with, such as the grip of a gun, luggage, a car's steering wheel, a victim's clothing, or a ligature used in the commission of a crime.

The collection of the skin cells can be accomplished in various methods, such as swabbing, cutting, tape-lift, and scraping.

In the past several years, this method of collecting evidence has resulted in a number of successful murder prosecutions, as well as aiding in establishing the actual innocence of a number of wrongfully convicted individuals.

A Search for George Hill Hodel's DNA

IN APRIL OF 2009, I contacted Bode Laboratories. After exchanging telephone calls, letters, and emails with Dr. Angela Williamson, Director of Forensic Casework, we decided on the best course of action to attempt to isolate and obtain my father's DNA.

I carefully packaged and forwarded to the Virginia-based lab a number of my father's personal effects, some of which had been in my possession for over forty years. They included a pair of his Bally dress shoes (size 10e) and four separate letters written by him over the past decades—all of which contained stamps and envelopes that might yield his DNA.

By July of 2010, over a year had elapsed, and three of the four items, including the shoes, had none of his DNA. We were down to the last item, a letter my father had mailed to me in 1971 from Manila, Philippines.

BINGO!

SUCCESS CAME ON THIS very last evidentiary item. The envelope contained his full genetic DNA profile!

George Hill Hodel Letter mailed from Manila in 1971

Fig. 15.0

George Hill Hodel's DNA profile remains in my possession and upon request will be made available to any legitimate law enforcement agency to help their cold case investigations.

George Hodel 1949 Booking DNA Full Profile Now Available

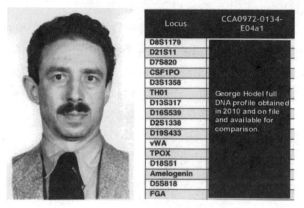

Locus	CCA0972-0134-E04a1
D8S1179	
D21S11	
D7S820	
CSF1PO	
D3S1358	
TH01	George Hodel full
D13S317	DNA profile obtained
D16S539	in 2010 and on file
D2S1338	and available for
D19S433	comparison.
vWA	
TPOX	
D18S51	
Amelogenin	
D5S818	
FGA	

Fig. 15.1

For those who have not read my sequel to *BDA, Most Evil: Avenger, Zodiac, and the Further Serial Murders of Dr. George Hill Hodel,* I will here provide only the briefest of summaries so you can understand that the following discussion about connecting George Hodel's newly-obtained DNA to other crimes in other cities is not simply arbitrary. Rather, it is based on compelling circumstantial evidence provided in that book.

Los Angeles DA Files—Elizabeth Short—The Chicago Lipstick Murders

AS I REVIEWED THE Los Angeles DA files, I discovered documents that showed that, in July of 1946, while my father was stationed with UNRRA in China, Elizabeth Short traveled to Chicago, Illinois and began her own personal investigation into three exceptionally high-profile crimes known as Chicago's "Lipstick Murders."

The three victims—Josephine Ross, Frances Brown, and Suzanne Degnan—had made national headlines in 1945 and 1946.

The third Lipstick victim gained the most notoriety. It involved the horrific kidnap-strangulation, murder, and surgical bisection of a six-year-old girl, little Suzanne Degnan. Her sadistic killer had kidnapped the sleeping child from her bedroom and carried her to a basement just a few blocks from her home. There he strangled her, performed a highly-skilled surgical operation known as a "hemicorpectomy," and divided the body by cutting through the second and third lumbar vertebrae—the exact same operation performed on Elizabeth Short one year later.

The killer then carried the body parts to six separate catch basins around that North Side neighborhood. Finally, he scrawled a message in lipstick on a post in front of the "murder room" that read:

"Stop Me Before I Kill More."

Lipstick printed sign on post near building where body of Suzanne Degnan was dismembered, discovered yesterday.

Fig. 15.2

Chicago's 1945 Frances Brown Lipstick Murder

Fig. 15.3

Written on an apartment wall in lipstick less than one month prior to the Degnan murder:

> *"For heaven's sake catch me Before I Kill more. I cannot control myself"*

The DA files document that Elizabeth Short spent three weeks in Chicago and slept with four separate Chicago newspaper reporters, apparently attempting to gain some inside information on the three separate Lipstick Murder investigations. She also informed the newsmen that "she knew a Chicago detective that was working the Degnan case."

The DA files also contained information indicating that the Dahlia's killer might have been an "Unknown Chicago Police Officer." Why?

The information was based on the fact that Elizabeth Short attended Jack Carson's CBS radio show in Hollywood in early January 1947, just days before being slain.

Chief Usher Jack Egger identified her as standing in line with an older "dapper male in his thirties" who identified himself to Egger as a Chicago police officer, showing Egger a police badge. Egger allowed both Short and the man to jump the line and enter the studio. Egger was familiar with Short because she regularly attended the shows, but this was the first time he ever recalled her being accompanied by a man.

Jack Egger went on to become a DA investigator, then joined the Beverly Hills Police Department, where he rose to command that department's Detective Bureau. After retirement, he became chief of security for Warner Brothers Studio in Burbank.

As detailed in my sequel, I discovered that Jack was still employed by Warner Brothers as their chief investigator, and I met with him in 2004.

After verifying the facts in his original 1950 DA interview, I showed Chief Egger a photograph of Dr. George Hill Hodel from around 1950. He positively identified my father as being the person he saw with Elizabeth Short at the CBS studio and the same individual who had shown him a Chicago police badge.

I also possess original Los Angeles Sheriff's Department investigative reports that show that the LASD, in 1946, was actively investigating the possibility that their 1944 Hollywood Lone Woman Murder of oil-heiress Georgette Bauerdorf might have been connected to the later 1945 Chicago Lipstick Murders. Those reports indicate that LASD requested prints and additional information to ascertain if the crimes were linked.

Photo Identification by Warner Brothers Studio Chief Jack Egger

Left: Dr. George Hodel; Right: Elizabeth Short

Fig. 15.4

John F. "Jack" Egger 1927 to 2010

Jack Egger (top and bottom left photos, 1945-1946); Captain Egger, Beverly Hills Police Department (center); Photo right shows Jack as Chief of Warner Brothers Security with LA District Attorney Steve Cooley in 2006. (Photographs courtesy of Jack's son, Brian Egger.)

Fig. 15.5

Jack Egger passed away in Los Angeles in 2010, at the age of eighty-three. His law enforcement service spanned more than five decades and included DA's investigator for four years, from 1949 to 1953, when he transferred to Beverly Hills Police Department. He rose to the rank of Detective Captain. Honorably retired, he then entered the private sector, and in 1979 he served at Warner Brothers Studio as Chief of Security, commanding a 400-man security force.

Up until his death, he remained active in the law enforcement community. In his final years, he served as a General Board Member of POALAC (Peace Officers Association Los Angeles County.) A few of his fellow board members were: Lee Baca, Sheriff, LA County; William Bratton, Chief LAPD; Steve Cooley, District Attorney, Los Angeles County; Sharon Papa, Assistant Chief, LAPD.

Thank you, Jack Egger for your key statements and assistance in the original and subsequent Black Dahlia investigation and for your decades of dedicated service in law enforcement to the citizens of both Los Angeles and Beverly Hills. May you Rest in Peace.

What's in a Name?
Another Black Dahlia Avenger Taunt

IN AN EARLIER CHAPTER, I described how I drove myself on what I believed was my father's probable original route from the Franklin house to the vacant lot on South Norton Avenue.

On arrival, I spent only four minutes at the vacant lot, just as the original witness had described it when he saw the black sedan pull up and stop on January 15, 1947.

I then resumed my drive home; again taking what I believed was my father's probable route. Driving north, I stopped halfway between the lot and the Franklin house and simulated placing Elizabeth Short's purse and shoes on top of a restaurant trash can in the 1100 block of South Crenshaw Boulevard—just where the witness had described seeing them. And then I went back home to Franklin and Normandie.

Some theorists and a few amateur profilers have argued there was a specific reason why the Dahlia killer selected the Liemert Park neighborhood. Maybe the killer had some connection to the neighborhood, they say.

In my sequel, *Most Evil*, I presented why I believe he selected that specific location. It was not because it "connects him to the neighborhood" but rather just the reverse—the placement of the body connects *her*, Elizabeth Short, to *his neighborhood*, his other crimes.

Another one of his diabolical "catch me if you can" clews, another of the Avenger's highly egotistical taunts that are, in the end, his signature. Pieced together they become his own undoing, and lead us directly to his identity.

Here is the explanation in brief.

The most direct route, the one I drove on January 16, 2011, and the one I believe was driven by my father, was: South on Normandie Avenue to Santa Barbara [now renamed Martin Luther King Jr. Boulevard], then a right turn on MLK Jr. Blvd for approximately two miles. I believe he then turned right on a residential street and drove north a few blocks to the vacant lot where he stopped, carefully posed the body parts, and was gone in just four minutes.

The name of the street he selected and turned right on? Degnan.

The very same name as that of his third Chicago Lipstick Murder victim.

Suzanne Degnan was the child who, just one year earlier, had been slain and a hemicorpectomy performed on her by a skilled surgeon/killer. Just as he had done with Elizabeth Short, he divided the little Degnan girl's body between the second and third lumbar vertebrae. The dissected body parts were then posed in a residential neighborhood with a taunting message written in lipstick, which was left near the body, promising, "There will be more."

I believe that Elizabeth Short had somehow made the connection of George Hodel, her "former suitor" and sometime boyfriend, to the Chicago Lipstick murders. She had gone to Chicago in June and July 1946 to investigate while he was away in China. The DA reports confirm it.

I suspect that Elizabeth later naively disclosed to George Hodel that she knew about or suspected his crimes. This might have caused his unexpected return to Los Angeles. She then fled in fear to San Diego. He pursued her. In time, she learned she had signed her own death warrant.

His choice of a dump site and the posing of her body on the street whose name related to a crime she was about to reveal was his own sardonic and macabre "poetry." It was his surrealistic homage—to add to his theme of murder as a fine art.

Norton vs. Degnan

THE SIMPLE FACT IS that George Hodel believed he had posed the body on Degnan. He likely didn't discover his mistake until reading the afternoon "extra" edition in the newspaper, which named the location as Thirty-Ninth and Norton.

What happened?

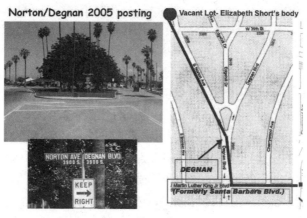

Fig. 15.6

The above photo exhibit gives us the answer. The fact is, this street has two names—Degnan and Norton. The arrow points to the exact location where the street magically changes its name from Degnan and becomes Norton.

Driving west on Santa Barbara Boulevard [MLK Jr.], George Hodel turned right on Degnan, the street he had previously selected. He drove north on Degnan looking for just the right spot. He came to the division and bore left, thinking he was still on Degnan. He simply zigged when he should have zagged. It was a fifty-fifty coin toss and he lost.

The above photographs show how the streets are currently marked, not how they appeared in 1947. Back then, there was no raised island or "one-way sign," just the simple choice. Bear right and remain on Degnan. Bear left and Degnan becomes Norton.

In later years, it had become so confusing that the city had to try and clarify it by adding the "KEEP RIGHT" sign for Degnan and putting in the one-way divider. Even today's Google maps, to try and help lessen the confusion, has the street split marked with an arrow.

Keep in mind that, in his youth, George Hodel was a Los Angeles cab driver, and with his perfect photographic memory, he could take you to any street in the city. He knew them all.

I previously described this unique act of George Hodel of connecting his victims to a street name as one of his criminal signatures. It was, and this example is just one of many. The additional signatures can be found detailed and summarized in the sequel, *Most Evil: Avenger, Zodiac, and the Further Serial Murders of Dr. George Hill Hodel* (Dutton, 2009).

Probable round-trip driving route from George Hodel's residence.

1. Dr. Hodel's Franklin house, 5121 Franklin Avenue

2. Vacant lot, 3815 South Norton (aka Degnan)

3. Elizabeth Short's purse and shoes left at 1136 South Crenshaw Boulevard (halfway between body and Franklin house)

Fig. 15.7

LA Lone Woman Murders

New "Touch DNA" Procedure Potentially Opens Door to Solving Many of the Forties' and Sixties' Serial Killings

IN ADDITION TO THE Black Dahlia murder, as has been noted in *BDA* and reviewed again in earlier chapters of this book, from 1943 to 1949, a number of other Lone Woman Murders occurred all in a tight geographical area between Hollywood and downtown Los Angeles.

LAPD's original on-scene detectives were convinced that many of these unsolved murders were committed by the same killer. Authorities released a summary to the press listing eleven points of similarity.

In six of those crimes, the killer left a taunting message, just as he had in the Elizabeth Short murder. This act alone is so unusual it raises the suspicion of linkage to the other murders.

The recent identification of Dr. George Hill Hodel's DNA profile, along with the newly developed "touch DNA" techniques, improve the chances of solving many of these additional LAPD and LASD murders, or at least proving whether George Hodel was involved.

All that is required is the attempt.

It would require minimal investigative manpower. A two-person team could oversee the collection of potential evidence for DNA testing. Those profiles could then be entered into state and federal CODIS (Combined DNA Index System) for inclusion or exclusion to the known George Hodel sample, as well as providing an automatic comparison to all DNA samples already in the data banks. The DNA collected by investigators from the various Lone Woman Murders cold cases could then also be compared not only to potential suspects but to other existent crime scene DNA already in the data banks for linkage to other unsolved crimes.

The names of some of the forties cold cases that remain unsolved and were actively investigated and suspected of possibly being connected and could—*if tested*—potentially yield suspect DNA are:

(Listed chronologically by investigating agency)

LAPD

- Miss Elizabeth Short, January 15, 1947. (It is unclear if the victim's purse, known to be handled by the killer, remains in evidence. Retired detective Brian Carr claimed all the physical evidence, letters, etc., had "disappeared," but did not specifically mention the victim's purse.)

- Mrs. Jeanne French, February 10, 1947

- Miss Evelyn Winters, March 11, 1947

- Miss Rosenda Mondragon, July 8, 1947

- Mrs. Gladys Kern, February 14, 1948

- Mrs. Louise Springer, June 13, 1949

LASD

- Mrs. Ora Murray, July 27, 1943

- Miss Georgette Bauerdorf, October 12, 1944

- Mrs. Gertrude Evelyn Landon, July 10, 1946

- Mrs. Dorothy Montgomery, May 2, 1947

- Miss Geneva Ellroy, June 22, 1958

- Miss Bobbie Long, January 22, 1959

Long Beach PD

- Laura Trelstad, May 11, 1947

San Diego PD

- Miss Marian Newton, July 17, 1947

Based on my investigation of the publicly known facts of these forties Lone Woman Murders, it is my belief that the best chance of obtaining positive DNA would most likely come from LAPD's Louise Springer murder.

However, all of the above-listed crimes are excellent potential sources for obtaining "touch DNA" due to the killer's extensive use of ligatures and the unusually rough ripping and tearing of the victim's clothing. Several included a man's handkerchief left at the crime scene.

Cold cases in the forties and sixties crimes summarized in my sequel *Most Evil* that could also potentially yield suspect DNA—*if tested*—include:

Chicago

- Miss Josephine Ross, June 5, 1945

- Miss Frances Brown, December 10, 1945

- Miss Suzanne Degnan, January 6, 1946

All three of the Chicago Lipstick Murders would offer a high probability of yielding "touch DNA."

In addition, Chicago PD hand-carried and booked into evidence at the FBI Laboratory a hair follicle found on Suzanne Degnan's body, which they insisted "had to belong to her killer." Additionally, Chicago PD detectives informed the press that victim Josephine Ross "was clutching in her hand some black hair follicles belonging to the killer which may help us in identifying him."

Does the hair follicle evidence in both the Ross and Degnan crimes still exist? Can DNA be obtained?

1945 Chicago Lipstick Killer Update

Attempted rape victim/witness confirmed the Lipstick Killer description as: "Tall, thin, with black hair, used clothesline rope to bind her."

IN A RECENT REVIEW of 1945 newspaper articles related to Chicago's Lipstick Killer, specifically the June 5, 1945 murder of Josephine Alice Ross, I discovered an interesting and hitherto unknown witness/victim account, long buried and forgotten, which should have had an important bearing on the later investigation. This is a new discovery, post-publication of *Most Evil*. Therefore, this was not discussed in that sequel.

This new information revealed that just a few hours before the brutal Lipstick Killer murder of Josephine Ross, another woman, Mrs. Eileen Huffman, age thirty-four, was accosted in her apartment house basement by a man armed with a handgun.

Described as "tall and thin, with black hair," he tied the victim's hands with clothesline and attempted to rape her, but fled when she screamed out.

Shortly after this assault, just a few hours later, and only five blocks away, the first Lipstick Killer victim, Josephine Ross, was attacked and murdered in her home. (See following diagram for victim locations.)

In the later, December 1945, murder of Frances Brown, the same killer used both a gun and a knife, stabbing her through the neck and shooting her twice.

Obviously, Chicago detectives made the connection between the Huffman and Ross crimes and, according to the article, delayed the murder inquest so that they could proceed with their search for a "tall, dark-haired man, wearing a light colored sweater; he was seen leaving the Ross apartment building," and closely fit the description provided by Mrs. Eileen Huffman.

"Tall, black-haired suspect" committed the Huffman and Ross crimes on June 5, 1945, just two hours and five blocks apart.

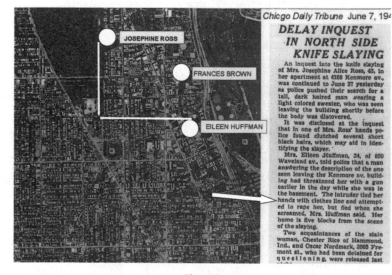

Fig. 15.8

Can DNA from the FBI Evidence Lab link George Hodel to the Chicago Lipstick Murders?

Does the FBI laboratory still have the hair follicle DNA evidence on the 1946 Degnan "Lipstick Murder" investigation?

FBI Receipt No. PC-16339-AO Q21

Dated January 8, 1946

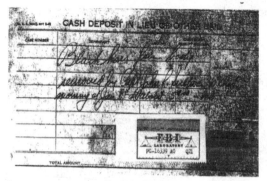

Original Jan 8, 1947 receipt from FBI on hair follicle booked in evidence

Fig. 15.9

Additional Potential Sources for "touch DNA"

Riverside PD

- Miss Cheri Jo Bates, October 30, 1966. (Hair follicles also found in victim's hand which reportedly have been tested. Do they contain a full DNA profile? Are they available for comparison?)

Manila PD, Manila, Philippines

- Miss Lucila Lalu, May 30, 1967

Solano County S.O.

- Miss Betty Jensen/Mr. David Faraday, December 20, 1968

Vallejo PD

- Mrs. Darlene Ferrin/Michael Mageau, July 4, 1969

Napa County S.O.

- Cecelia Shepard/Bryan Hartnell, September 27, 1969

San Francisco PD

- Mr. Paul Stine, October 11, 1969

Signature Crime

> *"SIGNATURE CRIME: (noun) any of two or more crimes that involve the use of a method, plan, or MO so distinctive that it logically follows that the crimes must have been committed by the same person."*
> —Merriam-Webster's Dictionary of Law

MODUS OPERANDI—OR MO—IS A very broad term and it is often mentioned in very general nonspecific terms when it comes to criminal investigations.

The squad-room roll call sergeant, when reading off crimes from the previous week, might say, "The suspect is a hot-prowl burglar and his MO is to enter upscale private residences during daytime hours."

That said, there are signature crimes and signature acts within those crimes that are so specific that they become extremely important in attempting to link serial crimes and serial killers.

In my *Most Evil* investigation, there are many such acts that I believe not only link the killer from crime to crime, but from city to city. As relates to the potential for "touch DNA," let's examine what I consider to be one of George Hodel's most significant *signature acts*—that being:

Bringing with him and use of pre-cut clothesline to either strangle or bind his victims.

Chicago's Lipstick Killer, Los Angeles's Black Dahlia Avenger, Manila's Jigsaw Killer, and San Francisco's Zodiac—each brought precut sections of clothesline with them and used them in connection with one or more of their crimes.

**Lipstick Killer, Avenger, Jigsaw, and Zodiac
All Used Precut Clothesline to Commit Their Crimes**

Fig. 15.10

In the 1967 bisection murder of Lucila Lalu in Manila, the killer used that country's version of clothesline rope. He bound her with "abaca," commonly known as Manila hemp. The photo seen above is a depiction and not the actual rope used in the Lalu crime. The other three photos do show the actual clothesline rope used in those murders.

"Touch DNA" processing could potentially result in obtaining suspect DNA skill cells on any or all of these ligatures.

Do LAPD and Riverside PD Letters Contain Zodiac's Full DNA Profile?

IN 2010, LAPD AND the DOJ teamed up to connect and solve a series of cold case murders that occurred in Los Angeles over a twenty-two-year period (from 1985 to 2007).

The suspect, Lonnie David Franklin Jr., whom the LA press dubbed "The Grim Sleeper," was arrested on DNA evidence that allegedly connected him to multiple victims. As of 2011, LAPD believes he might be responsible for as many as twenty separate rape-murders over twenty years in the south-central Los Angeles area.

Based on eleven years of investigation, new evidence reported in *Most Evil,* and now in this 2012 follow-up, I would suggest that George Hodel resumed his serial killing in California twenty years after the commission of his Black Dahlia Avenger crimes.

Setting aside for a moment the twenty or more Northern California Zodiac letters and evidence, let's just focus on the letters he sent to the police and press in the LA area.

There are four letters: Two mailed in Riverside in 1967, one to the *Los Angeles Times* in 1971, and one to KHJ-TV in 1978.

Do these four untested Southern California evidence letters contain
killer's DNA? Top: Killer mailed notes to both victim's father and
Riverside PD in 1967. Lower Left: 1971 Zodiac letter mailed to KHJ
TV booked into LAPD as evidence. Lower Right: 1978 Zodiac letter
mailed to the Los Angeles Times booked into LAPD as evidence

Fig. 15.11

1971 Zodiac Letter to *Los Angeles Times*

*"I do have to give them credit for stumbling across my
riverside activity, but they are only finding the easy one,
there are a hell of a lot more down there."*

—ZODIAC

I BELIEVE THIS LETTER offers the highest probability of yielding
actual suspect DNA. It is recognized as being a legitimate
letter written by Zodiac. In it, he acknowledged and took
credit for the 1966 Cheri Jo Bates murder, and informed the
public that he had killed a lot more victims "down there" [in
Southern California].

1971 *Los Angeles Times* Zodiac Letter

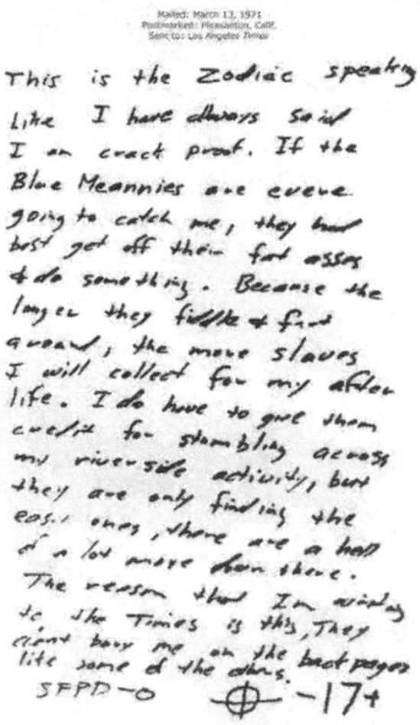

Fig. 15.12

1978 Zodiac Letter to KHJ-TV

WHEN I FIRST VIEWED this letter, I had mixed reactions as to whether this was a legitimate Zodiac letter. The handwriting in the body of the letter—though apparently disguised— seems a bit off when compared to other known writings. However, the handwriting on the envelope is much more consistent with known Zodiac samples. While focusing my attention on this letter, I have discovered what I believe to be new information that might well strengthen the case for the letter having actually been written by Zodiac. (My apologies if some of the information has been referenced elsewhere by other researchers/investigators. If it has been, I have not come across it.) Here's what I've discovered:

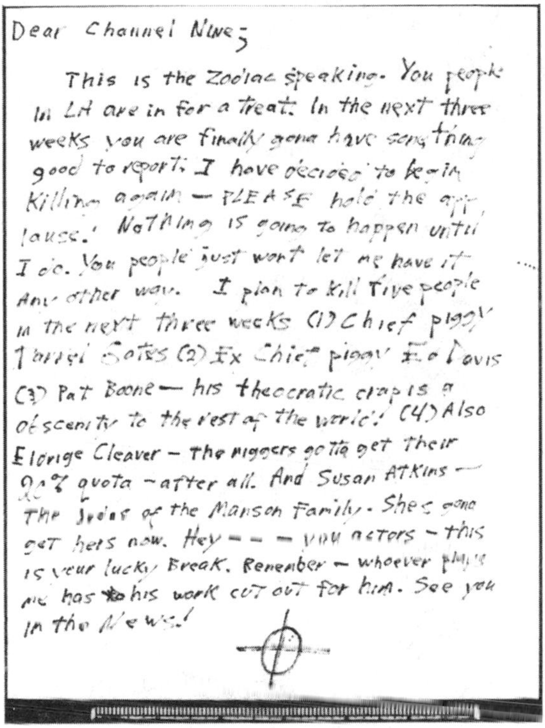

Fig. 15.13

This letter was received by KHJ-TV in May 1978 and turned over to the LAPD. It contains death threats against five individuals: Ex-LAPD Chiefs of Police Darryl Gates and Ed Davis; singer Pat Boone; black activist Eldridge Cleaver; and Manson Family member Susan Atkins. Specifically about Atkins, Zodiac writes:

> *"And Susan Atkins—the Judas of the Manson Family. Shes gona get hers now."*

The Envelope

ON THE OUTSIDE OF the envelope, where the return address should be, were written some backward letters and numbers. The top line reads "CIA" with the letter "C" reversed

Original 1978 Envelope in LAPD Custody

Fig. 15.14

Below, I have reversed the original printed information, which now reads:

"1, 2, 3, 4, 5, 6, 7" (7 reversed)

A.G.C.G.T.H!"

Fig. 15.15

Helter Skelter—Bugliosi/Manson

BASED ON ZODIAC'S REFERENCE to the Manson Family in the text of his letter, it becomes obvious that the source of the enigmatic message on the outside of the envelope is also a direct reference to Charles Manson.

Further, it is my belief that the person who wrote this letter had also read and was familiar with author Vincent Bugliosi's *Helter Skelter: The True Story of the Manson Murders*, published four years earlier in 1974.

Why?

Read this excerpt from Bugliosi's bestseller, page 294:

> *On May 25, I was going through LAPD's tubs on the LaBianca case when I noticed standing against the wall, a wooden door. On it was a multicolored mural, the lines from a nursery rhyme, "1, 2, 3, 4, 5, 6, 7—All Good Children Go to Heaven"; and, in large letters, the words "HELTER SKELTER IS COMING DOWN FAST."*

Stunned, I asked Gutierrez, "Where in the hell did you get that?"

"Spahn Ranch."

"When?"

He checked the yellow property envelope affixed to the door, "November 25, 1969."

"You mean for five months, while I've been desperately trying to link the killers with Helter Skelter, you've had this door, with those very words on it, the same bloody words that were found at the LaBianca residence?"

Gutierrez admitted they had. The door, it turned out, had been found on a cabinet in Juan Flynn's trailer. It had been considered so unimportant that to date no one had even bothered to book it into evidence.

Gutierrez did so the next day.

Photo of the Spahn Ranch Door in Evidence at LAPD Property

Writing on door reads:
"1, 2, 3, 4, 5, 6, 7—All Good Children (go to heaven)

Fig. 15.16

I believe the enigmatic reference on the 1978 envelope is classic Zodiac. He preferred to write it backward and in code—another of his cat-and-mouse games. A new taunt from the "master criminal." Let the cops try and connect these dots.

I know for a fact that my father had read and was familiar with Bugliosi's bestseller *Helter Skelter,* because during that time period he expressed an interest in the investigation. On one of his regular visits with me in LA, he told me he had read it and asked me directly, "What did you think about the book?" My response back then was, "Sorry, Dad, I haven't read it."

John Walsh—Anderson Cooper—More Zodiac Letters and DNA?

CNN *Anderson Cooper 360* "Notorious Crimes" July 22, 2011

2011 John Walsh and Anderson Cooper discussing Black Dahlia and Zodiac cases

Fig. 15.17

On July 23, 2011, CNN's *Anderson Cooper 360* aired an updated segment devoted to various "Notorious Crimes."

In September of 2006, Anderson had interviewed me on the Black Dahlia murder. On air, I eliminated the one photo in my father's album as Elizabeth Short and discussed the posing of the body and various signature connections of my father's crime to surrealism.

In the 2011 segment, Anderson updated my investigation and introduced the viewers to one of my most important new discoveries—the linking of physical evidence from my father's Sowden/Franklin house to evidence found near the body at the Thirty-Ninth and Norton vacant lot.

He presented the photographs and original receipts I had discovered at the UCLA Special Collections Department, linking the cement bags from the house to identical bags that LAPD determined were used to transport Elizabeth Short's body to the vacant lot. (All previously detailed in Chapter 5 of this book, "Scene of the Crime.")

In his update, he also mentioned the important fact that Dr. Hodel had fled the country before detectives were able to interview him about or arrest him for the tape-recorded admissions he made to killing Elizabeth Short and his secretary Ruth Spaulding, as well as personally admitting to "performing abortions at his VD clinic and to making payoffs to the police."

In the interview, John Walsh of *America's Most Wanted* expressed a strong conviction that, "in my heart and in my gut from doing this for so many years, I believe it was the doctor [George Hodel]."

Here is the excerpted exchange between Walsh and Cooper regarding the Black Dahlia Murder:

AC: The Black Dahlia case. This is a case that has been fascinating Hollywood and the country for decades.

JW: Bestselling book, movie, all that spin. But I do believe [he] killed the Black Dahlia, the main suspect they had. The doctor who is now deceased. I believe he got away with that case. They never charged him. He was a stalker. [Dr. George Hill Hodel] was the main suspect. They never had enough to indict him. She was dismembered by someone who had great knowledge of anatomy and skills in surgery. He was the logical suspect, but back in those days, they didn't have the tools that we have now.

AC: They obviously sensationalized the case not because she was beautiful, but because of the gruesome way that she was killed.

JW: The way that he displayed her. He displayed her as a trophy, like lots of serial killers and horrible narcissistic murderers do. He displayed her in the field for the whole world to see his work.

In my heart and in my gut from doing this so many years I believe it was that doctor.[51]

After discussing the Black Dahlia case, the program then reviewed the Zodiac murder. Here is an excerpt from that discussion where John Walsh described personally receiving multiple letters and death threats from a man identifying himself as "Scorpion," but who had identical handwriting and codes and ciphers to Zodiac.

...AC: The Zodiac Killer's probably the most famous cold case in the US. Why do you think there is so much fascination with it?

---

51   Author's note: Emphasis mine.

JW: Because he terrorized and held San Francisco captive for so long. They locked down that city when he said, "If you keep looking for me, I have a sniper's rifle, I will kill the kids getting off of the buses." He claimed to have killed multiple victims. They believe he killed seven people. It actually paralyzed a city. A United States city. One low-life coward paralyzed that city. People were fascinated. He always sent this cryptic code around, and everybody analyzed it. When I first profiled the Zodiac Killer, I got a letter sent exactly like his code. Sent to me in exactly the same kind of envelope that he sent others. I had to give it to the FBI. It was signed in blood. In human blood. He said, "I will kill you. You will be the ultimate victory. I got away with it. I've committed mayhem since I murdered those other people. You will be my ultimate prize. I still have the ability to kill people." It's fascinating. We don't know if it was the Zodiac Killer? Nobody knows. It fascinates people when somebody gets away with murder and they brag about it.

AC: The Zodiac Killer had seven confirmed victims. Five of them died. But he's suspected possibly to have dozens more.

Several years prior to this interview, John Walsh had published the actual letters on his *America's Most Wanted* website, informing the public that the letters and ciphers containing the death threats were sent to him in 1990. The killer signed his letters "Scorpion." (That is the same year that George Hodel relocated from Asia back to San Francisco.)

Both the hand-printing and ciphers are similar to those of the original Zodiac, and in his Anderson Cooper interview John Walsh informed us "that the envelopes were the same kind [the Zodiac] sent others."

"Scorpion Letters" Mailed to John Walsh in 1990

Fig. 15.18

Clearly, based on Walsh's information these letters should be examined and processed for potential DNA.

John Walsh has been a dedicated fighter for victims' rights for twenty-three years, and his success as the host of *America's Most Wanted* has resulted in more than 1,200 "solves." He has been a major force in helping law enforcement take so many vicious criminals "off the streets." His crime-fighting efforts have also resulted in an incalculable number of crimes being prevented.

He has my highest respect and personal congratulations for an outstanding job in standing up for victim's rights and his long years of assistance to law enforcement.

Zodiac—San Francisco Paul Stine Murder Shirt and Gloves

IN MY OPINION, THE best potential for hard physical evidence in the unsolved Zodiac murders can be found in the physical evidence booked in connection with the Paul Stine cabbie shooting in San Francisco.

The killer's bloodstained gloves and the section of shirt torn from the victim's body and mailed to SFPD both remain untested. Both items are highly likely to yield a full Zodiac profile, if tested.

The gloves (men's size seven) apparently contain the victim's blood splatters. They were inadvertently left behind, or maybe fell out of Zodiac's pocket before the shooting. The 1969 police and DOJ reports confirm that law enforcement believes that they were owned and worn by Zodiac.

In addition, there remain some fifteen to twenty notes mailed by Zodiac that could be retested using today's much-more-sophisticated techniques.

I find it incredible that no confirmed Zodiac DNA has yet been obtained. There is no Zodiac DNA entered into any state or national CODIS data banks.

The last report I am aware of from law enforcement sources dates back to 2002, and that sample reportedly is highly suspect and contains only a partial DNA profile which is insufficient to include or exclude anyone. That sample only contains three out of the thirteen loci found in a full DNA profile.

California DOJ Meet and the Zodiac DNA Evidence

IN NOVEMBER OF 2009, two months after the publication of my book *Most Evil*, I met with two agents from the California Department of Justice.

The agents, I'll call them, X and Y, flew down from the DOJ San Francisco Regional Office to Los Angeles for a morning meet. I presented them with a PowerPoint summary of my overall investigation.

I focused on the Zodiac connections and what I believed were the best potential sources for obtaining Zodiac DNA with special emphasis on the size seven gloves left by Zodiac inside the murder victim's taxi.

Both Agent Y (a retired SFPD detective) and Agent X, his supervisor, seemed impressed with my findings. Agent X said she would be back in contact with me after they had a chance to review the various written materials I had provided.

Six months later, in May of 2010, I contacted Agent Y by e-mail and inquired if he had been able to test the gloves. He responded that the SFPD homicide commander "had given him permission to have them tested, and he was in the process of attempting to locate the evidence."

I recontacted Agent Y in August of 2010, and he indicated that he was hoping to meet with the SFPD detective and "track down the gloves and get the process going."

My last communication with Agent Y occurred in November 2010. In that exchange, he said he was "still trying to make contact with his contact at SFPD and continue the search for the gloves," assuring me that "at some point, this will all come together." (As a side note, Agent Y advised me that their DOJ handwriting expert "had examined and compared George Hodel's handwriting to known Zodiac documents and was unable to include or exclude him as the author of the Zodiac letters." Their Questioned Document Expert requested through Agent Y that I provide them with some additional samples of George Hodel's "lowercase handwriting." Unfortunately, I have no additional samples in my possession as my father rarely wrote in lowercase. I am currently attempting to locate additional writing samples. Despite the "inconclusive" finding, the fact that the DOJ expert could not eliminate George Hodel as the writer of the Zodiac notes and letters is, by itself, significant.)

It has now been two years since my original meeting with the two DOJ agents. It is unknown if the gloves have been found or tested, or still remain missing. In criminal investigations, "No news is bad news." We can only hope that in Agent Y's optimistic words, "this will all come together."

Have the SFPD Stine Gloves Been Located and Tested for DNA or is the Evidence Still Missing?

Left: SFPD Paul Stine evidence includes suspect's bloodstained gloves and victim's shirt.
Right: George Hodel is pictured putting on his size-seven gloves on a visit to me on Orcas Island in Washington State in 1995.

SFPD evidence photo showing Stine shirt and men's black leather gloves (size 7) at the bottom of the frame in clear plastic evidence bag (arrow points to gloves).

George and June Hodel Rosario Retreat, Orcas Island, Washington 1995.

Fig. 15.19

Bottom Line:

I believe that the potential for obtaining the suspect's DNA on many of the forties' unsolved Los Angeles Lone Woman Murders exists.

I believe that analysis of those samples will prove linkage like they did in the Grim Sleeper Murders.

Once DNA is obtained, cold case detectives can enter the samples into state and federal CODIS data banks and very possibly identify a suspect and clear many of the cases.

At the very least, detectives should make the attempt to obtain DNA from the Los Angeles-area Zodiac letters booked in evidence at LAPD and Riverside to see if they *can be linked to a killer already entered in CODIS.*

With the recent advancement of "touch DNA," I am extremely confident that the forty-year-old unsolved Zodiac serial murders can be solved.

All that it requires is one dedicated cold case investigator in any of the many jurisdictions to take the initiative and make the first step forward! That detective might now be assigned to any of the following: Riverside PD, LASD Homicide, LAPD Homicide CCU, Long Beach PD, San Francisco PD, Napa or Solano Sheriff, or Vallejo PD.

The solution is there, just a simple phone call away. As an old-time homicide detective who has been there and done that, I strongly urge that detective to pick up the telephone and make the call to his or her crime lab.

I'll close with a quote from SFPD Inspector Mike Maloney, who was one of the last detectives actively assigned to work Zodiac. He died in 2005, believing that DNA would one day solve the case.

In an open letter to the public, written shortly before his death, he said:

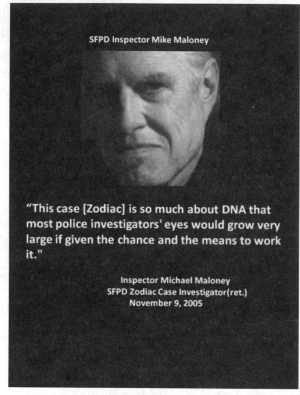

Fig. 15.20

I believe Mike's assessment was absolutely correct!

Rest in Peace, Mike

BIBLIOGRAPHY

1. Anger, Kenneth. *Hollywood Babylon*. San Francisco: Stonehill Publishing, 1975.
2. ———. *Hollywood Babylon II*. New York: NAL Penguin, 1984.
3. Bonelli, William G. *Billion Dollar Blackjack*. Beverly Hills: Civic Research Press, 1954.
4. Borchard, Edwin M. *Convicting The Innocent*. Garden City, NY: Garden City Publishing Company, 1932
5. Blanche, Tony, and Brad Schreiber. *Death in Paradise: An Illustrated History of the Los Angeles County Department of Coroner*. Los Angeles: General Publishing Group, 1998.
6. Breton, Andre. *Manifestoes of Surrealism*. Ann Arbor: University of Michigan Press, Ann Arbor Paperbacks, 1972.
7. Bruccoli, Matthew J., and Richard Layman. *A Matter of Crime, Vol. I*. San Diego: Harcourt Brace Jovanovich, 1987.
8. Caen, Herb. *Herb Caen's Guide to San Francisco*. Garden City, NY: Doubleday & Company, 1957.
9. Caen, Herb. *Hills of San Francisco*. San Francisco: Chronicle Publishing Company, 1959.
10. Carter, Vincent A. *LAPD's Rogue Cops*. Lucerne Valley, CA: Desert View Books, 1993.
11. Chandler, Raymond. *The Blue Dahlia: A Screenplay*. Chicago: Southern Illinois University Press, 1976.
12. Cohen, Mickey. *In My Own Words*. Englewood Cliffs, NJ: Prentice-Hall, 1975.
13. Connell, Richard. *The Most Dangerous Game*. New York: Berkley Highland Books, 1957.
14. Conrad, Barnaby. *The World of Herb Caen*. San Francisco: Chronicle Books, 1997.
15. Cox, Julian. *Spirit into Matter*. J. Paul Getty Trust, Los Angeles, 2004.

16. Davis, Howard. *The Zodiac Manson Connection*. Costa Mesa: Pen Power Publications, 1997.

17. deFord, Miriam Allen. *Murders Sane & Mad*. New York: Avon Books, 1965.

18. Delson, Susan. *Dudley Murphy, Hollywood Wild Card*. Minneapolis: University of Minnesota Press, 2006.

19. Demaris, Ovid. *The Last Mafioso*. New York: Times Books, 1981.

20. De Quincey, Thomas. *Murder Considered as One of the Fine Arts*. New York and London: Nickerbocker Nuggets.

21. De Rivers, J. Paul, MD. *The Sexual Criminal: A Psychoanalytical Study*. Burbank, CA: Bloat, 1949; rev. ed. 2000.

22. Dickensheet, Dean W. *Great Crimes Of San Francisco*. New York: Ballentine Books, 1974.

23. Domanick, Joe. *To Protect and to Serve: The LAPD's Century of War in the City of Dreams*. New York: Pocket Books, 1994.

24. Douglas, John, and Mark Olshaker. *The Cases That Haunt Us*. New York: Lisa Drew Books/Scribner, 2000.

25. –––. *Mind Hunter*. New York: Lisa Drew Books/Scribner, 1995.

26. Dmytryk, Edward. *Odd Man Out: A Memoir of the Hollywood Ten*. Carbondale: Southern Illinois University Press, 1996.

27. Ellroy, James. *The Black Dahlia*. New York: Mysterious Press, 1987.

28. –––. *My Dark Places*. New York: Alfred A. Knopf, 1996.

29. –––. *Crime Wave*. New York: Vintage Crime/Black Lizard Vintage Books, 1999.

30. Fetherling, Doug. *The Five Lives of Ben Hecht*. Toronto: Lester & Orpen, 1977.

31. Finney, Guy W. *Angel City in Turmoil*. Los Angeles: Amer Press, 1945.

32. Freeman, Lucy, *"Before I kill more..."*. New York: Crown Publishers Inc., 1955.

33. Fowler, Will. *The Young Man from Denver*. Garden City, NY: Doubleday & Company, 1962.

34. –––. *Reporters: Memoirs of a Young Newspaperman*. Malibu, CA: Roundtable, 1991.

35. Giesler, Jerry, and Pete Martin. *The Jerry Giesler Story*. New York: Simon & Schuster, 1960.

36. Gilmore, John. *Severed: The True Story of the Black Dahlia Murder*. San Francisco: Zanja Press, 1994.

37. Goodman, Jonathan. *Acts of Murder*. New York: Lyle Stuart Books, Carol Publishing Group, 1986.

38. Granlund, Nils T. *Blondes, Brunettes, and Bullets*. New York: David McKay, 1957.

39. Graysmith, Robert. *Zodiac*. New York: Berkeley Books, 1987.

40. Graysmith, Robert. *Zodiac Unmasked*. New York: Berkeley Books, 2002.

41. Gribble, Leonard. *They Had a Way with Women*. London: Arrow Books, 1967.

42. Grobel, Lawrence. *The Hustons*. New York: Charles Scribners's Sons, 1989.

43. Halberstam, David. *The Powers That Be*. New York: Alfred A. Knopf, 1979.

44. Hall, Angus, ed. *Crimes of Horror*. New York: Phoebus, 1976.

45. Halleck, Seymour L., MD. *Psychiatry and the Dilemmas of Crime*. New York: Harper & Row, 1967.

46. Harris, Martha. *Angelica Huston: The Lady and the Legacy*. New York: St. Martin's Press, 1989.

47. Henderson, Bruce and Sam Summerlin. *The Super Sleuths*. New York: Macmillan, 1976.

48. Hecht, Ben. *Fantazius Mallare: A Mysterious Oath*. Chicago: Pascal Covici, 1922.

49. ———. *The Kingdom of Evil: A Continuation of the Journal of Fantazius Mallare*. Chicago: Pascal Covici, 1924.

50. Heimann, Jim. *Sins of the City: The Real LA Noir*. San Francisco: Chronicle Books, 1999.

51. Hodel, George Hill. *The New Far East: Seven Nations of Asia*. Hong Kong: Reader's Digest Far East, 1966.

52. Hodel, Steve. *Black Dahlia Avenger: A Genius for Murder*. New York: Harper, 2006.

53. Hodel, Steve. *Black Dahlia Avenger: A Genius for Murder: The True Story*. Arcade Pub, 2015.

54. Hodel, Steve, with Ralph Pezzullo. *Most Evil: Avenger, Zodiac, and the Further Serial Murders of Dr. George Hill Hodel*. New York: Dutton, 2009.

55. Huston, John. *An Open Book*. New York: Alfred A. Knopf, 1980.

56. ———. *Frankie and Johnny*. New York: Albert and Charles Boni, 1930.

57. Jeffers, Robinson. *Roan Stallion, Tamar, and Other Poems*. New York: Boni & Liveright, 1925.

58. Jennings, Dean. *We Only Kill Each Other: The Life and Bad Times of Bugsy Siegel*. Englewood Cliffs, NJ: Prentice-Hall, 1967.

59. Kelleher, Michael D. and David Van Nuys. *"This is the Zodiac speaking"*. Westport, CT: Praeger Publisher, 2002.

60. Kennedy, Dolores. *William Heirens: His Day In Court*. Chicago: Bonus Books, 1999.

61. Kennedy, Ludovic. *The Airman and the Carpenter*. New York: Viking Penguin, 1985.

62. Keppel, Robert D. *Signature Killers*. New York: Pocket Books, 1997.

63. Klein, Norman M., and Martin J. Schiesl. *20th Century Los Angeles: Power, Promotion, and Social Conflict*. Claremont, CA: Regina Books, 1990.

64. Knowlton, Janice, and Michael Newton. *Daddy Was the Black Dahlia Killer*. New York: Pocket Books, 1995.

65. Krupp, Dr. E.C. *In Search Of Ancient Astronomies*. New York: McGraw-Hill Book Company, 1978.

66. Lane, Brian, and Wilfred Gregg. *The Encyclopedia of Serial Killers*. New York: Diamond Books, 1992.

67. Martinez, Al. *Jigsaw John*. Los Angeles: J. P. Tarcher, 1975.

68. Morton, James. *Gangland International: An Informal History of the Mafia and Other Mobs in the Twentieth Century*. London: Little, Brown & Company, 1998.

69. Mayo, Morrow. *Los Angeles*. New York: Alfred A. Knopf, 1933.

70. Nelson, Mark and Bayliss, Sarah Hudson. *Exquisite Corpse,: Surrealism and the Black Dahlia Murder*. New York: Bulfinch Press, 2006.

71. Nickel, Steven. *Torso: The Story of Eliot Ness and the Search for a Psychopathic Killer*. Winston-Salem, NC: John F. Blair, 1989.

72. Pacios, Mary. *Childhood Shadows: The Hidden Story of the Black Dahlia Murder*. Downloaded and printed via electronic distribution from the World Wide Web. ISBN 1-58500-484-7, 1999.

73. Parker, William H. *Parker on Police*. Springfield, IL: Charles C. Thomas Publisher, 1957.

74. Parrish, Michael. *For the People*. Los Angeles: Angel City Press, 2001.

75. Penn, Gareth. *TIMES 17*. Foxglove Press, 1987.

76. Phillips, Michelle. *California Dreamin': The True Story of the Mamas and Papas*. New York: Warner, 1986.

77. Poe, Edgar Allan. *Edgar Allan Poe Reader*. Philadelphia, IL: Running Press, 1993.

78. Rappleye, Charles, and Ed Becker. *All American Mafioso: The Johnny Rosselli Story*. New York: Doubleday, 1991.

79. Reid, David. *Sex, Death and Gods in LA*. New York: Random House, 1992.

80. Reid, Ed. *The Grim Reapers: The Anatomy of Organized Crime in America.* Chicago: Henry Regnery, 1969.

81. Reinhardt, Richard. *Treasure Island: San Francisco's Exposition Years.* San Francisco: Scrimshaw Press, 1973.

82. Richardson, James H. *For the Life of Me: Memoirs of a City Editor.* New York: G. P. Putnam's Sons, 1954.

83. Roeburt, John. *Get Me Giesler.* New York: Belmont Books, 1962.

84. Rothmiller, Mike, and Ivan G. Goldman. *LA Secret Police: Inside the LAPD Elite Spy Network.* New York: Pocket Books, 1992.

85. Rowan, David. *Famous American Crimes.* London: Frederick Muller, 1957.

86. Sade, Donatien-Alphonse-François de. *Selected Writings of de Sade.* New York: British Book Centre, 1954.

87. Sade, Donatien-Alphonse-François de. *The Complete Justine, Philosophy in the Bedroom and Other Writings.* New York: Grove Press, 1965.

88. Sade, Donatien-Alphonse-François de. *The 120 Days of Sodom and Other Writings.* New York: Grove Press, 1966.

89. Sade, Donatien-Alphonse-François de. *120 Days of Sodom, or the School for Libertinage.* New York: Falstaff Press, 1934.

90. Sakol, Jeannie. *The Birth of Marilyn: The Lost Photographs of Norma Jean by Joseph Jasgur.* New York: St. Martin's Press, 1991.

91. Seaver, Richard, Terry Southern, and Alexander Trocchi, eds. *Writers in Revolt: An Anthology.* New York: Frederick Fell, 1963.

92. Sjoquist, Arthur W. *Captain: Los Angeles Police Department 1869–1984.* Dallas: Taylor, 1984.

93. Smith, Jack. *Jack Smith's LA.* New York: McGraw-Hill, 1980.

94. Starr, Kevin. *Inventing the Dream: California through the Progressive Era.* New York: Oxford University Press, 1985.

95. ———. *The Dream Endures: California Enters the 1940s.* New York: Oxford University Press, 1997.

96. Stevenson, Robert Louis. *The Strange Case of Dr. Jekyll and Mr. Hyde and Other Stories.* New York: Barnes & Noble, 1995.

97. Sterling, Hank. *Ten Perfect Crimes.* New York: Stravon, 1954.

98. Stoker, Charles. *Thicker'n Thieves.* Santa Monica: Sidereal, 1951.

99. Stoker, Charles. *Thicker'n Thieves,* Los Angeles: Thoughtprint Press, 2011.

100. Storm, Hyemeyohsts. *Seven Arrows.* New York: Ballantine Books, 1972.

101. Tejaratchi, Sean, ed. *Death Scenes: A Homicide Detective's Scrapbook*. Portland: Feral House, 1996.

102. Terman, Lewis M. *Genetic Studies of Genius. Vol. 1*. Stanford: Stanford University Press, 1925.

103. Terman, Lewis M., and Melita H. Oden. *The Gifted Group at Mid-Life: Thirty-Five Years' Follow-Up of the Superior Child*. Stanford: Stanford University Press, 1959.

104. *True Crime—Unsolved Crimes*. Alexandria, VA: Time-Life Books, 1993.

105. Turvey, Brent, *Criminal Profiling: An Introduction To Behavioral Evidence Analysis*. San Diego, CA: Academic Press, 1999.

106. Tygiel, Jules. *The Great Los Angeles Swindle*. New York: Oxford University Press, 1994.

107. Viertel, Peter. *Dangerous Friends: At Large with Huston and Hemingway in the Fifties*. New York: Nan A. Talese/Bantam Doubleday Dell, 1992.

108. Viertel, Peter. *White Hunter Black Heart*. New York: Doubleday, 1953.

109. Underwood, Agness. *Newspaperwoman*. New York: Harper & Brothers, 1949.

110. Waldberg, Patrick. *Surrealism*. New York: Thames & Hudson, 1997.

111. Walker, Clifford James. *One Eye Closed the Other Red: The California Bootlegging Years*. Barstow, CA: Back Door Publishing, 1999.

112. Webb, Jack. *The Badge*. Greenwich, CT: Fawcett, 1958.

113. White, Leslie T. *Me, Detective*. New York: Harcourt, Brace & Company, 1936.

114. Williamson, Ray A. *Living The Sky: The Cosmos of the American Indian*. Norman, OK: University of Oklahoma Press, 1987.

115. Wilson, Colin. *Murder in the 1940s*. New York: Carroll & Graf, 1993.

116. Woods, Gerald. *The Police in Los Angeles*. New York: Garland Publishing Inc., 1993.

117. Wolf, Marvin J., and Katherine Mader. *Fallen Angels: Chronicles of LA Crime and Mystery*. New York: Facts on File, 1986.

118. Weintraub, Alan. *Lloyd Wright: The Architecture of Frank Lloyd Wright Jr*. New York: Harry N. Abrams, 1998.

119. Work Projects Administration. *Los Angeles: A Guide to the City and its Environs*. New York: Hastings House, 1941.

Man Ray Research-Related Books

120. Foresta, Merry. *Perpetual Motif: The Art of Man Ray*. New York: Abbeville Press and the National Museum of American Art, 1988.

121. Man Ray. *Self Portrait*. Boston: Little, Brown & Company, 1963.

122. ———. *Man Ray Photographs*. New York: Thames & Hudson, 1991.

123. Penrose, Roland. *Man Ray*. New York: Thames & Hudson, 1975.

124. Robert Berman Gallery. *Man Ray: Paris–LA*. New York: Smart Art Press Art Catalog, 1996.

125. Butterfield and Dunning. *Fine Photographs*. Catalog, November 17, 1999.

126. ———. *Fine Photographs*. Catalog, May 27, 1999.

Newspaper Sources

127. *San Francisco Chronicle,* 1969-1978

128. *San Francisco Examiner,* 1969-1970

129. *Vallejo-Times Herald,* 1969

130. *Los Angeles Record,* 1925

131. *Riverside Press Enterprise,* 1966-1971

132. *Los Angeles Times,* 1941-1972

133. *Los Angeles Mirror,* 1947

134. *Los Angeles Herald Express,* 1945-1951

135. *Los Angeles Times,* 1947

136. *Los Angeles Mirror,* 1947

137. *Los Angeles Examiner,* 1947

138. *Chicago Daily Tribune,* 1946

139. *The Manila Times,* 1967

Magazine Articles:

140. "He Wants Slave Girls Waiting For Him In Paradise." *Front Page Detective,* September 1975.

141. "Are They Closing In On Zodiac?" *Detective Cases,* April 1974.

142. "Is The Zodiac Killer Still At Large?" *Coronet,* October 1973.

143. "The Zodiac Killings—California's No. 1 Murder Mystery." *True Detective,* August 1971.

144. "Zodiac—California's Blood-Thirsty Phantom." *Argosy*, September 1970.

145. "Zodiac Casts A Stranger's Shadow." *Startling Detective*, March 1970.

146. "Has The Zodiac Killer Trapped Himself?" *Front Page Detective*, February 1970.

147. "Your Daughter May Be Next." *Inside Detective*, January 1969.

148. "The Zodiac Killer." *Real-Life Crimes*, 1994 Vol. 5 Part 64.

149. "Savage Rage of the 'Lipstick Killer'" *Real-Life Crimes*, 1993, Vol. 3 Part 43.

150. "Mystery Of The Medicine Wheels." *National Geographic*, January 1997.

151. "The Case Of William Heirens." *Life Magazine*, July 29, 1946. Page 30.

152. "Portrait of the Artist as a Mass Murderer." *California Magazine*, November 1981.

Miscellaneous

153. Department of Justice- Zodiac Investigation, Case No. 1-15-311-F9-5861, 35 pages.

154. Department of Justice- Special Report, "Zodiac Homicides: Napa Co., San Francisco, Solano Co., Vallejo, Riverside," 10 pages.

155. F.B.I. Files on "Zodiac"

156. F.B.I., FOIA Files on Elizabeth Short.

157. Los Angeles District Attorney, Bureau of Investigation, "Black Dahlia and Dr. George Hill Hodel Files"; Electronic Surveillance Files on George Hodel, and Investigative summaries on Black Dahlia by DA Lt. Frank B. Jemison; 146-page Hodel-Black Dahlia transcripts; Frank Jemison/ Dorothy Hodel 6-page interview transcripts.

158. Sowden House, Historic American Survey, National Park Service, Department of Interior 1969.

Websites

159. www.stevehodel.com

160. www.zodiackiller.com

161. www.lapl.org

162. www.lmharnisch.com

Black Dahlia Avenger Television Documentaries & Shows

163. *Dateline NBC,* "Black Dahlia" Josh Mankiewicz (2003, twenty minute segment)
164. *Court TV,* "Who Killed the Black Dahlia?" Josh Mankiewicz (2003, one hour)
165. *CBS 48-Hours Special,* "Black Dahlia Confidential" (2004, one hour)
166. *A&E Bill Kurtis Cold Case Files,* "Black Dahlia" (2006, one hour)
167. *NBC Universal* (France), "The Truth about the Black Dahlia" (2006, one hour)
168. *CNN Anderson Cooper-360,* "Black Dahlia" (2006, eight minute author interview)
169. *Discovery Channel, Most Evil* (2007, one-hour)

Video Sources

170. Bygone Video: *Charlie Chan At Treasure Island,* 1999
171. Columbia Pictures Film Noir: *The Sniper,* 1952, Directed by Ed. Dmytryk
172. United American Video: *Most Dangerous Game,* Charlotte NC, 1991
173. *American Justice: Who Is the Lipstick Killer?*

For More Information, Visit:

www.stevehodel.com

www.stevehodel.com/blog

INDEX

D

E

F

I

J

K

L

M

W

Y

Z

ACKNOWLEDGMENTS

I WOULD LIKE TO take the opportunity to here acknowledge the following individuals for their important contributions to this book and the investigation.

Across the pond, a huge "MERCI" to M. Yves Person, in Paris, who, by thinking outside-the-box, "cracked the code" and gave us the solution to Zodiac's 1970 Halloween Card cipher.

Also, my deep gratitude to his neighbor, Detective Chief Inspector Susan Wilshire, in the UK who handed me the clews and "thoughtprints" concealed in the 1948 collaborative *Alphabet for Adults* publication by Man Ray and Bill Copley.

In Texas, my good friend and retired Dallas P.D. detective, Robert "Dr. Watson" Sadler who has unselfishly contributed both his time and critical thinking in helping me examine potential linkage and evidence, along with his recent essay, "Scratching the Surface of the Zodiac Ciphers" included as addenda in this book.

Also, in Texas, kudos to my editor/clean-up man, bestselling novelist, journalist, and true-crime writer, Ron Franscell. Thank you once again Ron for your invaluable assistance in helping separate the wheat from the chaff.

Here in Los Angeles, I am most fortunate to have the ongoing support of my "full time partner," Roberta McCreary, who continues to amaze and inspire me with her grace and ability to overlook and understand my many post-retirement obsessions.

Big thumbs-up to my amigos, Los Angeles historian, Dennis Effle, and my pooka-like scholar, Hermann H., both of whom continue to provide objective thoughts and contributions to "the cause."

Finally, my gratitude and appreciation to my new friends at Los Angeles' RARE BIRD BOOKS. To all of the hardworking staff hanging out in their very cool and very noirish downtown office, (think Sam Spade's working digs in *Maltese Falcon*) along with their intrepid publisher, Tyson Cornell, (the former marketing and publicity director at the legendary, Book Soup, on the Sunset Strip.) Special thanks to the flocks, wing-commander Tyson, and his copilot, Managing Editor Alice Elmer, and navigators Julia Callahan and Winona Leon, along with the rest of the ground crew.

Steve Hodel
Los Angeles
August 2015